THE PERFECT TIE

THE PERFECT TIE

The True Story of the 2000 Presidential Election

JAMES W. CEASER
AND
ANDREW E. BUSCH

ROWMAN & LITTLEFIELD PUBLISHERS, INC.
Lanham • Boulder • New York • Oxford

ROWMAN & LITTLEFIELD PUBLISHERS, INC.

Published in the United States of America
by Rowman & Littlefield Publishers, Inc.
4720 Boston Way, Lanham, Maryland 20706
www.rowmanlittlefield.com

12 Hid's Copse Road
Cumnor Hill, Oxford OX2 9JJ, England

British Library Cataloging in Publication Information Available

Library of Congress Cataloging-in-Publication Data

Ceaser, James W.
    The perfect tie : the true story of the 2000 presidential election / James W. Ceaser and
Andrew E. Busch.
        p. cm.
    Includes bibliographical references and index.
    ISBN 0-7425-0835-8 (alk. paper)—IBN 0-7425-0836-6 (pbk. : alk. paper)
    1. Presidents—United States—Election—2000. I. Busch, Andrew. II. Title.

    JK526 2000f
    324.973'0929—dc21

                                                                                2001020455

Printed in the United States of America

 ∞™ The paper used in this publication meets the minimum requirements of American
National Standard for Information Sciences—Permanence of Paper for Printed Library
Materials, ANSI/NISO Z.39.48-1992.

To

Daniel Christopher Busch

and

Harvey, Richard, and Martin Ceaser

Contents

Acknowledgments

We would like to thank the following people for their help in writing this book: Ben Bogardus, who prepared the graphs and tables; Kari Anderson, Reginald Bauer, Kathleen Grammatico, Robert Hume, Mark McNaught, and Hannah Bradley St. Leger, who provided research assistance; and Spencer Wellhofer, Shamira Gelb, and the graduate students in the 2000 election seminar at the University of Virginia, who read and commented on parts of the manuscript over the course of a much longer than anticipated election campaign.

Our appreciation also goes to Mindy Busch in Denver for her kind patience and support in Denver and to Blaire French in Charlottesville for her help in editing and proofreading. Finally, the editorial staff at Rowman & Littlefield gave us its usual support and encouragement, and our special thanks go to Executive Editor Steve Wrinn and our production editor, Lynn Gemmell.

Prologue
Election Eve, 2000

On the evening of October 29, 1991, meteorologists on the East Coast gazed into their computer monitors and observed three mighty weather systems, one a veritable hurricane, converging over the North Atlantic. No one had seen anything like it before. It was a natural event of such rarity and force that one experienced weatherman called it the Perfect Storm.

The equivalent of this phenomenon in American electoral history took place on the night of November 7, 2000. As the election returns for Congress showed the House and Senate moving toward parity between the two parties, the presidential race edged, eerily, toward an astonishing outcome: two candidates separated in the national popular tally by a few hundred thousand votes, an Electoral College result that without the state of Florida produced no majority, and a popular-vote margin in Florida of under 2,000 ballots. It was the Perfect Tie.

Compared to the results of other general elections in American history, the contest in 2000 ended with the closest possible division of seats between the parties in the Senate (50 senators from each party), the fourth closest division of seats (by percentage) in the House, and the second closest presidential race by the electoral vote.[1] Observers of politics who emulate the meteorologists' precision in measuring natural phenomena might consider a closeness index for American elections. If the differences in these three instances, expressed in percentage terms, are averaged together and subtracted from 1, the 2000 election rates a remarkable score of 0.991. It is by far the closest election in American history.[2]

Events like a perfect storm or a perfect tie possess a terrible beauty that can remind people of the tremendous power of nature and of fate. Just as the Perfect Storm swept aside the structures man built to shield himself from the environment, so the Perfect Tie overwhelmed the institutions that

1

were designed, in the words of *The Federalist Papers*, to prevent "tumult and disorder" and to produce a legitimate presidential victor.[3] One by one, parts of the electoral system teetered and gave way. Trouble began on election night with the collapse of the television networks' vote projection system, which is relied on today, informally, to declare presidential winners. Trouble spread next to disputes about the accuracy and reliability of election and balloting machinery in Florida, and by implication in the nation as a whole. It then finally moved on to confusion over Florida's election laws and, more ominously, to controversy over the rightful powers of state judicial and political institutions.

In the end, the nation's political system held up. Or at least it held up in the sense that a president of the United States, George W. Bush, was finally chosen, albeit more than five weeks after election day. Though there were demonstrations, accusations of mob rule, and heated rhetoric, actual civil unrest and violence were avoided, owing in part, it would seem, to the good fortune of an election that had taken place in times of plenty, without any highly divisive issues. But the stress placed on the political system was evident. It took a highly controversial decision by the U.S. Supreme Court (determined by a five to four vote) overruling a highly controversial decision by the Florida Supreme Court (determined by a four to three vote) to assure George Bush his election. Bush assumed the presidency with the formal blessings of almost everyone in the political class, and with general support from the American people. But the very fact that issues of legitimacy were raised meant that his title to the office fell short of being universally acknowledged.[4] If there is any solace for George W. Bush in the postelection events, it is probably that the intense focus on this contest diverted attention from what many had worried would be another crisis: winning the electoral vote while losing the national popular vote. George W. Bush was the first president since Benjamin Harrison in 1888 to have clearly been elected in this way.

The problems that began on November 7 seemed to most Americans to be at first the stuff of history books, drawn from a more primitive political era. Journalists found themselves searching for accounts of the last disputed presidential election, the Hayes-Tilden contest of 1876, when a close national election result led to a revisiting of the votes in a few of the reconstruction governments in the southern states, including Florida. According to a classic description: "The Republicans controlled the state governments and the election machinery, had relied upon the Negro masses for votes, and had practiced frauds as in the past. The Democrats used threats, intimidation, and even violence when necessary to keep Negroes from the polls; and where they were in a position to do so they resorted to fraud also."[5] Charges of a similar kind were raised in 2000, but most people realized that fraud in the literal sense was not really the main source of problems in the 2000 election. Instead, it was the exceptional way the vote was distributed around the country, coupled with an unexpected technical challenge that by chance occurred in the state of Florida, where the difference in vote totals between the two main candidates was smaller than the margin of error that the electoral mechanisms could handle. It was more than Florida had planned for, more perhaps than it might reasonably have been expected to plan for. But now that this result has occurred, important questions will have to be raised about what should be done to achieve greater reliability (or perhaps "uniformity") in election results, not only within each state, but also across the nation as a whole. Is reform to consist chiefly of improving voting machinery and revising individual state electoral laws, or will it involve major changes in national electoral laws and perhaps a constitutional amendment to alter the entire Electoral College system?

Much of the devastation of 2000 occurred after the night of the Perfect Tie on November 7. Just as the Hollywood movie *The Perfect Storm* devoted a good deal of attention to the rescue efforts that followed the disaster, so in this case it will be important to consider how different political institutions and actors responded to the extraordinary challenges they confronted after the election. These questions go well beyond what is usually covered in electoral studies and extend into realms that assess prudence and statesmanship. Here, alas, political science has developed no index to assist us.

Forecasting the Perfect Tie

Could the improbable results of the election of 2000 have been foreseen? As the evening of November 7, 2000, approached, signs of what was to occur were already detectable, although, as in so many disasters, their full significance became apparent only in retrospect.

Political scientists in the middle of the last decade began to suggest that the general electoral condition of our era made a perfect tie conceivable. Even to think in such terms, it must be said, required a conceptual breakthrough in the study of elections. Historical patterns had led analysts to conclude that "normal" electoral alignments consisted of one party gaining a clear long-term advantage over the other, as the Democrats had managed to do for the two or three decades following the elections of 1932 and 1936. Electoral observers in the 1990s were therefore on the lookout for one of the parties to establish clear dominance, as some thought the Republican Party might have done after its vaunted "revolution" of 1994, and as others believed the Democrats might be on the verge of doing after Bill Clinton's second "third-way" victory in 1996. But there was another way of viewing matters. Could not a situation of parity between the parties also be an alignment? After repeatedly observing in the middle 1990s that Democratic and Republican partisans were fairly evenly balanced in the electorate, a few analysts awoke to declare that this arrangement, far from being some kind of transitional phase, *was* the contemporary alignment, pure and simple. According to a well-known political scientist, Paul Allen Beck, this most modern alignment consists of "a more even balance in electoral strength between the two major parties than the nation has ever seen, at least for a century." Democrats now are about a third of the electorate (perhaps a bit more) and Republicans also about a third. The large remaining slice of the modern electoral pie contains the grouping of nonpartisan voters, also roughly a third of the electorate, therefore equal to each of the two partisan slices. This segment floats between the two parties and is easily attracted to independent candidates and third parties. Modern elections accordingly display a good deal of volatility from one contest to the next. Each outcome, to cite Beck again, reflects "election specific movements of a large nonpartisan electorate around a 50-50 'normal vote' baseline."[6]

In our two previous books on the 1992 and 1996 presidential elections, we sought to identify the short-term forces at work on the electorate in each contest, in particular those acting upon the segment of floating voters that is most sensitive to these time-dependent pressures.[7] In 1992 a powerful animus against "insiders" and a deep concern over economic conditions pushed voters away from President George H. W. Bush, giving the election to Bill Clinton. In 1996 Bill Clinton was reelected not only on the strength of the economy, but also as a reaction against the Republican Congress and its visible leadership, largely in the person of House Speaker Newt Gingrich. For readers looking for dramatic long-term trends deriving from each election, such an approach is admittedly unsatisfactory. Given the importance of the short-term factors operating on large numbers of floating voters, it is a mistake to read too much into the division of votes on election day. A good part of their support is "soft," and under only slightly different conditions many voters could easily have gone the other way. Modern elections, we said, are a bit like mayflies, living only for the day.

This does not mean that the floating vote is entirely without structure or direction. Although a portion of the vote in every election is predicated on responses to evanescent moods and an evaluation of personality and leadership traits, it is still possible to discern the outlines of what the floating voters appear to want, or more precisely, what they do not want. The floating vote, understood here to include most of the nonpartisans as well as a portion of weaker partisans, has made known its dislikes at least twice in the last decade: in 1994, when it reacted against a strong Big Government agenda and a cultural politics of permissiveness from the left; and in 1996, when it reacted against a strong antigovernment agenda and a strident culture-war rhetoric from the right. Floating voters have therefore previously rejected the intellectual packages and worldviews that are embraced by the strong partisans of both parties. Successful presidential candidates have been those who have found a way to maintain the enthusiasm and support of their core supporters, while managing to appeal to a larger portion of this floating vote.[8]

Now imagine an election in which almost all of the partisans stick by the candidate of their own party and in which the short-term factors pressure the floating voters equally in different and ultimately offsetting directions. Given the basic shape of the modern electorate, the result would approach parity. This is just about what happened in 2000. Party adherents voted overwhelmingly for "their" candidates, a result that probably had less to do with any extraordinary appeal of Gore and Bush among the candidates' own supporters than with their inability to generate much cross-partisan interest. Whatever the cause, partisan faithfulness in 2000 reached the highest level for any modern election and netted each candidate a roughly equal number of votes by partisans. Next, the net effect of short-term forces split the nonpartisan or floating voters about down the middle. In some instances these forces pressured different groups of voters in opposite directions, though in approximately equal amounts. In other instances these forces pulled and tugged the same people in different directions, causing cross-pressured voters, by far the greatest number of whom were women, to swing greatly back and forth between the candidates.

Describing how and why this equilibrium of forces was reached in 2000 will be a large part of our task in this book. For the moment, however, it is worth exploring further the parity that exists today in American politics. There are two basic ways of measuring relative party strength, one (just referred to) that looks at how people respond in *surveys* to the question of which party they identify with (Democratic, Republican, or Independent), and the other that looks at which party's candidates people actually vote for in real *elections*. By this last measure, as we have seen, the results in 2000 show the two parties at near parity for each of the national institutions. It is also important, of course, to consider how people vote for the three major political offices at the state level: governor, the state Senate, and the state House. The results here are striking. For the state legislative chambers, Democrats in 2000 control 25 state Houses to 24 for the Republicans, while Republicans control 24 state Senates to 21 for the Democrats. Four Senates are tied between the two parties.[9] There is, however, one office today where one of the parties holds a clear advantage. Among the governors, 29 are Republican and 19 are Democrats. And therein lies a tale. It is surely no accident that the president, George Bush, not only came from the ranks of the Republican governors, but also was nominated with their support and campaigned for the presidency, conspicuously, with their help.

These figures make clear that an important change in relative party strength has taken place over the past decade. At the beginning of the decade, the Republican Party was predominantly a presidential party. Republicans held the presidency (as they had since 1980), but both houses of Congress were in the hands of the Democrats. In the states, the Democrats had the edge in governors (30D-20R) and the decided advantage among state Senates (38-11) and state Houses (40-9). By 1994 the contours of partisan control had begun to change. Democrats now held the presidency, while Republicans captured the House and Senate. Republicans in 1994 gained their large advantage among governors (30R-19D), and had pulled almost even among state Senates (25D-24R) and close among state Houses (26D-22R). The elections of the 1990s therefore did indeed realign American politics. But they did so not by placing a single party in control, but by bringing one of the parties (the Republicans) from an overall minority status into a position of parity. A large part of this change, as many have observed, has been the transformation of southern politics, in which the change from Democratic to Republican voting that showed earlier in presidential races worked its way down to the lower levels of officeholding. But the picture is in many ways more complicated.

A statistician might object to these measurements by saying that they tell us which party has won an office or institution, but not by how much. (You can win a governor's race by a handful of votes or a landslide, or control a state Senate or House by a few seats or by a comfortable margin.) Once again, therefore, an index may help, an index that we call the Comprehensive Index of American politics. It is an attempt to capture the strength of the two parties in a single number, by calculating how well each party has done in each state for all six of the major elective offices: president, Senate, House, governor, state Senate, state House.[10] The results, with the states weighted by population, are presented below in graph form. The graph shows a nation that at the outset of the decade was more Democratic than Republican, but that in 1994 moved into and has since remained in a perfect tie.

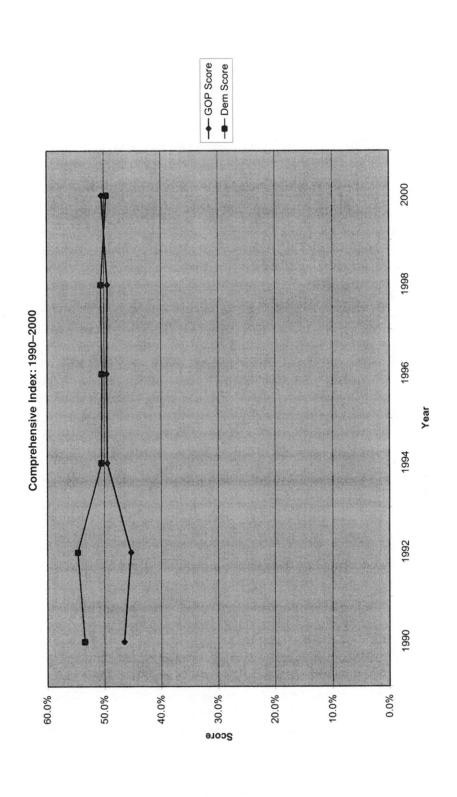

Comprehensive Index: 1990–2000

But enough of the past. Let us return to the 2000 presidential race and observe the short-range forecasters working much closer to the final event. As the campaign entered late October, forecasters with help from the hot new instrument of daily tracking polls became even more deeply impressed with the sustained closeness of this race, constantly calling it a "dead heat." And what a peculiar kind of dead heat it was—not just close, but oscillating. The Gallup tracking poll showed the lead changing no fewer than nine times over the course of the fall campaign. Although similar data are not available from past elections, the best guess is that previous close races have tended to follow the pattern of a horse race or marathon, in which one candidate is consistently in the lead, and at the very end the trailing candidate makes a single upward bid, either managing to pull ahead or ending up just short. But the 2000 race continually moved back and forth in September and October, with George W. Bush generally maintaining an ever so slight lead in the final week or so of the campaign. At the last possible moment in early November, however, the polls began to close with momentum swinging in the direction of Al Gore.

Final results of four of the most respected polling firms were as follows: Zogby/MSNBC (Gore plus 2), Gallup (Bush plus 2), Washington Post (Bush plus 1), CBS (Gore plus 1).[11] All of these results, of course, were well within the margin of error that allowed victory for either candidate. And averaged together, they just happen to make a Perfect Tie.

Election Night 2000

The great seventeenth-century French thinker Blaise Pascal, himself a mathematician before he became a philosopher, described two basic ways of analyzing human affairs: a mathematical or quantitative approach, and a humanistic or qualitative approach. What we have described above was the Perfect Tie on the night of November 7 as looked at from a mathematical point of view. But election eve 2000 was no less improbable from a qualitative point of view. Anyone hardy or foolish enough to have stayed awake the whole evening, from the first reports of election results at 7 P.M. EST to the strange and inconclusive speeches of the campaign managers after 5 A.M., watched a drama that was so full of twists and turns that no writer would ever have dared to offer it as a piece of fiction. It was all simply too implausible to be true.

The citizen settling down before the television set on November 7 probably had a slight expectation of a George Bush victory, given the prognostications of the previous month. Our viewer was therefore treated to an immediate (albeit mild) surprise when the television commentators, who were privy to the early returns of the national exit polls, let it be known at 7 P.M. that this election was going to be close—very, very close. And to eliminate any suspicions that this claim was just media hype or feigned impartiality, some took the unusual step of saying that they really meant it. If this was disappointing news for Bush supporters, things shortly would turn much worse. Just before 8 P.M. the networks declared Al Gore to be the winner in Florida. Within the next hour and a half, Gore was also awarded Pennsylvania and Michigan. Bush had thus lost all three of the big battleground states. Almost every scenario for a Bush victory depended on his carrying at least one of them. What hope remained now for Bush was the slim prospect of winning almost all of the remaining states where the outcome had been considered doubtful. That, or else the miracle that only George Bush himself had predicted: winning California.

The viewer now began to sense the contest moving toward a quick end. Gore's supporters in Nashville, gathered at the Legislative Plaza, were shown to be celebrating. Reports leaked out from the Loews Vanderbilt Hotel, headquarters of the Gore senior campaign staff, that his advisers were breaking out the champagne bottles. Television commentators, too, hinted at the vice president's impending victory, but spoke only guardedly for fear perhaps of later being branded biased or partisan. On election night television anchors are highly conscious of performing a quasi-public function, and their studied tone and bearing reveal how seriously they take this role. Still, anyone flipping from network to network could hear, as it were, between the lines. Al Gore was to be the 43rd president of the United States. The story line of this victory had been written. It was a version of Harry Truman's come-from-behind win in 1948, this time with Fighting Al, having defied the pundits and the (slight) odds, coming back at the last moment to prevail.

Under these circumstances, a good many sensible citizens, with jobs to attend the next morning and with children to awaken for school, took the cue and went off to bed.

But there was a problem. Governor Bush, who skipped a planned early election victory party at an Austin hotel, returned to the governor's mansion and took the unusual step of granting a brief interview in which he questioned the networks' call of Florida. His sources on the ground, he insisted, were reporting something very different. Viewers no doubt regarded this statement as understandable spin, designed to buoy supporters in the West, where voting was still going on. The networks, as the anchors assured viewers, make calls only when they are certain. As Dan Rather put it, "If we call a state, you can take it to the bank. Book it!"[12] But to everyone's astonishment, Bush's claim, not Dan Rather's, proved correct. The networks soon discovered that they had miscalled Florida, based, so it was later explained, on important errors and miscalculations made from their combined pool source of information, the Voter News Service. Shortly before 10 P.M. EST the networks pulled Florida from Gore's column and placed it back among the undecideds.

Viewers were now witnessing a near television equivalent of the famous media debacle of 1948, when major newspapers declared Dewey the victor over Truman. Only this time there were real consequences to the error. A wrong call had been made not only before voters in other states had voted, but also—contrary to general network policy—while some of Florida's own polls were still open. The western part of the Florida panhandle lies in the central, not the eastern, time zone. Were some Florida voters discouraged from turning out at the last moment in areas of the state that strongly favored George W. Bush? This claim was to be frequently cited, no doubt with embellishment, when Bush supporters in the next days joined in the initial debate over the fairness of the Florida election.[13] The shift of Florida brought a complete reversal to the drama. It was George Bush's miracle—more miraculous to the viewer than a victory in California could be. Lazarus-like, George Bush's campaign had arisen from the dead, and with Bush now actually ahead in the vote count in Florida, CBS News anchor Dan Rather commented at 10:06, "It's beginning to look increasingly like the advantage is going to George W. Bush." By 10:10 he had Gore "hanging, hanging by a thread."[14] Still, after what had just happened no one was ready to call Florida again—not just yet, anyhow.

Along with the change in status of Florida from Gore to undecided, over the next few hours Bush either won or remained in the running in enough of the states to keep alive the possibility of his winning an electoral victory without carrying Florida. This possibility, greater than most had earlier expected, surged and then faded as more states were called. At one point, indeed, NBC's Tim Russert, who had abandoned high-technology graphics for makeshift calculations with a Magic Marker, sketched a highly plausible scenario under which each candidate would win 269 electoral votes, a tie that would throw the election into the House of Representatives. But by about 1 A.M., the possibility of Bush winning without capturing Florida ended, as Gore closed in on the contested states of Iowa, Minnesota, and Wisconsin. Everything finally narrowed down to just Florida. Like the classic drama, in which all of the subplots must first be resolved before turning back to the central story line, whoever now carried Florida would pass the threshold of 270 electoral votes and become the 43rd president of the United States.

In the actual vote count in Florida, George Bush now held a modest lead, although commentators noted that some of the Democratic-leaning areas in large southern Florida counties had not yet reported. Bush's lead began to dwindle, but so too did the number of precincts outstanding. It was a race between Bush's vote margin (his distance ahead) and the precincts remaining (the distance to the finish line). Would Bush be able to hold on? His lead, once 130,000 votes, shrank to 30,000. Then, just after 2 A.M., his lead ballooned again to 59,000, a seemingly insurmountable advantage. One network after another announced Florida for George W. Bush, making him the 43rd president of the United States. Television anchors at this moment all have a way about them, interrupting whatever analysis is taking place and, in a solemn, if excited tone, announce that a new president has been chosen. Immediately, a new network graphic, long in preparation, is flashed on the screen, showing a picture of the victor against the backdrop of patriotic symbols coupled with heroic music. For everyone brought up in the television age, this moment is the modern act of the investiture, the equivalent of the prince's kneeling and having his shoulder touched by the prelate's sword. Something mysterious occurs that describes the real meaning of legitimacy, however else it may be defined in textbooks or legal treatises. At once, in the souls of millions of citizens, there is an acknowledgment of the victor's right to the office, whatever their previous preference might have been. The people have spoken, and a verdict has been rendered.

Following the investiture, the lead commentators offered their first pronouncement on the "meaning" of the election, a meaning now shaped by the new reality of a victorious candidate. Then came casual talk about Cabinet appointments and presidential priorities as well as some initial and delicate speculations on the political future of the defeated candidate. Everyone was merely marking time until the candidates gave their concession and victory speeches.

What remained of a drenched and shivering crowd in Austin, where it was an exceptionally chilly night for November in Texas, grew lively with warmth and excitement. It had been a long evening, from the moment—was it just a few hours ago?—when Bush's supporters were in despair after losing Florida, Pennsylvania, and Michigan. Meanwhile in Nashville, where the cold rain from Texas was just now arriving, the scene was the complete opposite. The disappointment was palpable, all the more so for having been transformed from the joy that went through this crowd a few hours earlier. The large television screens in front of the War Memorial in Nashville were then turned off.

But this drama was nowhere near being over.

Having watched the network's declaration of Bush's victory, Vice President Gore called Governor Bush and graciously offered his congratulations in what was reported as a brief, but correct and pleasant, conversation. Gore said that he would be making his way shortly from his hotel to the Legislative Plaza, where he would offer his public concession. Governor Bush began to go over his victory comments.

As Vice President Gore's motorcade made its way to the plaza, the television anchors proceeded with their soothing narrative. They were now clearly more relaxed with everything in the studio once again under control, even as they felt compelled, with a great deal of relief, to mention the turbulence earlier in the evening. As the various pundits, commentators, and anchors continued on, Bush's vote margin in Florida, displayed on the boards behind the anchor desks, began to shrink dramatically. Some took note of this fact in passing, as if it were a small curiosity. It was inconceivable that their system for calling elections could fail a second time. But suddenly, when the margin fell beneath 6,000 votes, the actual vote totals could not be ignored.

Meanwhile back in the real world, frantic calls were placed from Gore supporters in Florida to his headquarters, and then from his headquarters to the motorcade, trying to get the message through to the vice president not to go ahead with a public concession. On arriving at the plaza and learning of the closeness of the vote, a decision was made to wait. Shortly thereafter, the vice president made a second call to Governor Bush, which from all accounts lacked the cordiality of the first one. It included Al Gore's "You don't have to get snippy about this" rebuke that evidently came in response to Mr. Bush's incredulous "Let me make sure I understand, you are calling to retract your concession?" And to the governor's assurance that Florida's governor had him ahead, the vice president evidently had the chilly response, "Let me explain something, your younger brother is not the ultimate authority on this." Whatever the two men said to each other, it was certainly fully understandable under the tensions of the moment. A month later, when George W. Bush was trying to be conciliatory to Gore, he responded to a question of whether he had been "snippy" on the telephone: "We don't use that word too often down here in Texas. So I'm not exactly sure what that means, but if he meant abrupt, I was abrupt. I wasn't, you know, I wasn't warm and fuzzy on the telephone, let me put it to you that way."[15]

For the second time that night, the networks now had to retract their Florida call. George Bush had been president-elect, at least so far as the networks were concerned, for about two hours. Unlike the first miscall, this one could have no material effect on the balloting, as the voting was over. But it did create a clear disadvantage for Vice President Gore. No one could erase the "fact" that George W. Bush had been declared president-elect, complete with new graphics, music, and two hours of pundits lauding his campaign strategy. It was thereafter Vice President Gore who was in a position of reversing the presumption. True enough, George Bush was ahead in the counting of the ballots in Florida, and this result was—and would have to be—the most important material fact. But with a lead this narrow, nobody could have expected the vice president to forgo the automatic recount to which he was entitled under Florida law, and no one would have expected that he should concede until that recount had taken place. The only "real" story, then, was that no definitive result had yet occurred. The networks' call helped to set in motion a different story, where one candidate (Gore) now seemed to have to go further to change a "result," while the other (Bush) was pushed into an awkward position of groveling for the office that had been "awarded" to him.

At just about this point, as if to relieve momentarily the gathering tension, another singular event, unrelated to the main drama, intruded itself. All night long, George Bush had been ahead in the national popular vote, even as he trailed at times in the electoral vote. This result corresponded to a scenario that had been widely discussed before the election: a race that would be close enough to enable Al Gore to win the electoral vote while losing the popular. Gore, in fact, had been queried on this matter in a number of television interviews. Very few thought that the race could ever turn out the other way, with Bush losing the popular vote but winning the presidency. Yet now, with the returns from California coming in, Al Gore for the first time pulled ahead in the national popular vote, and it was a safe bet that he would remain so. If Bush were to win the presidency, he would be the one, strangely enough, to be the "minority" president. Commentators took note of this striking fact, important politically because the Democrats would by the next day begin to use it to Gore's advantage. But its significance for the moment paled next to the outcome of the real drama.

Having now "unconceded," Al Gore returned to his hotel room reportedly to go to sleep. The emotional swings of what remained of the two crowds were on the surface a near reversal of what had taken place a couple of hours earlier: in Gore's camp, renewed hope and chants of "recount, recount"; in Bush's camp, frustration. Probably a fairer description of the scenes was that partisans on both sides were more dazed than energized. There had been one twist of fortune too many. Instead of the vice president arriving to deliver his concession, it was William Daley,

Gore's campaign chairman, who appeared before the crowd. Daley made clear that the election was not over, and that "until the results, the recount, is concluded and the results of Florida become official, our campaign continues." An hour later Donald L. Evans briefly addressed the few remaining Bush supporters, "We hope and believe we have elected the next president of the United States."

What had begun was another phase of the 2000 race, a postelection campaign that would last five more weeks and that would be filled with as many ups and downs as the melodrama of election eve.

Notes

1. This excludes the election of 1800, when Jefferson and Burr tied. The nation operated then under a different system of electoral vote counting under which each elector had two votes for the presidency. The change to a single vote for each elector for president came with the Twelfth Amendment, ratified in 1804, which was a direct response to the problems with the system revealed in 1800.

2. The next three closest elections were 1876 with a score of 0.955, 1916 with a score of 0.939, and 1880 with a score of 0.921. The formula for creating the "closeness index" is Index Value = 1 − [(positive percent difference between the two largest parties in the House) + (positive percent difference between the two largest parties in the Senate) + (positive percent difference between the two largest parties in the Electoral College) ÷ 3].

3. *The Federalist Papers*, number 68.

4. Almost a third of those who voted for Al Gore refused in the aftermath to accept George Bush as the legitimate president, and the Democratic House Minority Leader, Richard Gephardt, would only sidestep questions on this issue (Gallup poll of Dec. 18, 2000).

5. Cited in Congressional Quarterly's *Guide to U.S. Elections* (Washington, D.C.: Congressional Quarterly Press, 1975), p. 209.

6. Paul Allen Beck, "The Changing American Party Coalitions" in *The State of the Parties*, John Green and Daniel Shea (Lanham, Md.: Rowman & Littlefield, 1999), p. 28.

7. James Ceaser and Andrew Busch, *Upside Down and Inside Out: The 1992 Elections and American Politics* (Lanham, Md.: Rowman & Littlefield, 1993), and *Losing to Win: The 1996 Elections and American Politics* (Lanham, Md.: Rowman & Littlefield, 1997).

8. These themes have been developed in depth and traced back over the whole postwar period by Byron Shafer, most succinctly in "The Partisan Legacy" in *The Clinton Legacy*, ed. Colin Campbell and Bert Rockman (New York: Seven Bridges Press, 1999).

9. Legislatures total only 49 because Nebraska has a nonpartisan and unicameral sytem.

10. The Comprehensive Index of Competition measures the relative performance of the Republican and Democratic Parties for major constitutional and state offices. It is measured biennially and takes into account party performance for the presidency, governor, Congress, and the state legislature. The index counts state and federal offices equally and legislative and executive offices equally (25 percent of the average derives from the presidential vote in a state, 25 percent from the gubernatorial vote, 25 percent from the congressional vote in a state, and 25 percent from the seat allotment in the state legislature). The index expressed as an equation is

Comprehensive Index for (X) State in (Y) year for (Z) party = [(party Z's two-party presidential vote in the most recent election) * 0.25] + [(average two-party percentage for party Z in the two previous U.S. Senate races) * 0.125] + [(two-party percentage of the cumulative raw vote for party Z for each U.S. House district in the state) * 0.125] + [(two-party percentage of the vote for party Z in the previous gubernatorial race in the state) * 0.25] + [(two-party percentage of party Z's seats in the State Senate) * 0.125] + [(two-party percentage of party Z's seats in the State House) * 0.125].

From the values obtained from each state, a national average of competition, weighted to the state's proportional share of the electoral vote (roughly population) is then constructed, and the state totals are then added to arrive at a national measure of competition that reflects the values of the states in national politics. The national weighted average of index scores does not include the District of Columbia. If it were factored in, the differences in party scores in 2000 would become even closer than the miniscule 0.8 percentage point difference—perhaps even closing the gap to a almost perfect 50–50 tie in competition.

11. For Washington Post, "Race Too Close to Call," Nov. 7, 2000, A17. For CBS, http://cbsnews.com/now/story/0,1597,247530-412,00.html. For Zogby, http://zogby.com. For Gallup, http://gallup.com.

12. Sandy Grady, "Winners and Losers of Y2K, and a Semi-Good-bye," *Houston Chronicle*, Jan. 1, 2001, A35.

13. It was also used as a material fact in at least one of the myriad lawsuits that were brought in Florida courts.

14. Glen Johnson, and Anne E. Kornblut, "A Night of Highs and Lows for Gore and Bush," *Boston Globe*, Nov. 9, 2000, D1.

15. "Contesting the Vote," *New York Times*, Dec. 6, 2000, A27.

Chapter One

The Politics of the Perfect Tie

The 2000 election was unusual, even unprecedented, in that all three of the elected national institutions—the presidency, the House, and the Senate—were considered to be "in play" for both parties during the campaign. No other general campaign in modern American history has offered this range of choice. Any one of the eight logical partisan combinations for organizing the governing institutions was a genuine option. (For those who have never before bothered to consider these combinations, they are a Republican President with a Republican House and a Republican Senate or RRR; RRD; RDR; RDD; DDD; DRD; DDR; and DRR.)

The election results only confirmed that any of these combinations was possible. The outcome for each contest could just as easily have gone to the other party. The presidency was decided by a chad, the Senate ended with a tie, and the House left the two parties only a few seats apart. If there was any deviation from the most commonly expected results, it was in a reversal of the expectations for the Democrats' performance in the elections for the two houses of Congress. The results in the House of Representatives were a bit of a disappointment for Democrats. The 2000 election was the third contest since the Republican revolution of 1994, and in each one the Democrats chipped away at the Republican majority. The Democrats gained nine seats in 1996, five seats in 1998, but only two in 2000, falling short of their strong hopes of winning a majority. The Senate outcome moved in the other direction, with Democrats doing very well, picking up a net of four seats. This result overcame part of the huge Republican surge of 1994, when the Republicans gained eleven seats. Three Republican incumbents from that class—Spencer Abraham of Michigan, Rod Grams of Minnesota, and John Ashcroft of Missouri—went down in defeat.

There was also something almost uncanny in the *way* the Senate result paralleled what was happening in the presidential election. On election night two of the networks called the race in the state of Washington for the Democrat, Maria Cantwell, which meant a 50-50 division in the Senate. But by morning, they withdrew the call, and in the actual counting of ballots, the Republican incumbent, Slade Gorton, was in the lead, and remained so for nearly two weeks. Finally, as the post-presidential contest in Florida was entering its third week, Maria Cantwell took the lead for good and, following a mandatory recount, was awarded the seat by a 2,229-vote margin—a veritable landslide in comparison to the presidential contest in Florida.

Although a single partisan majority was attainable for all three institutions, voters showed little sign during the campaign that they were ready to give, in one fell swoop, one party a single national majority. Political professionals, of course, were intensely aware of the stakes involved. The national parties and various special interest groups and labor unions waged huge and impressive efforts to either hold on to or win majorities in both houses. Large sums of money were raised and organizational support created by the parties and by supporting partisan groups, and poured into competitive House and Senate races. But the professionals' obsession with national majorities was never quite matched by the public. Individual voters both denationalized and separated congressional races from the presidential contest. There was no galvanizing theme running across all competitive districts like there was in 1994 and 1998. The presidential and congressional contests took place in remarkable isolation from each other. In the press in 2000, the term "coattails" turned up more often in occasional references to outmoded fashions in formal clothing than it did in reference to political contests.

This separation of the presidential and congressional races resulted in part from a strategic choice by both candidates. Neither one, especially George W. Bush who was running from "outside" of Washington and who offered himself as a pragmatic candidate from the gubernatorial wing of his party, wanted to tie himself too closely to the congressional wing of his party. The separation was strikingly illustrated in the candidates' convention speeches, in which neither man asked for a party majority in Congress or used his party label to rally a national majority.[1] To be fair, the presidential candidates did not totally run away from their congressional running mates during the campaign. They offered modest support where it was possible. But no national, partisan-related theme was trumpeted simultaneously by the presidential and congressional candidates as it had been in 1992, when Bill Clinton urged voters to vote for him in order to end "gridlock," or in 1996, when Bob Dole's campaign initially urged voters to vote for him in order to "finish the job" begun by the Republican Congress in 1994.[2]

Political conditions in 2000 made it difficult to connect the presidential and congressional races, for the simple reason that no one could know for certain which party would win the majority in any of the contests. The striking point here is that foreknowledge of what party would control which of the institutions has become a major factor influencing voter behavior. This fact really only became apparent in the light of an extraordinary change in voter attitude that began (or was first noticed) during the 1996 election, when a large part of the electorate, it seemed, wished to prevent entrusting all the branches of government to the same political party. Instead of voters beginning with a natural bias of voting for all candidates for national office from the same party, which was the premise of the "party government" or "mandate democracy" theory made so popular by Woodrow Wilson, it now appears that a known majority in one institution might have the widespread effect of repulse voting—denying that party power in another institution. Voters, or a significant portion of them, have recently expressed a positive desire for divided rather than for unitary government. One of the few to take a stab at connecting the presidential and congressional voting in this way in 2000 was Bill Clinton, the master of repulsion politics. In one of his few forays onto the stump for Al Gore, he declared: "I think we're going to win the House and the Senate. But if we don't, someone needs to be doing what I've done for the last six years, which is to stop extremism in Washington, D.C., and you certainly only have one choice—Al Gore."[3] But any such result was nearly impossible for voters to execute in 2000, for with the presidential race in constant doubt, no judgment about congressional control could correspondingly be made.

A political contest in which congressional elections are nationalized and strongly connected to the presidential race is more likely to occur when the Congress itself is prominent in the public mind. Congress certainly held such a position in 1996 when Newt Gingrich, locked in an ongoing personal duel with Bill Clinton, introduced a dramatic nationalizing and polarizing effect into congressional elections. As Sherlock Holmes would insist, the search for the understanding of any election result should begin with a dog-that-did-not-bark explanation. Clearly the Great Dane that did not show in 2000 was Newt Gingrich. While Bill Clinton's shadow still loomed over this election, Newt Gingrich's was largely absent.[4] Republicans as a collective entity in Congress managed to assume a far lower profile than in the elections of 1994, 1996, or 1998, and in the person of Speaker Dennis Hastert, they had clearly found the perfect invisible man.

The one national institution that is not elected, of course, is the Supreme Court. It was nonetheless considered to be every bit as much "in play" in the 2000 elections as were any of the elected institutions. Although majorities on the Court vary from issue to issue, in recent years there has been a fairly consistent conservative and liberal bloc, with a couple of justices swinging between them. Five to four votes, generally favoring the conservatives, have been a frequent occurrence. Not surprisingly, therefore, the future majority on the Court also became an important issue in 2000, and judicial robes rivaled congressional coattails as a direct concern of those interested in presidential politics. As Al Gore pointed out in a speech during the last week of the campaign in Michigan: "The Supreme Court is at stake. There are going to be three, maybe four justices of the Supreme Court appointed by the next president of the United States. That means a majority on the court that will interpret our rights under the Constitution for the next 30 to 40 years."[5] The Court, Gore was saying, would follow the results of the election. Never could he have then imagined, as some later wryly remarked, that it would actually *decide* the results of the election.

The Politics of the Perfect Tie: Governing without a Mandate

Electoral analysts sometimes offer speculation on the meaning of an election for governing, trying to discern the signals voters have sent to politicians about the opportunities and constraints under which they will operate. Usually, however, election results contain enough ambiguity to allow for a number of different interpretations. Political operatives are naturally quick to embrace the version that is most favorable to promoting their party's agenda. Some elections nevertheless have outcomes so clear that even the most adept of political spinners must acknowledge a palpable reality. The Democrats' landslide victory in 1936, which provided a mandate to proceed with the New Deal, is the most striking example.

In its own way, the election of 2000 falls into this same category. It delivered an unambiguous and unmistakable message: that there is no popular mandate of any kind. George W. Bush received nothing more than a key to his office. Neither party could make a plausible claim to be unambiguously in power. The reaction to the election on the part of party leaders was remarkable. Spokespersons of the two parties were strangely subdued, and few on either side even tried to argue for any kind of grand electoral victory. All they laid claim to were the races they had actually won—nothing less, yet also nothing more.

On November 8, 2000, Americans awoke to the realization that the nation had entered a period of political equilibrium characterized by the politics of the Perfect Tie. An analysis of underlying political forces, as noted, could have suggested that parity was *already* in effect before the 2000 election. Since 1994 the electorate had achieved political balance by distributing different majorities among the different institutions. But until 2000 leaders of both parties had some reason to think (or publicly claim) that, except for some temporary and inhibiting factor, their party owned the "real" advantage. In 2000 the party leaders acknowledged that for now neither party is ahead. Obviously, this situation does not mean that the party leaders will cease combat. Rather, each side will be looking, as it is supposed to, for ways to break the deadlock.

Political leaders today are adjusting to this unusual situation of politics without a mandate. Alexis de Tocqueville once remarked that a presidential election is just as important for showing which doctrines hold the majority as for putting into office someone who will work to put those doctrines into effect.[6] Elections carry a kind of moral authority in a democratic society, settling for the moment which views are on top and arguably "right." This natural effect of democratic elections was elevated into an extraconstitutional theory of governance by (among others) Woodrow Wilson, who sought to derive additional governing legitimacy from mandates expressed (or more often discovered) in the election results. But in this election neither side can claim that authority, and both parties seemed almost humbled by the realization that neither one has been able to win an outright majority (more than 50 percent) of the votes cast in a presidential election since 1988. Far from constituting a crisis, however, this situation may offer some new possibilities for governance. With politicians operating without the overhang of any claim to a mandate, they are free to consider patterns of conduct unrelated to an extraconstitutional source of authority. Depending on what techniques and tone President Bush adopts, he could reintroduce institutional models, both for the presidency and for dealing with Congress, that have a closer affinity to the spirit of constitutional government.

The politics of the Perfect Tie take place, paradoxically, under a situation of unitary government, with each branch scheduled to be in the hands of the Republicans. This situation represents, in one sense, a high watermark of Republican influence in the past half-century. Since 1954, all the other basic combinations of partisan arrangements have been tried except for a Democratic president with one house of Congress Republican, and this one (see table 1.1). But while unitary government describes the formal situation of the national government, it does not capture the reality. Republicans clearly have no reason to apologize for their precarious "control" of the government, but the truth is that the results of 2000 have nothing in common with the other moments of achieving unitary government (1964, 1976, and 1992), when at a minimum a claim of a "party" victory could plausibly be entertained. In

Table 1.1.   Years of Various Partisan Divisions: 1954–2000

Type	Number of Years	Years Listed
Unified Democratic Control	14	1960–1968; 1976–1980; 1992–1994
Democratic President and One House of Congress Republican	0	
Democratic President and Two Houses of Congress Republican	6	1994–2000
Unified Republican Control	0	
Republican President and One House of Congress Democratic	6	1980–1986
Republican President and Two Houses of Congress Democratic	20	1954–1960; 1968–1976; 1986–1992

2000, the Republicans took control of the government after losing seats in both houses of Congress and losing the popular vote for president.

How much the Republican Party will actually be judged by the public to be running the country over the next two years is an interesting question. Robert Samuelson best stated the conventional wisdom when he observed, "Bush and the Republicans will have enough power to be blamed for anything that goes wrong—but not enough to accomplish much."[7] It is traditional, in any case, for the president's party to be held accountable in midterm congressional elections, regardless of whether or not it is in the majority. But there is reason now to wonder how much the traditional rules for parceling out party credit and blame in elections still hold in American politics, especially when so many voters have begun to question the idea of mandate democracy.

Electoral analysis also often tries to place too much significance on the role of election results on the ability to govern. Other factors affecting the political context soon come into play that have had equal, if not greater, influence. The skill (or the lack thereof) that a president displays in office, and the impact of major national and world events, for example, can affect the power and energy of the executive. Extrapolating power relationships between the branches of government from election results therefore represents at best a crude attempt to understand some of the possibilities for governance for the next two years. At this point, analysts have outlined three different scenarios or models.

One scenario foresees a period of intense and open partisan contestation in which the Democrats, acting as the out party, find it in their interest to obstruct major governmental action, appealing to public opinion for vindication in the next election. The general idea is that if little by way of legislation is accomplished, it will rebound to the benefit of the out party. Obstruction would, of course, be concealed under claims that the president was not offering bipartisan proposals, a definition the Democratic leadership would solely define. This strategy might also encourage questioning of the legitimacy of the Bush presidency, which in turn would lend further justification to an "outside" appeal to the people in a political referendum in 2002. This approach would parallel the tactics pursued by followers of Andrew Jackson during John Quincy Adams's presidency and by some Democrats in the aftermath of the disputed election of Rutherford B. Hayes in 1876.

A second scenario envisages a substantial degree of bipartisan cooperation and legislative action. President Bush would work largely with and through the established congressional leadership of the parties, negotiating in particular with the official leaders of the opposition, who would be recognized to speak for their party. Democrats would cooperate based on a calculation that voters are not in a mood to condone partisanship and would penalize either party if it were perceived as too obstructionist. Faced with this kind of uncertainty, Democrats might think that they have as much to gain as Republicans by a record of legislative accomplishment for which they could claim equal credit.

A third scenario foresees "underpartisan" coalitions that accomplish modest legislative action through a series of majorities composed largely of Republicans and different Democrats, depending on the bill being debated. The president would deal here through individual members of Congress, especially certain sympathetic Democrats, rather than through the Democratic Party leadership. This scenario reminds us that although everyone in Congress is a member of a party, in fact much of the action in Congress follows from individuals considering the interests of their own constituencies and their own particular electoral situation. Different coalitions can be forged on different issues, often taking place underneath the official party leadership. Bill Clinton employed this strategy after 1996, often securing the backing of "pressured" Republicans from constituencies where the president had strong support. Similarly, Bush may look to the example of Ronald Reagan, who won passage of his tax and spending plans in 1981 with this kind of approach.

Interpreting Presidential Campaigns

Most of the political postmortems on the presidential election, after acknowledging that the race ended in a virtual tie, focused on why the candidate who "should have won" actually did not. Nearly all of these accounts bestowed this dubious honor of losing a sure-win on Al Gore. According to one Democrat: "Everything was going for Gore—a great economy with no desire for change, a weak Republican opponent. This is the worst presidential campaign that I have seen in my lifetime. It's the candidate. He's horrible. How could he lose Tennessee? How could he lose West Virginia?"[8] A leading columnist reported, "Democrats are furious at him for blowing an election that, given the peace and prosperity and domestic tranquility he inherited, Gore should have won by 20 points."[9] Gore in this view stands as the first clear should-have-won loser since Thomas Dewey in 1948.

There was, of course, a dissenting view. It was best presented by Al Gore himself, which by itself is no reason to dismiss it out of hand. In an interview given just before the election Gore pointed out: "Well, we started out 20 points behind, and it's close because it's taken us all year to make up that 20-point gap."[10] Gore had, in fact, trailed George W. Bush by 19 points in the January 13, 2000, Gallup poll, and by 16 points in the Gallup poll taken after the Republican National Convention in August. While Gore's critics might insist that his initial deficit had something to do with the candidate himself, this certainly was not what Gore had in mind. His point was rather that the 2000 race was not really so favorable for Democrats—due to an obvious reason that Gore, out of civility, chose not to mention in public.

For the moment let us set aside Al Gore and consider the general concept that is being employed here in the study of elections. Central to most journalistic and scholarly treatments of presidential campaigns is a notion that there is a candidate who "should win." Actually, going back further in the chain of reasoning, there is a notion that a certain *party's* candidate "should win," whomever he may be. This idea is expressed in such diverse phrases as it is X's "election to lose," that the "fundamentals" favor X, or that X is "running downhill" (as opposed to the underdog's "running uphill"). The importance of this a priori assumption cannot be overemphasized. Adopting it means that the story of a campaign virtually writes itself. If the candidate of party X "should win" but is unfortunate enough not to do so, there must be something dramatically wrong either with the candidate himself (he was unlikable, boring, arrogant, etc.) or with his strategy of the campaign (it changed courses too often, it stressed the wrong themes, etc.) or with both.

What is the basis for making such an assumption in the first place? The core, it seems, is a rule-of-thumb judgment about the prevailing conditions in the country and how these conditions favor (or hurt) an incumbent or an incumbent's party. Prosperity, peace, and domestic tranquility (mentioned in the quotes cited above) are obvious components of good conditions. Good conditions mean that people will be inclined to vote for the incumbent party. This view is echoed by an academic theory of voting known as retrospective voting. It holds that when things are going well, voters will stick with the same party, whether because they wish to reward that party or because they calculate that good conditions are more likely to continue if that party remains in power (and that, correspondingly, a change of parties might endanger these conditions). A similar notion lies behind the many mathematical models that have been developed by political scientists to predict the final results and that received so much attention in the press in 2000. Although many hard-core modelers dismiss a concern for intuitive ideas of causal explanation as irrelevant, preferring to focus on what is found to work, these models nonetheless constitute mechanical efforts to quantify the basic idea of retrospective voting. The models select, in the words of Larry Bartels, "the most crucial factors influencing the outcome of presidential elections: the state of the country and the state of the economy."[11] An equation is then developed to predict the share of the popular vote a candidate should receive. In the estimates of all of the major academic models that were run in 2000, Al Gore was the computer's clear choice, with an expected victory margin varying between 4 and 20 points.[12]

But of course Al Gore did not win the election (although he did receive more votes than George W. Bush). Gore's defiance of these theories leaves two responses to this approach. The first, which is the way that has been discussed up to now, is to accept the validity of the rule-of-thumb reasoning and the models and then proceed to locate the inevitable and massive faults in the loser's (Gore's) campaign to explain why he did not perform as expected. The other is to question the adequacy of the rule-of-thumb reasoning and the models in general, or at least in this case, on the grounds that they may have wrongly specified certain things or that they missed other particular aspects of this election.

Most political operatives, as already observed, followed the first path, in the timeworn political tradition of faulting the defeated candidate, and not themselves. Joining them as members of this Blame Al Gore (BAG) school were many political science modelers, who, it seems, have a professional interest in supporting this view. In a social scientific version of shoot the messenger, they conclude that because the models are right, the candidate must be wrong. According to Michael Lewis Beck, "One reason why the model didn't work this time is that Gore didn't engage in the behavior that is implicit in the model functioning properly, which is to make the link between himself and the leader of the party."[13] Helmut Norpoth concurred, arguing that Gore committed the sin of "not running a campaign consistent with the model."[14] Although the models themselves do not specify anything about the content of campaign strategy—indeed, some have gone so far as to argue that campaigns do not matter to election outcomes—we now learn that campaigns can be decisive and that the models have all along implicitly held the key to how to wage an effective one.

A large number of political analysts, by contrast, have raised questions about the adequacy of the rule-of-thumb approach.[15] Especially during the summer, when George W. Bush had a large lead in the polls, many tried to explain this fact by arguing that a fundamental change of the political and economic context had taken place, such that the conditions of prosperity in 2000 did not help the incumbent party in the same degree as it had in the past. Among the reasons cited were that the current prosperity had gone on for so long that the public now took it for granted; that Americans were crediting prosperity to the activity of entrepreneurs in a dynamic economy and not to the government; that the strength of the economy, to the extent government policies were involved, was due to decisions made by Alan Greenspan; and that credit for economic performance should go as much to Republicans as to Democrats, as power had been shared for the past six years.[16]

Another line of argument was that rule-of-thumb reasoning, while correct as far as it went, missed a crucial aspect of the situation in 2000: a concern for the moral state of the nation as embodied in Bill Clinton's presidency. While voters do indeed reward the party that brings good conditions, what constitutes good conditions is not exhausted solely by prosperity and peace. In 2000, morality was another huge factor. If not any Democrat, then any Democratic vice president, especially one as loyal as Al Gore, would have faced the burden of Clinton's negatives. Perhaps this was the background Al Gore had in mind when he spoke of beginning the race from 20 points behind.

In the degree that either of these arguments questioning the validity of rule-of-thumb reasoning is given weight, the view that Al Gore "should have won" is weakened and his responsibility for losing mitigated by the above statement. Any kind of in-depth analysis of the 2000 campaign must, obviously, come to terms with the theoretical issue involved in the "should win" thesis. The position we adopt in this book is nuanced. Because so much rides on an initial assumption, it seems unwise to allow it to carry too much weight unless one can be almost certain of its accuracy.

This is not the case here. At the same time, it is impossible—and it would be highly artificial—to avoid making a judgment of some kind about political conditions operating during an election year. Our own reading of the evidence is that Al Gore should be considered the favored candidate, although to a much smaller extent than proponents of the BAG school so casually contend. But given our own doubts, we plan to invoke this assumption with caution and use it only sparingly.

Our assessment of the race is that Al Gore did indeed lose it in the campaign and because of the campaign. This is a conclusion that is based not on a deduction from an a priori premise, but on an examination of the events themselves. George W. Bush ran the better campaign. Or, if this sounds too admiring, Al Gore ran the poorer one. At the end of the day, in a race that either man could have won, Al Gore made more mistakes that had a negative influence on the outcome for him, even as he almost balanced these out by some bold—and successful—moves. It hardly stirs controversy to assert that George W. Bush was neither a scintillating campaigner nor a charismatic figure. But Bush and his campaign team—which, in striking contrast to Gore's, remained intact over the entire campaign period—developed a sound strategy for winning the 2000 election and then executed it with great steadiness. Bush's campaign, while certainly not flawless, made a minimum of mistakes, or at least fewer mistakes than his opponent. The Bush campaign did not seek to be flashy or bold, but surefooted and steady. If some wars, especially wars of attrition, are won by those who make the fewest errors, then there is much positive to be said for the Bush campaign of 2000.

What Decided the 2000 Presidential Campaign

One of the first great interpreters of American elections, Lord James Bryce, began his treatment of voting behavior with a simple question: "Upon what does a presidential election turn?" He answered by specifying two general categories: personal qualities (what we refer to as "persona") and political professions ("issues and ideology").[17] Our study of campaigns has suggested the need for a third category, national mood, that takes into account broad and, sometimes, vague currents running through the electorate, such as a hostility to "insiders" (as was so prominent in 1992) or a desire for "reform." Moods are different from—although they can overlap with—ideology and issues.

The outcome of the 2000 presidential race, which was a virtual tie, can be described and accounted for by the balances and offsetting advantages between the two candidates among these three categories. Measurements in these matters are far from exact. Yet it appears that for the category of national mood, where one category (the nation being on the right track) worked for Gore, and the other category (a concern over political dishonesty) worked for Bush, Gore had the slight advantage. The category of issues and ideology was also split, with Gore having the advantage on issues, and Bush on ideology—with perhaps a slight over-all edge going to Bush. Judgments of persona favored Bush. Neither candidate, then—obviously—dominated the race. The analysis of these categories shows why.

During the 2000 campaign, three different national moods had an important effect on the vote (see table 1.2). The first was a feeling that conditions in the country were good, and that the nation was on the right track in matters generally, and on economic matters specifically. More than two-thirds of the voters (65%) judged the nation to be "on the right track."[18] As conventional deductions from the retrospective theory of voting indicate, this mood worked to Al Gore's benefit, both in his primary campaign against Bill Bradley, where Gore was from the incumbent administration, and in the final election campaign against George W. Bush, where Gore was from the incumbent party. Gore received the strong, though not over-whelming, support of six in ten of the "right track" respondents. True enough, Gore offered to give away this advantage in his convention speech ("I'm not asking you to vote for me on the basis of the economy we have"), but that offer was never as generous as it seemed. It was intended to put some distance between himself and Bill Clinton. All along, Gore argued

Table 1.2.   2000 Exit Poll Data on National Moods

Question	All Voters	Vote of Those Giving Positive Answers	Vote of Those Giving Negative Answers
Is the Country on the Right or Wrong Track?	65% Right Track 31% Wrong Track	61% Gore 36% Bush 2% Nader	36% Bush 74% Bush 4% Nader
Is the Country on the Right or Wrong Moral Track?	39% Right Track 57% Wrong Track	70% Gore 27% Bush 2% Nader	33% Gore 62% Bush 3% Nader
What is Your Opinion of Bill Clinton as a Person?	36% Favorable 60% Unfavorable	83% Gore 13% Bush 2% Nader	26% Gore 70% Bush 3% Nader

Source: 2000 VNS Exit Poll.

that George W. Bush's policies, in particular his tax cut, would endanger the economy. And Gore closed the race with a crescendo appeal to the right-track mood: "Prosperity is on the ballot." How much of the vote Al Gore lost by not pushing this theme more explicitly during the whole campaign is a matter that will long be debated.

But this element of the national mood was not completely hostile to George W. Bush.[19] Bush worked to position himself as a moderate, not one inclined to pursue radical measures that would endanger prosperity. As a governor of a large state, he claimed—in conjunction with other Republican governors who were his strongest supporters—to be a competent manager of economic affairs and deserving of some of the credit for many of the policy successes the nation was enjoying. Bush's overall position was designed to assure those who felt things were going well on practical matters that they could vote for him without endangering this sense of well-being.[20] In addition, Bush cleverly managed to inoculate himself from the phrase "risky scheme" in a humorous part of his own convention speech. Gore stuck with the substance, but he was forced to abandon the specific charge.

The second mood having an important effect in the 2000 campaign was a feeling that the nation was on the wrong moral track. For many this mood centered on the Clinton administration—on its lawlessness, dishonesty, spin politics, and disrespect for the "forms" or character of the presidential office. Nearly 60 percent of the voters considered the nation to be going in the wrong direction in regard to the moral condition of the country, and about half judged the Clinton scandals to be important. This mood tracked opinion that had developed during the Clinton impeachment proceedings in 1998 and 1999. But it was broader this time, as no wrenching or extreme measures were involved. Capitalizing on this discontented moral mood was a central part of Bush's campaign. It was also intended to dovetail with other subthemes having some resonance, including the wish to elect someone from outside of Washington who had not been part of the bitter personal warfare of the past years so as to offer a fresh start.

In order for this appeal to the moral mood to be effective, Bush had to make sure, first, that he did not push anti-Clintonism too far and appear to be vindictive. Provoking the reaction of anti-anti-Clintonism had been the Republicans' clear mistake at least twice before (in 1995 and 1998), and each time Bill Clinton made it the springboard for a remarkable personal comeback. Anti-Clintonism was a sentiment that had to be allowed to grow largely on its own, gently cultivated, but never killed by supplying too much fertilizer. Of all of the Republican politicians in America, George W. Bush came closest to finding just the right tone in this matter. He was

suggestive of the problems, but did not appear to be too harsh in his con-
demnations. Bush's positive appeal was encapsulated in the "oath of office" peroration of his campaign speeches, in which he proclaimed, "So
when I put my hand on the Bible, I will swear to not only uphold the laws
of our land, I will swear to uphold the honor and dignity of the office to
which I have been elected, so help me God." If there was any problem in
this appeal, it may only have been that, in a campaign so long, a constant
repetition of the same message grew a bit wearisome.

Next, Bush had to ensure that his own integrity did not come seriously
into question. Nothing can precipitate a harder or quicker fall than an ac-
cuser who is guilty of sins of his own. Integrity or honesty necessarily became, so to speak, the coin of the realm for Bush. Bush, overall, managed
to convey a picture of integrity. No doubt this was slightly compromised
in the last week of the campaign with the "surprise" revelation of a Driving Under the Influence arrest many years before that Bush had tried to
keep secret. Although arguably minor—that was Bush's argument—it
might have raised just enough questions at just the right moment to have
an impact. Of course, almost any unpleasant incident in 2000, no matter
how minor, could be said to have made the difference.

Finally, Bush had to be able to connect Al Gore to the mood of concern
about the moral condition of the country. Before the party conventions, the
link between Clinton and Gore seemed almost to form on its own accord.
As number two in the administration, Gore was by definition bound to the
president. Yet it went beyond definition. Their connection had been sealed,
as it were, in blood, by Gore's own campaign finance problems, still lingering on Clinton's behalf from the 1996 campaign. It was affirmed by
Gore's enthusiastic profession of fealty and admiration on the White
House lawn following Clinton's impeachment and it was then put on ex-
hibit in Gore's political campaign against Bill Bradley, where Gore was
widely accused of displaying the substance of Clintonism without any of
its style. Republicans at their convention made clear that the connection of
Clinton to Gore held one of the keys to their success. In the words of Dick
Cheney's acceptance speech: "Mr. Gore will try to separate himself from
his leader's shadow. But somehow we will never see one without thinking
of the other."

The greatest shock to the Bush campaign—and the greatest tactical
achievement of the Gore campaign—came in August, when Gore almost
managed to sever the connection. He did so in a brilliant three-step strategy of first choosing a vice presidential candidate, Joe Lieberman, who
had condemned Clinton; then embracing a populist-style campaign that
broke from Clinton's New Democratic orthodoxy; and finally planting an

eternal kiss on Tipper, showing that alpha-male sexuality could be tied to marital fidelity. To make his declaration of independence more explicit still, Gore proclaimed in his convention speech: "I stand here tonight as my own man, and I want you to know me for who I truly am." The sudden and stunning success of this strategy left the Bush campaign discomfited, tilting futilely at Bill Clinton when the real opposition candidate was now Al Gore. Bush was only able to recover the use of the anti-Clinton theme when, in October, Gore provided grounds for reforging the connection.

Perhaps the best indicator of the strength of this moral mood in the campaign was to be found in the strategy adopted by the Gore campaign. Gore barely used Bill Clinton, seeking for the most part to keep him, against his will, in a closet under lock and key. A good deal of Gore's campaign, including not just matters of image and style but even of basic content, was influenced, if not dictated, by Gore's judgment of his need to escape his "shadow." To be sure, as many from the BAG school insist, it can be said that Gore erred in this judgment and did not make a close enough connection with Clinton or use him enough in the campaign. Yet few have demonstrated how Gore could have won all of the supposed benefits of making the link between himself and Clinton without suffering any of the penalties. As Thomas Mann of the Brookings Institution wrote, "The evidence was overwhelming that Clinton would have done more harm than good with swing voters in battleground states." [21]

The final national mood that played a role in 2000, especially during the contest for the party nominations, was a desire for "reform." Insofar as this mood invoked a desire for integrity and a need to break from the prevailing climate of bitter partisanship, it overlapped with the mood for putting the nation on the right moral track. But "reform" as used in the context of the 2000 race, in the sense in which it was championed by John McCain and Bill Bradley, had a more distinct focus. It emphasized the themes of honesty and integrity as they were to be manifested by a kind of politics that promised to eliminate the influence of money and special interests on the political system and that promised to revitalize the political order by changes in political procedures. The central issue, and chief symbol, of this mood was campaign finance reform.

As party establishment candidates who had raised huge sums of money for their campaigns, neither Bush nor Gore was in a strong position to tap the reform mood. Bush never made much pretence of trying. After losing to John McCain in the New Hampshire primary, he took a stab at offering himself as a "reformer with results." But procedural issues were never really at the core of even this rhetorical foray. Reform for Bush was always related more to changes in policy areas such as education and social security. Bush then passed up any idea of opening a reform dimension to his final election campaign when he decided not to ask John McCain to be his running mate. Although Al Gore, plagued by charges of campaign finance irregularities stemming from the 1996 campaign, tried early on to appeal to this reformist mood by vigorously supporting campaign finance reform, he could never make headway as a plausible crusader for the cause. As such, his references to it grew fewer and more perfunctory as the campaign went on.

How broad the mood of reform actually was, or might have become, in the final election campaign remains an open question. Only one of the candidates, the Green Party nominee Ralph Nader, could lay serious claim to the reform mantle. Nader made the issue of the influence of money on politics a central theme of his campaign, and it struck a chord with a part of the electorate, although his appeal was limited by his third-party status and by other parts of his program.[22] Otherwise the reform sentiment went largely untapped, with those potentially concerned with this theme having to make their choice on other grounds.

A second category of voter decision making is the electorate's assessment of the candidates' personae (see table 1.3). Persona is sometimes discussed in terms of mere "personality" traits, and there were certainly more than enough efforts expended by both camps in 2000 to display each candidate's warm and fuzzy qualities. In keeping with the era of intimacy and informality inaugurated by Bill Clinton, Bush and Gore both hit the talk-show circuit, including appearances on the Oprah Winfrey and Regis Philbin shows. Bush had the chance to show off his highly touted qualities of charm and likability, while Gore had the opportunity to put to rest—sometimes by deadpanning—his reputation for being wooden, boring, and arrogant. All and all, both candidates spent a good

Table 1.3.   2000 Exit Poll Data on Candidate Persona

Question	All Voters
Will Gore Say Anything to Become President?	74% Yes
	24% No
Will Bush Say Anything to Become President?	58% Yes
	40% No
Does Gore Know Enough to Be President?	67% Yes
	30% No
Does Bush Know Enough to Be President?	54% Yes
	44% No

Source: 2000 VNS Exit Poll.

deal of time on these types of shows in order to court voters, especially the large number of undecided women.

There is no doubt that these personality issues played some role in the voters' decision. But the more important assessment of persona concerned serious questions about the candidates' qualifications and temperaments, even if these were sometimes raised and discussed only in crude or frivolous ways. A remarkable facet of the 2000 race was the emergence very early on of a consensus about the matters of qualification and temperament that each candidate held. This consensus sprang in part from spontaneous reactions to the candidates, which were picked up and crystallized by the media and then hammered away at, as interest dictated, by each of the campaigns. The two images were as follows: Viewed from a perspective favorable to Gore, the great question about George W. Bush was not only whether he had the preparation and experience to be president of the United States, but also if he had the intellectual heft and depth. To put it simply, the basic question was, is George W. Bush just an amiable "empty suit" who had climbed to his position on the strength of being the son of a former president? By contrast, Gore was seen as highly experienced, fully in command of the issues, and as possessing a significant intellect, a conception proven in part by his strong past debate performances.

From the Bush side, the question turned positive entirely on the quality of sincerity (understood in its largest sense as the freedom from dissimulation or duplicity), straightforwardness, and a quality of being centered or grounded as a person. Gore's problem was insincerity, a willingness to do whatever was necessary to become president and an absence of a genuine core to his character. Gore's own advisers, in an internal memo, summarized matters this way: "The Bush campaign's mantra is that Gore will say or do anything it takes to win. This description is effective because it encapsulates the core criticism of Gore in a single, easily repeated sentence."[23] This facet of persona had the additional quality, potentially so dangerous to Gore, of merging with many voters' objections to Clintonism, and evoking the mood of being on the wrong moral track. By contrast with this image, the positive portrayal of George W. Bush was one of being steady, in possession of himself, and centered, both as a person and as a political leader.

The negative characterizations of the two candidates hold the key to the battle over persona in the 2000 election. Each candidate was placed on national probation and asked during the final election campaign to demonstrate to the American people his ability to refrain from displaying his flaws. It was Al Gore who most obviously violated the terms of this probation. It occurred at a time when he was in command of the race, during his

first television debate, when he was caught in a few exaggerations and misstatements and displayed an attitude of arrogance and disrespect toward his
opponent. Immediately his problem of persona came to the foreground
along with the old criticism that the only problem with the Gore campaign
was Gore himself. Alone, this was not enough to turn the tide. But it opened
the door to Bush's other appeals, allowing him once again to make the case
for the need for a change in the tone of the presidency, and enabling him to
restate his position on the issues. It is difficult to say how important the category of persona was relative to the others in deciding the election. The
truth is that these categories are only distinct and independent in the studies of electoral analysts; in actual life they often blend into and evoke each
other in a way that makes separation impossible. But what can be said with
some assurance is that the judgment about Gore's character was decisive at
the margins, and sparked the turning point in the campaign.

A final category of voter behavior consists of positions taken on specific
issues and a general ideological orientation (see table 1.4). These two elements, while obviously interrelated, are also somewhat independent. The
whole is slightly different, and sometimes greater, than the parts. This distinction is nicely captured by an assessment made by Gerald Pomper about
the 1988 presidential race. Pomper says, "On most specific issues,
Dukakis's position won more favor from the voters than [George H. W.]
Bush's, but elections are not public opinion polls on discrete topics. They
are generalized judgments, on men as well as measures."[24]

The core of Al Gore's campaign, by his own reckoning as well as that
of most commentators, was his strong appeal on specific issues. As an antidote to whatever difficulties might ail the Democratic campaign, many in
the party offered the same prescription: "issues, issues, and issues." Gore
was only too pleased to take his medicine. His convention acceptance
speech was advertised in advance to be crammed with "specifics," and it
did not disappoint. Throughout the fall campaign, Gore pounded away
daily on the details of his various plans. And by all accounts Al Gore won
on specific issues. Voters were asked to list their views of the issues of top
priority. Of the top four cited (education, tax cuts, Social Security, and prescription drugs), Gore was the favored candidate among the voters on all
of them except tax cuts. Of course this does not mean that these citizens
voted for Gore or Bush *because* of their stand on these issues. Many of
these voters may have already been disposed to someone's candidacy. And
what is occurring during a campaign is sometimes the reverse of what
seems to be the case. People who decide to vote for a candidate for reasons
other than specific issues then quite naturally tend to adopt the priorities

Table 1.4.   2000 Exit Poll Data on Issues and Ideology

Question	All Voters	Vote of Those Giving Positive Answers
What Is the Top Priority for the Next President?	26% Tax Cut	27% Gore 71% Bush 1% Nader
	11% Prescription Drugs	56% Gore 39% Bush 3% Nader
	30% Education	58% Gore 37% Bush 4% Nader
	23% Social Security	58% Gore 40% Bush 1% Nader
What Is Your Ideology?	20% Liberal 50% Moderate 29% Conservative	
What Is Gore's Position on Issues?	43% Too Liberal 9% Too Conservative 44% About Right	
What Is Bush's Position on Issues?	13% Too Liberal 34% Too Conservative 47% About Right	

Source: 2000 VNS Exit Poll.

and positions of their selected candidate. Indeed, across the board, poll responses on a variety of measures echo what the campaigns are saying. But in this case, and from experience with a number of recent elections, it is clear that some of the issues mentioned were in fact "working" well for Al Gore.

Yet it is just here, on issues, where George W. Bush lost ground to Al Gore, that he may have won the election. The core of Bush's campaign theme of compassionate conservatism was, in its strategic aspect, to take on the Democrats on certain issues where Democrats were known to have the edge. To be sure, the Republicans had "their" major issues — tax cuts and military preparedness — as points of large mass appeal, as well as their smaller items — opposition to gun control and promotion of coal development — underneath the radar screen for specialized appeals, but Bush's campaign was predicated on an acknowledgment that the

traditional way of winning elections—identifying "your" issues and trying to make them prevail in the campaign—would simply not work in
2000.[25] Bush entered the race accepting that the campaign would be
fought in large part on terrain traditionally chosen by Democrats, because these issues were among the ones of greatest concern to the American people. Bush's aim was to win on some of these issues with Republican counterproposals, or, if not to win, then at least to cut down
dramatically on the margins by which Republicans had been losing on
these issues in the recent past. Education, which is the traditional Democratic issue that Bush emphasized the most during the campaign,
serves as the best example of this strategy. Among those who ranked education the most important issue in 2000, Gore won 52 percent of the
voters as opposed to 44 percent for George W. Bush. Compare this to
the results in 1996, when for the same issue Bill Clinton won 82 percent
of the vote against 12 percent for Bob Dole.

Elections are won at the margins, either by building on and increasing
the advantages that one side naturally holds, or by decreasing the advantages on issues held by the other side. In domestic politics over the past
decade, Republicans watched as many of their traditional issues—crime
and welfare, for example—were skillfully neutralized by Democrats,
while many of the Democratic issues—education, Social Security, and
health care—were growing in significance in the public's mind. What
Democrats had managed to do on many of the heavy-load Republican issues, Bush would seek to do on the heavy-load Democratic issues. In a
sense, Bush even went further—no doubt because he had to—by conceding that these issues would be among the most important in the campaign.
Bush fought the election on Democratic territory. He knew that he was going to lose on the issues, but hoped, as turned out to be the case, that he
would lose there by an acceptable margin, while at the same time maintaining the support of the Republican issue voters.

The other element in this category, ideological orientation, locates the
voters' assessment of the candidates' positions in a more general sense. At
the beginning of the year, while the candidates were engaged in their primary races, it was widely expected that the campaign would be between
two candidates who vied for the center of the electorate. Bush was running
to the left of his Republican rivals (until John McCain emerged as his principal opponent), and Al Gore was running a bit to the right of Bill Bradley.
In one sense, this initial expectation was borne out in the end. An analysis
of the two candidates' stands on many of the issues clearly shows that not
only were they not very far apart, but also that they moved closer to each
other over the course of the year. For example, Bush adopted a prescrip-

tion drug program in order to match Gore's plan, and Gore added many features to his education policy that borrowed from Bush's plan. But by the time the fall contest was under way, the campaign became decidedly more ideological in tone than almost anyone had anticipated. George W. Bush was able to draw a clear line between the two candidates in a way that Bush found helpful to his prospects for victory, and that Al Gore, although he had precipitated the division, clearly would have preferred to avoid.

The decisive step was taken by Gore in July. For a number of reasons — a flagging campaign, a plan to quell a surge by Ralph Nader, the need to separate his candidacy from Bill Clinton, and others — Gore launched a more polarizing campaign, opting for a populist style of "fighting for" the little guy against the "powerful interests." Whatever the fine print of Gore's specific issue positions, his general rhetorical posture presented Bush the opportunity to identify Gore as a "Big Government" candidate. Although Gore achieved much by his move to the left in the short term, he could not, as he hoped, gain all of the benefits of this move while avoiding paying any costs. Gore certainly planned to have it both ways; or else — in what amounts to almost the same thing — he planned a two-phase campaign that would start on the populist side and then return to the center. But these plans were foiled by a Bush campaign that raised the stakes of ideological confrontation, driving Gore from the center and not allowing him to ever fully recapture it. While Gore held the clear edge on the issues, Bush captured the advantage on ideology.

A New Republican versus an Old Democrat

Ideology may not always be the principal factor in how citizens decide to vote, but it often has the most important consequences for political life. The ideological orientation of the winning candidate not only influences the direction of governing by the incoming administration, but it can also create ideas and doctrines that define a political party's long-term public philosophy.

With some allowance made for the exaggeration of a slogan, the 2000 presidential race turned out in the end to be one between an Old Democrat and a New Republican. Many analysts contended that what the American people really wanted in 2000 was a continuation of Clinton's policies — actually centrist policies — without Bill Clinton. George W. Bush may have come as close to this formula as Al Gore.

To label Al Gore an Old Democrat requires surveying the recent ideological shifts within the Democratic Party. The pride of Bill Clinton's presidency, and what many have counted as his greatest legacy, was the transformation of the Democratic Party into a more moderate or centrist party, described by the labels of "New Democratic" thinking or of the "Third Way." This legacy, it has been argued, extended well beyond an effect on American politics into a reshaping of leftist politics and parties throughout the West. Tony Blair's transformation of the Labour Party to "New Labour" in Great Britain, Gerhardt Schroeder's change of the SPD to "die Neue Mitte" in Germany, and Ehud Barak's efforts to alter the Labor Party in Israel not only borrowed from "New Democrat" thinking, but also used New Democratic consultants and adopted New Democratic electoral stratagems. Insofar as many have seen these parties as representing the wave of the future, with their ideas and policies being best adapted to a new technological age, many viewed Bill Clinton as the prince of this new era.

This New Democratic legacy was, in some ways, on the ballot in 2000. A victory for Al Gore as a New Democratic candidate—even a victory for Al Gore running a campaign that distanced himself tactically from New Democratic thinking—as well as a victory for the Democrats in the Congress, would have helped to seal the success of the movement. Its status now may be in some trouble, as New Democratic thinking has never managed to capture the hearts of many on the left. Its appeal has been to the head—that it worked, both in winning votes and in solving problems. The longer it could remain in control, the more it would be able to demonstrate that it was the only rational way to govern a modern society from the left. Democrats have now begun the debate over what caused their defeat in the 2000 election: Was it New Democratic ideas, or was it the partial abandonment of New Democratic ideas?

The New Democratic movement began in the 1980s, with the support of many moderate (and southern) Democrats who were reacting against the loss of the presidential contests of 1984 and 1988. These Democrats, mostly elected officials, rejected many of the liberal positions held by the Democratic Party in the 1970s and 1980s, positions that, under the label of "new politics," had thrown overboard a good part of the liberalism of the 1960s. The New Democrats in certain areas were actually returning to some of the older, 1960s, liberal positions. The movement at first was largely an elite affair based on these elected officials' assessment of the need to develop an independent institutional base that could help them formulate and promote moderate ideas. These leaders created the Democratic Leadership Council (DLC), which in turn spawned a network of supporting policy institutes that aimed to redefine the Democratic Party. Functioning after a while as a free-standing entity, the DLC and its intellectual apparatus became a player of its own inside of Democratic Party politics, often finding itself in conflict with elements from labor, women's groups, and the black leadership.[26]

The DLC challenged Democratic orthodoxies in a number of areas. In foreign affairs, where the Democratic Party of the 1970s and 1980s had adopted positions critical of the U.S. military tinged with pacifism, New Democrats sought to reinstitute a more vigorous internationalist posture. They criticized old-style Democrats for being isolationist when it came to employing force, while remaining vaguely internationalist when calling for humanitarian changes and imposing economic sanctions. Democrats in Congress, for example, voted overwhelmingly against the authorization of the use of force in the Gulf War. Foreign affairs, it is true, had little to do with Clinton's 1992 presidential campaign, which focused on the economy like, in Clinton's words, "a laser beam." Clinton's stance on foreign affairs, though vaguely New Democratic, was compromised by his problems with his military service. But once in office, the Clinton administration followed policies that were broadly consistent with New Democratic thinking. Transforming the Democrats' position in the area of foreign affairs was made easier, of course, by the ending of the Cold War just before Clinton assumed office. The dangers attached to the use of military power were greatly reduced, and American military might, after the buildup of the previous decade, enjoyed clear superiority in most theaters. Under these circumstances Democrats could now back their promotion of broad internationalist values with an assertion of American power.

In the area of foreign affairs, Al Gore was clearly and decisively a New Democrat. Indeed, he had been a New Democrat in this arena well before Bill Clinton. Gore had made an unsuccessful run for the presidency in 1988 as a prototype of a New Democratic candidate, where he had taken forceful positions on issues of foreign policy. Gore later became one of only 10 Democratic senators to have voted for the Gulf War. His selection of Joe Lieberman, himself a leading New Democrat spokesperson on issues of foreign affairs and early supporter of the Gulf War, solidified this position. Gore also gave a strong defense of the New Democratic foreign policy thinking in the 2000 presidential debates, to which Bush responded with a more modest, older-style Republican brand of internationalism.

In the area of cultural matters (or "social issues"), New Democrats broke with many of the lenient and expressivist policies that were associated with the liberalism of the 1970s and 1980s. Democrats had seen a large defection of voters to Republicans in previous presidential elections—the so-called Reagan Democrats—because of the party's stand on issues related to the death penalty, welfare, and crime prevention. New Democrats adopted more conservative positions on these issues, and they added a new and appealing theme of promoting "personal responsibility" to support their position. New Democrats did not, however, follow conservative positions across the board. They steered clear where conservative stands had little support among Democratic elites, such as abortion and gun control. Their strategy was, then, to isolate conservatives on cultural matters by arguing that it was the conservative positions that were extreme or out of the mainstream.

The Clinton administration wavered initially on cultural matters, going back and forth between instituting a federal death penalty and supporting a surgeon general who condoned masturbation. But by the end of his first term, especially with his embrace of the welfare reform bill, Clinton was clearly following New Democratic thinking. Yet the president was obviously hampered in delivering a broader thematic message on personal responsibility because of stories about his own conduct and his often too easy relationship with the Hollywood scene. In his second term, the Lewinsky affair along with the president's public deceptions and possible perjury made a mockery of this message. Even though many Democrats decried Clinton's behavior, too many of his friends were excusing him to avoid reigniting a huge cultural conflict. The New Democrats' hopes of returning the party to a more sober position in support of "family values" were dealt a serious blow.

In the area of cultural issues, Al Gore tried to reconnect his campaign with New Democratic thinking. The selection of Joe Lieberman, the voice of New Democrats in cultural matters, was intended to send just this signal. Indeed, some of Lieberman's statements at the outset of the campaign on the role of religion in public life placed him more to the traditional side on this issue than many in the Republican Party, a stance that could have the effect of blunting future Democratic criticisms of the Christian right. Gore continued with New Democratic themes in other areas as well, and to the shock of Europeans from the left, he echoed George W. Bush entirely in Bush's support for the death penalty, even if he seemed to display a bit less conviction. But even with these stands, the difficulty Gore faced in the broad area of the culture question was credibility. Try as he might, Gore was unable to persuade many Americans that the Democrats remained in solidarity with traditional values. His association with Bill Clinton spoke as loudly as his positions, and Lieberman became less helpful as he shifted leftward to Gore.

On the role of government, the Democrats of the 1970s and 1980s were accused by Republicans of favoring "Big Government," a label that quickly became one of general opprobrium. For every social problem, it was said, Democrats believed that there needed to be a corresponding public policy and federal program, not to mention an interest group that depended on a special government benefit. New Democrats never wholly accepted this caricature, but they did call for a more modest role for the federal government and sought to reduce the link between the party and its interest group supporters. Bill Clinton campaigned on this theme in 1992, only to begin by attempting to govern on the old basis of a Big Government agenda. The defeat of his ambitious health care plan followed by the Republicans' huge victory in the 1994 election prompted a shift of positions, at least tactically. Clinton proclaimed that the "era of big government is over" and ran his 1996 campaign supporting a moderate view of government that appealed to many of the new wealthy and to those in the growing technology sector. As opinion in the nation turned against the Republicans' views, Clinton moved again, proposing new initiatives and castigating the Republicans for their cramped and ideological opposition to government. The wheel had clearly turned, and Republicans were now increasingly on the defensive. But Clinton pursued his expanded government agenda while generally avoiding a rhetoric that suggested an instinctive attraction to large-scale new programs.

It was here that Al Gore's campaign made an important change. Over the objection of many New Democrats, Gore in his convention speech embraced a populist theme, making one direct promise after another to assist different groups. To many Americans, the program suggested a return to Big Government. Gore's leadership style was also different. New Democrats counseled a consensual approach on economic matters that avoided overtones of conflict among different economic groups or classes. They had targeted the new wealthy and the growing upper middle class as key sectors to solidify a permanent electoral majority. Gore's rhetoric played up the idea of division and was based on the theme of "fight[ing] for the people, not the powerful." He used the word "fight" no fewer than twenty times in his convention speech, leaving the impression that some would be able to benefit only by taking away from others. He lost the subtlety or ambivalence that Clinton had effected: no talk of the end of Big Government to balance the laundry list of new programs, no talk of making abortion "safe, legal, and *rare*."

Gore's style did succeed in energizing a large part of the Democrats' following. And unlike the "tax and spend" label that attached automatically to Big Government advocates just a few years before, the huge government surpluses allowed Gore to promise to spend and spend, with money still left over for a "responsible" tax cut. It was a much more appealing agenda in 2000 than it had been a decade before. Yet the appeal also risked losing some of Clinton's cross-partisan support. Budget surplus or no, many Americans continued, at least on a general ideological level, to harbor deep suspicions toward Big Government. George W. Bush was able to duplicate many of the themes of the Republican campaigns of 1980, 1984, and 1988 by running explicitly against "Big Government," although he made sure to point out that he was not necessarily against government, only that Gore was for Big Government.

The shift of Al Gore from a New Democratic stance to an Old Democratic stance was one part of the ideological story of the 2000 campaign; the other, and perhaps more important, part was the change that took place in the Republican Party, with George W. Bush fashioning a new kind of Republicanism based on the theme of "compassionate conservatism." George W. Bush, in fact, was the only candidate in the race in 2000 who had a memorable descriptive label or theme to identify his position. Just as Bill Clinton had been a "New Democrat" in 1992, George W. Bush was a "compassionate conservative" in 2000. As Bush liked to repeat early in his campaign, in a bit of an evangelistic style, "On this ground [compassionate conservatism], I'll take my stand." Because this theme left a great deal yet to be defined, however, Bush was really not committing himself to very much just yet.

The evolution of the theme of compassionate conservatism shares some similarities with the development of New Democrat thinking. In both cases, many people—critics, in particular—have asked whether the impetus for the change derived more from practical considerations of electoral benefits, or whether it came from a genuine reconsideration of philosophical doctrine. The only plausible answer in both cases is that both elements were involved. The relative levels of each motivation, however, can be determined only by a casuist. If a public philosophy, as Samuel Beer once stated, is "an outlook on public affairs which is accepted within a nation by a wide coalition and which serves to give definition to problems and directions to government policies dealing with them," then both doctrine and electoral strategy must be considered.[27]

One thing is sure. Republicans coming into the 2000 race were in the throes of a major intellectual crisis about what the conservative movement stood for and what message would be palatable enough to sell to the American people. The existence of this crisis so soon after the spectacular Republican revolution of 1994 was in itself a shock to many in the party. The Republican revolution had seemed to resolve this question decisively in favor of an aggressive antigovernment, populist conservatism. But the turn of fortune that occurred in the 1996 presidential election and the 1998 congressional elections left Republicans reeling. Whatever might be said for the accomplishments of the revolutionaries of 1994, there was no question that something now was wrong with either the message or the messengers.

Every bit as much as the Democrats after 1988, Republicans after 1998 were engaged in trying to define, or redefine, the meaning of their party's core ideology.

The Republican Party has traditionally been a party that has sought to protect individual rights, especially in the area of economic activity. It has also championed the dignity and worth of the private sphere, often, but not always, against government activity. Yet a defense of the market and the private sphere has never been enough to capture the imagination of the voting public, and the Republican Party has been most successful when it has been able to tie or wed this theme with a broader public purpose or national mission. Going back to the Republican revolution of 1980, for example, the public purpose that the party articulated was supplied in part by the national mission of anticommunism and by saving the country from what many believed was the proven incapacity of liberalism to govern. But by 1990 the Cold War was over, and, apart from the president's personal problems, Democrats had clearly shown to many that they could govern sensibly and manage the affairs of the nation.

A number of proposals for a direction of the Republican Party were put forward after 1998. One was a renewed or restored moral conservatism that would be more vigorously and honestly pressed than in 1996 or 1998, and that would proceed without carrying the baggage connected to Newt Gingrich. Another idea was "national greatness conservatism," which called for a renewed emphasis on America's international role and for government activism in a few areas. It found its roots in the vigorous virtues of Alexander Hamilton and Theodore Roosevelt. Finally, there was the plan of "compassionate conservatism." Many conservatives took this label to be an insulting redundancy, implying incorrectly that conservativism before Bush had lacked compassion properly understood. Others saw it as a contradiction in terms, validating the very emotion of compassion that had been the engine for liberalism's indiscriminate advocacy of Big Government. Indeed, George W. Bush was roundly attacked for advocating "Clintonism without Clinton" within the Republican Party. But as Bush defined the theme, it became clear that his idea of compassion found its roots more in a religious than a secular spirit, and that it was aimed more at trying to find ways of helping distinct individuals facing particular problems than at transferring resources to groups considered at need. The message here was that in many situations only community institutions and faith-based organizations, not Big Government or the administrative state government, can effect a change. As Bush put it in his "Duty of Hope" speech delivered in Indianapolis on July 22, 1999:

> In every instance where my administration sees a responsibility to help people, we will look first to faith-based organizations, charities and community groups that have shown their ability to save and change lives. . . . We will rally the armies of compassion in our communities to fight a very different war against poverty and hopelessness, a daily battle waged house to house and heart by heart. This will not be the failed compassion of towering, distant bureaucracies. On the contrary, it will be government that serves those who are serving their neighbors. . . . It will be government that both knows its limits, and shows its heart. And it will be government truly by the people and for the people.[28]

This idea spoke in general terms to the importance of voluntarism and community institutions and to the fundamental limitations of Big Government. But at the same time, it was clear that such organizations and activities might need resources from government. As Bush said in the same speech, "It is not enough to call for volunteerism. Without more support—both public and private—we are asking them to make bricks without straw." Bush was signaling by his combined attention to the poor and social problems and by his willingness to call on government that he was breaking from the reigning image of conservatism that was associated with the congressional Republicans.

Like many of the Democratic moderates who rejected the liberalism of their party in the late 1980s, it was the Republican governors who took the lead in trying to change and save the Republican Party. Many of these governors, of course, came from the larger states with Democratic majorities. They had to deal with the problems of people living outside of Republican constituencies and find ways of appealing to independent and Democratic voters. Looking back to the election of 1994 in light of the events of 2000, the winning "section" or wing of the Republican Party may not have been, as everyone once believed, the congressional wing, but the gubernatorial wing. Many of these governors had borrowed much from New Democratic ideas. But, as New Democrats had clearly borrowed much from Republican ideas, the debate over intellectual ownership of this new politics can obviously continue forever without resolution.

The Republican governors in effect agreed among themselves to select the party's nominee, subordinating individual ambitions and agreeing to coalesce behind one person. In George W. Bush they found one of the most conservative of their group, and therefore one most sellable to the conservative base of the party, yet still someone who endorsed their more pragmatic and positive views of the use of government. Apart, however, from this more moderate or pragmatic understanding of the role of government and their conviction that congressional Republican conservatism would lead the party to disaster, the governors had not developed a positive theme of their own. As governors, their focus was still on the states and lacked a general or synoptic national view. Compassionate conservatism supplied that view, or at any rate, provided a very compelling label.

A discussion of parallels between the path of development of New Democratic thinking and compassionate conservatism should not lead one to overlook the very different relationship that exists in these two cases between the main political leader and his relationship to an intellectual movement. Bill Clinton was not the first New Democratic presidential candidate (Al Gore may well have been in 1988) and in no sense did Clinton develop its ideas (though he played some role). New Democratic thinking had a large institutional and intellectual base of its own, and the leading figures in this "establishment" sought out Bill Clinton after 1988 and offered him a full package, from which he subsequently picked and chose, according to his own political instincts. By contrast, George W. Bush is the first major New Republican politician espousing the compassionate conservative theme. Although the term was occasionally used before 1999 by a few Republican senators, it had no resonance until George W. Bush adopted it. While Bill Clinton embraced New Democratic thinking, George W. Bush created compassionate conservatism—though not by himself, of course. He drew on a number of intellectuals—quite a few of them from outside of the Washington conservative think tank mainstream—and combined their ideas with his own strong religious orientation. It is always easy, of course, to exaggerate how much there is that is really "new" in any of these doctrines. Just as a good many of the themes of New Democratic thinking were already present in what many moderate and southern Democrats were saying in ordinary language, so too were many elements of compassionate conservatism present in the practice of many of the Republican governors. Yet George W. Bush was the politician to put the concept together and to give it his unique slant.

This situation, wherein George W. Bush is the new prince of this compassionate conservative movement, has certain consequences. The New Democratic movement had a large independent institutional life of its own, which has spawned much philosophic thinking and developed many agenda items. Compassionate conservatism has no organized institutional existence and hardly exists apart from its connection to a political figure. In form it is therefore more political and less intellectual. It is interpreted in light of the political needs of its political leader. It is impossible to imagine a revolt of compassionate conservatives against George W. Bush or a concerted effort by the compassionate conservative movement to try to make him adhere to its program, as New Democrats did with Bill Clinton. This situation gives Bush more flexibility in respect to his guiding intellectual theme, which is therefore made more fully his own. Yet this situation also means that he may have less support and backup. New Democrats had a whole agenda of their own and a reservoir of intellectual ideas from which to draw. Compassionate conservatism does speak to many fundamental conservative themes, and there are a number of important conservative intellectuals who have articulated its general premises. But the question remains: Has the intellectual capital been invested for planning the next phase of a compassionate conservative political agenda?

Notes

1. Gore never even used the words Republican or Democrat. Bush used them only when saying, "I worked with Republicans and Democrats to get things done."

2. Ronald Brownstein, "What a Difference Two Years Makes for Dole," *Los Angeles Times*, Oct. 29, 1996, A5.

3. Michael Hedges, "Clinton Woos Swing Seats for Congress," *Houston Chronicle* Nov. 5, 2000, A1.

4. A notable exception occurred in the Senate race in New York, where Mrs. Clinton frequently invoked Newt Gingrich in her contest against Rick Lazio.

5. Katharine Q. Seelye and Richard Perex-Pena, "Gore Team Renews Criticism of Bush As Inexperienced," *New York Times*, Oct. 30, 2000, A1.

6. Alexis de Tocqueville, *Democracy in America*, ed. J. P. Mayer (New York: HarperPerennial, 1988), p. 135.

7. Robert J. Samuelson, "Clinton's Third Term," *Washington Post*, Nov. 15, 2000, A39.

8. Robert Novak, "Dems say no Gore in 2004," *Chicago Sun-Times*, Dec. 7, 2000, 43.

9. Charles Krauthammer, "Lingering Myths About the Election Need to be Banished," *Pittsburgh Post-Gazette*, Dec. 9, 2000, E1.

10. Ceci Connolly and John F. Harris, "Putting On a Blitz; For Gore, It's a Five-State Finale in 30 Hours," *Washington Post*, Nov. 7, 2000, A1.

11. Robert G. Kaiser, "Academics Say It's Elementary: Gore Wins," *Washington Post*, Aug. 31, 2000, A12.

12. Robert G. Kaiser, "Academics Say It's Elementary: Gore Wins," *Washington Post*, Aug. 31, 2000, A12.

13. Allan Bernstein, "Political Forecasters Sticking with Gore Despite Polls," *Houston Chronicle*, Nov. 1, 2000, A13.

14. D. W. Miller, "Election Returns Leave Political Scientists Defensive Over Forecast," *Chronicle of Higher Education*, Nov. 7, 2000.

15. They were joined by a few political scientists who have a reflexive hatred of models and seem to spend much of their careers looking for any occasion to discredit them. As will become clear in chapter 4, we have a certain way of using models and a certain view of how they should be used. Models focus attention on the aspect of human reality and history that is repetitive and homogenous. They serve, in Larry Bartels's

words, as an "antidote to the press's overwhelming focus on candidates' personalities, campaign tactics and other 'unique,' campaign-specific factors which are more interesting to write about but much less important to the outcome of the election" (*Washington Post*, Aug. 31, 2000). On the other hand, the models miss another dimension of human reality and history that involves the unique and the heterogeneous. A combination of approaches is accordingly needed.

16. The list of those speculating on this thesis included Robert Samuelson, George Will, and Charles Krauthammer.

17. James Bryce, *The American Commonwealth*, vol. 2. (London: Macmillan, 1889), p. 207.

18. VNS 2000 National Exit Polls, from http://cnn.com.

19. Bush received 36 percent of the votes from those who judged the nation to be on the right track.

20. Robert J. Samuelson, "Clinton's Third Term," *Washington Post*, Nov. 15, 2000, A39.

21. *Wall Street Journal*, "Notable and Quotable," Jan. 2, 2001, A22.

22. Nader's appeal was both bolstered and limited by his leftist positions, so that his candidacy is only partly reflective of the reform sentiment. He received 2.7 percent of the vote, although he polled considerably higher during most of the campaign.

23. Howard Kurtz, "Gore's Masters of Disaster; The Campaign Behind the Campaign: The Secret Media Blueprint that Nearly Captured the Presidency," *Washington Post*, Dec. 17, 2000, F1.

24. Gerald M. Pomper, "The Presidential Election," in *The Election of 1988: Reports and Interpretations*, ed. G. M. Pomper (Chatham, N.J.: Chatham House, 1989), p. 139.

25. The prevalence of this way of thinking, incidentally, is why many political campaigns tend to speak past one another, with one side addressing the other only when it is forced to.

26. For a full history of the New Democratic movement, see Kenneth Baer, *Reinventing Democrats* (Lawrence: University of Kansas Press, 2000).

27. Samuel Beer, "In Search of a New Public Philosophy" in *The New American Political System*, ed. Anthony King (Washington, D.C.: AEI Press, 1977), p. 87.

28. George W. Bush, Duty of Hope speech, Indianapolis, July 22, 1999.

Chapter Two

The Invisible Primary:
The Marathon Begins

The presidential nomination campaign for 2000 was unusual for having three different nominating contests. In addition to the two normal major party contests between Al Gore and Bill Bradley in the Democratic Party and between George W. Bush and (chiefly) John McCain in the Republican Party, there was also an informal, cross-party contest between Bill Bradley and John McCain. The Bradley-McCain race, which became a primary of sorts for the independent and reform-minded voters, was perhaps the most intriguing of the three. While recent nominating history has not been completely devoid of cases of cross-party competition—Jerry Brown battled Pat Buchanan for a portion of the "outsider" constituency in 1992, and Ronald Reagan competed with George Wallace for disaffected Democrats in 1976—never have two candidates from different parties so directly influenced the major party results. When McCain defeated Bradley in the "primary" for independent reform candidates in New Hampshire, he did more than enliven the Republican race beyond all expectations; he guaranteed that Al Gore would be the Democratic nominee.

In the two official party contests, the results that seemed so clear before the nomination campaign got under way, and so logical after they were over, were far from obvious in the interim. The favorites, Al Gore and George W. Bush, emerged from their respective campaigns as decisive winners, but in the crucial period between the predictions and the predictable, neither outcome appeared certain, and one misstep here or one break could have changed everything.

The Nominating Context

Serious politicians contemplating a race for the presidency generally think long and hard before entering the fray. A poor showing can endanger an existing career or end further hopes for seeking the presidency. While less well-known figures may continue to compete and stay in the race in order to advance their careers or represent a certain political view, real politicians will heavily weigh the prevailing political context and attempt to gauge their prospects of actually becoming the party's nominee.

The political context of the choice to enter the nomination campaign, treated as an analytic concept, can be broken down into five basic elements: the selection rules and procedures, the results of the preceding midterm elections, the structure of the choice (whether an incumbent is seeking reelection), the factional balance within the parties, and the mood of the nation. Discerning the trends for each element is not always easy, and politicians and their advisers accordingly engage in a good deal of assessment, reassessment, and guessing. Thus, spending some time looking at these elements is a good way to understand the main issues of nomination politics.

Rules

The nomination process since the 1970s is best described as a popular or plebiscitary system in which individual candidates appeal directly to a large and mostly partisan electorate in a series of state primary elections. While the basic system has remained unchanged for the past quarter-century, in each election there have been second- or third-order revisions of the rules, some of which have had very significant effects. The rules for the 2000 nomination race fall into this category, even though—and this has been true of previous instances as well—their impact was not always anticipated or fully understood in advance. No one can really say whether these revisions altered the final outcomes, but they certainly influenced candidate strategies and the way the race unfolded.

The most notable development in 2000, identified and studied by all of the participants, was the acceleration of a process known as "front-loading." Front-loading, for those unaware of the jargon of nominating politics, refers to the scheduling of primary elections as early as possible (this is the "front" part), with the result that many of the primaries are packed together in a short time (the "load" part). The consequence of this is a dramatic compression of the meaningful period of the primary calendar. Around 75 percent of the delegates in 2000 were selected by the end of March, compared

with 45 percent in 1992. Going back all the way to the last year of the previous nominating system in 1968, less than 10 percent of delegates were
chosen during the six weeks after the first primary.[1]

The mad rush to the front in 2000 was triggered by California's decision
to advance its primary to March 7. California, now by far the most delegate-rich state in the Union, used to hold its presidential primary near the
end of the campaign season, on the first Tuesday of June. Frustrated after
1992 by their state's lack of influence, California lawmakers moved their
1996 primary to March 26. But even this date proved to be too late, as the
Republican race of 1996 was essentially determined by March 12 (Democrats had no contest in 1996). In 1998 the California legislature made another try, changing the state's primary day to the first Tuesday in March.
This step opened the floodgates. When California speaks, other states in
the nation listen. Realizing that their primaries could have virtually no influence if they came after California, many states decided to reschedule
their dates as well.

The front-loaded schedule has been widely criticized on the grounds
that it limits the field of entrants and decreases deliberation in the decision-
making process. Under the first and most commonly cited scenario, the
front-loaded system gives an almost insuperable advantage to candidates
who do well in the "invisible primary," the period in the year preceding the
election when candidates attempt to raise money, win endorsements and
media attention, and build organizations. Accruing these assets has of
course always been helpful, but it becomes more so under a heavily front-
loaded system. To compete in so many primaries right at the beginning,
candidates must raise huge sums of money ($20 million is a figure fre-
quently mentioned) before the first vote is cast—a very difficult task,
given federal contribution limits of $1,000 per individual. Those unable to
raise this kind of money cannot seriously compete, depriving voters of the
chance to survey some potentially strong candidates. More and more, critics charge, it is the elites in the major party establishments—that is to say,
large donors, professional fund-raisers, and officeholders (whose views influence the donors)—who control the process.[2]

Under a second and less likely scenario, some say that front-loading
might open the possibility for an underdog to pick up an early win and then
parlay the resultant momentum into a rapid series of decisive victories under the compressed primary schedule. Facing the electoral equivalent of
blitzkrieg, the race might be over before the previous front-runner or anyone else has a chance to recover, leaving no opportunity for a second look
and further deliberation. Under this scenario, if the Gary Hart–Walter
Mondale race of 1984 had occurred under 2000 rules, Hart might well

have ridden his New Hampshire momentum all the way to the nomination. While still plausible, this prospect seems dimmer after the campaigns of 1996 and 2000, in which Pat Buchanan and John McCain scored important early wins but then were ultimately overwhelmed by the superior resources of front-running opponents.[3]

Another important feature of the rules in 2000 was the asymmetry that emerged between the primary schedules of the two parties. Most importantly, throughout the entire month of February Republicans were holding primaries while Democrats were not. Not since the nomination race of 1936, when Democrats abolished their rule requiring the nominee to receive a two-thirds vote of the convention's delegates, has the difference in selection methods between the parties been as great. This development was a classic case of an unintended consequence, one that emerged, ironically, from efforts that were made to limit front-loading. To reduce front-loading, both Democrats and Republicans established dates (referred to as "windows") before which delegate selection was not permitted. But the parties adopted different windows: February 1 for Republicans and March 1 for Democrats (with exemptions granted to Iowa and New Hampshire to allow them to keep their traditionally early positions). A virtual one-party Republican primary schedule for all of February was the result (see table 2.1).[4]

The consequences of this arrangement under the political circumstances of 2000 were striking. The loser of the Democratic New Hampshire primary, Bill Bradley, was denied an opportunity for quick redemption. Although Bradley received 43 percent against Al Gore—an impressive showing against a strong front-runner—he found himself almost completely ignored by the media. The Democratic race was pushed to the sidelines as the nation focused on the Republican contest. Faced with the prospect of waiting five weeks until Super Tuesday (March 7) and contesting Gore in 16 states at once, Bradley decided instead to campaign in the nonbinding "beauty con-

Table 2.1.   Primary Schedule for February

Republican Party	*Democratic Primary*
Feb. 1 New Hampshire (Open)	Feb. 1 New Hampshire (Open)
Feb. 8 Delaware (Open)	Feb. 5 Delaware (Beauty contest, Open)
Feb. 19 South Carolina (Open)	Feb. 29 Washington (Beauty contest, Open)
Feb. 22 Michigan (Open) Arizona (Closed)	
Feb. 29 Virginia (Open) Washington (Part open, part closed)	

test" in Washington State, making that unlikely setting his last real stand of the 2000 campaign. One may speculate on how this arrangement would have worked if Bradley had managed to defeat Gore in New Hampshire. Surely, with Gore still the favorite, the Democratic race would not have been so easily ignored in February, even in the absence of any primary contests. But for a challenger with his poll ratings sinking, this schedule proved fatal, and Bill Bradley was widely written off.

The flip side of this arrangement was that the Republican race drew almost all of the attention during this crucial period of the primary process. This effect obviously depended on there being a real contest, which was assured when John McCain scored his upset victory over George Bush in New Hampshire. From then on, almost all of the news coverage in February was about Bush and McCain. This attention was clearly helpful for McCain. Whether it was ultimately beneficial or harmful to George Bush's prospects for the general election is another matter. For instance, Bush's controversial speaking engagement at Bob Jones University probably received more coverage than if the media attention had been equally divided with the Democratic race.

A final important feature of the 2000 primary rules was the large number of states holding open primaries, where nonparty members are permitted to vote. Open primaries have a long history, being the favored arrangement of many of the progressives who originated presidential primaries in the early 1900s. The Democratic National Party tried to ban them in the 1970s and 1980s on the grounds that non-Democratic voters diluted the "full and meaningful participation" of Democrats. But the national party ultimately backed down under protests from some of the states that had a long attachment to the institution, especially Wisconsin. For their part, Republicans in the South enthusiastically embraced open primaries as a means of gradually moving conservative white southern Democrats into the Republican Party. Elsewhere in the nation, most notably in California, there was sentiment to go beyond the open primary and employ the more radical "blanket primary," in which all voters receive the same ballot and may choose a candidate from either party without needing to declare whether they are participating in a Democratic or a Republican primary.

The large number of open primaries had a notable impact on the 2000 race, especially when combined with the fact that many of them happened to be scheduled during February, when only Republicans were holding contests. Independents as well as a substantial number of Democrats became fair game for a Republican candidate with a strong appeal beyond his party. Such a candidate, of course, was John McCain. After New Hampshire, an open primary state, McCain almost overcame Bush in South

Carolina, and then he defeated him by a significant margin in Michigan, both open primary states. McCain was competitive in these races only because of the votes of independents and Democrats. Although John McCain as the underdog was arguably disadvantaged by the general movement of front-loading, within the limits of that system it is difficult to imagine an arrangement that could have been more to his benefit, unless the Republican National Committee had allowed him to choose the order of primaries. Conversely, Bill Bradley's drive for the Democratic nomination was adversely affected. The voters who gravitated to McCain in this period in February were many of the same voters Bradley needed later. When the Democratic primaries started up again five weeks after New Hampshire, they were already spoken for.

The effects produced by the combination of the campaign schedule and the open primaries could not all have been fully calculated before the campaign got under way. They depended on a certain sequence of events. But the effects nevertheless explain a good deal about the 2000 nominating race. As for what might be the general tendency of these rules for future years, there is little reason to figure it out. Whatever else may happen, we are unlikely to see the same schedule in 2004.

Midterm elections

Presidential nomination contests are often affected by the results of the most recent midterm elections, which can send very strong signals about which kinds of candidacies are viable. The general rule (almost always evident) in midterm congressional elections is that the president's party loses a certain number of seats. A greater than average loss can weaken a president or the faction of his party that supports him, and in fact most of major intraparty challenges to incumbent presidents in the twentieth century were preceded by larger than average midterm election losses in the House and Senate.[5]

In 1998, the normal midterm pattern was broken. Not only did Democrats perform better than average, but they also defied the normal midterm pattern of losing seats in midterm elections. Democrats held their own in the Senate and actually gained five seats in the House, the first time since 1934 that a president's party had picked up House seats in a midterm election. This strong performance came despite (or perhaps because of) the scandals that surrounded President Clinton, and the result was a reconfiguration of the landscape of nominating politics in both parties.

On the Democratic side, Al Gore was strengthened by the 1998 midterm election in several ways. The election was widely read as an endorsement for how the administration was managing the country, notwithstanding the president's personal problems. Al Gore was in an enviable position of representing Clintonism without being Clinton. And because of the Lewinsky scandal, Clinton had assumed a low profile during the 1998 campaign, avoiding most public campaigning except for fund-raising appearances before Democratic audiences. Gore therefore carried a greater than usual share of the campaign burden, which enabled him to collect a larger than usual number of IOUs from lower-level Democratic officeholders and party officials. Gore also benefited from the 1998 election because House Minority Leader Richard Gephardt, Gore's strongest potential rival, decided not to run for the presidency. He was deterred from making a presidential run by Gore's newly revealed strength, but also, with the Democratic gains, he was enticed to remain in the House by the prospect of becoming Speaker. Comparing his chances of becoming Speaker in 2000 to giving up his House seat and risking a long-shot race against Gore, Gephardt opted to stay put. Finally, in spite of their strong showing, Democrats were acutely aware that they had narrowly averted a disaster: Clinton had almost been forced to resign. Following Nixon's resignation in 1973, Republicans lost 48 House seats and 5 Senate seats in the 1974 elections. Sensing the precariousness of their situation, Democrats responded by circling the wagons. This sentiment spilled over into a desire to avoid a major battle for the presidential nomination that almost surely would have to put an unfavorable spotlight on the administration's scandals.

To engage a moment in the "what if" game, if Republicans had performed in their "expected" range in 1998, winning 10 to 15 House seats, more Democrats would probably have been emboldened to enter the race against Al Gore. Only one alternative midterm election scenario could have strengthened Gore more than the actual outcome: Republican gains so enormous as to have changed the impeachment or resignation equation, making Al Gore the 43rd president of the United States. But even in this case, Al Gore would have been an incumbent in the fashion of Gerald Ford running in 1976, facing Democratic opposition that sought to give the party a new direction—hardly the most enviable or secure position to be in.

On the Republican side, the midterm elections left party members stunned. Entering the campaign with expectations of huge gains, Republicans finished by losing seats. If ever anxiety or fear gripped a party, it did so to the Republicans in 1998. The biggest losers were House Republicans and social conservatives, who were widely viewed as responsible for the election debacle. Democratic gains, it appears, were the result of the attractive set of issues that they put forward, while Republicans seemed to sit back and wait for Clinton's woes to help them. As the Republican pollster and analyst Richard Wirthlin wrote after the campaign, "The biggest lesson of the '98 elections is that there is no substitute for a compelling message. . . . [T]he Democrats successfully outmaneuvered Republicans on issues of greatest importance to voters and largely neutralized many of their own key vulnerabilities."[6] Democrats used these issues, as well as Republican missteps in the impeachment process, to mobilize their key constituencies (blacks and organized labor), while Republicans failed to turn out their supporters in anything like the same numbers.[7] Insofar as national personalities influenced the race, the administration somehow managed to turn the election into a referendum not on Bill Clinton but on Newt Gingrich. In truth, Clinton and Gingrich, without ever directly confronting each other, had squared off three times in national campaigns: in 1994 when Gingrich led the Republican revolution against Bill Clinton; in 1996 when Clinton made his presidential race against Bob Dole a kind of test of Newt Gingrich; and finally in 1998 when all signs pointed to Clinton's defeat. When Clinton nevertheless won, Gingrich drew the inevitable conclusion and immediately resigned the speakership and announced his retirement from Congress.

In the aftermath of the elections, many Republicans became convinced that the party had to adopt a different course from the leadership of the congressional branch, even if they did not yet know exactly what that direction should be. At the very least, the party had to acquire a different look. Party leaders began looking for a unifying candidate, one who could prevent the party from going into a free fall and losing all the ground that had been gained in the 1990s. Sentiment grew in the higher echelons of the party, among both officeholders and money givers, to avoid open divisions and put ideological differences aside. Many rank-and-file Republicans desired to try and settle the presidential nomination in advance of the primaries, thereby avoiding a divisive winter and spring in 2000.

Besides the signals midterm elections send about the political situation, the standings of prominent individuals in highly visible races for the Senate or for governorships can also influence nomination politics. Two notable examples from the past were Woodrow Wilson, who was catapulted to the front ranks of 1912 Democratic contenders when he won the New Jersey governorship in 1910, and Franklin Roosevelt, who became the front-runner for the 1932 nomination following his crushing reelection victory for governor of New York two years earlier. Conversely, as recently as 1991, New Jersey Senator Bill Bradley and New York Governor Mario Cuomo were forced to reassess their nascent presidential bids by uninspiring showings in the midterm elections.

Clearly, the big winner for Republicans in 1998 was George W. Bush, whose reelection as governor of Texas provided a bright spot that contrasted with the discouraging results of the congressional Republicans. In fact, the 1998 elections appeared to indicate that the gubernatorial wing, not the congressional wing, was now the Republican Party's greatest source of strength. Although the GOP lost the governorship in California, other big states either elected or reelected major Republican governors, among them George W. Bush's brother Jeb in Florida, George Pataki in New York, Tommy Thompson in Wisconsin, and Tom Ridge in Pennsylvania. These governors began to see themselves as a group within the party having its own approach to governing. Bush's victory in Texas exemplified and confirmed their general strategy. His personal standing was bolstered not only by the size of his victory, but also by its shape. He showed strong appeal among traditionally Democratic groups: Hispanics (winning about two of five), women (winning a significant majority), and blacks (winning about three in ten). He also tested a platform of "compassionate conservatism," emphasizing education and voluntarism along with tax cuts and crime fighting, all with an optimistic tenor. This platform was meant to overcome the more negative perception that many people had developed about congressional Republicans. Here, many Republicans believed, was the new message coming from a different place than the Congress.

The structure of the choice

One of the most important elements in the nominating context is the structure of the choice, most specifically whether an incumbent president is running for reelection or not. The race in 2000 was for an open seat, the first time since 1988. (Other open-seat elections in recent times have been in 1968, 1960, and 1952.) All other things being equal, these races are more attractive to potential candidates. Certainly this is true in the party of the incumbent, where aspirants can run without facing the nearly insuperable task of unseating a sitting president.

Potential candidates on the Democratic side did, however, face what was probably the closest approximation of incumbency ever witnessed in the person of Al Gore. As vice president, Gore enjoyed the support of Bill Clinton and served as an active and trusted member of the administration. In the style of modern vice presidents, he was assigned many important responsibilities and took part in most of the crucial decisions. Clinton chose Gore in 1992 not least because their political views were similar. The two were joined at the hip politically, to the detriment of intraparty challengers.

In the last half of the twentieth century, vice presidential incumbency has been an advantage to those seeking their party's nomination. In addition to George Bush in 1988, sitting vice presidents won nominations in 1968 (Hubert Humphrey) and 1960 (Richard Nixon). No sitting vice president who has tried to win a nomination has failed since 1940. Then John Nance Garner lost to his own boss, Franklin Roosevelt, when Roosevelt at the last moment broke with tradition to seek a third term. If one counts both presidents seeking reelection and their vice presidents seeking to ascend, the last race without an incumbent of some sort winning a party nomination was 1952.

Yet vice presidential incumbency is not as weighty as presidential incumbency, and the nomination races when a sitting vice president decides to run generally draw more numerous and serious opposition. And in the end, though Vice President Gore was not challenged in 2000 by a large field or by the most prominent of potential opponents, Bill Bradley was a credible foe with a good reputation and was fairly well known. Gore's nomination race was therefore not a cakewalk.

The condition of the parties

A fourth element of the nomination context is the constellation of prevailing forces within the political parties. Nomination races involve voter decisions based on both assessments of candidates (who they are) and their positions and ideology on issues (what they believe). Prospective candidates must assess the relative power of ideological and organizational factions within their party to determine if they fit the prevailing party mood, or how they might alter conditions to reshape the party more in their own image.

The Democratic Party over the past decade has displayed two broad ideological tendencies: left and center. One of Bill Clinton's most notable efforts as a so-called New Democrat was directed at remaking the Democratic Party, leading it to adopt positions more compatible with centrist ideas both on certain cultural programs and on part of his domestic agenda. While Clinton introduced these themes in his 1992 presidential campaign, once in office, he moved to a more leftist or "Big Government" position when he launched his health care proposal in 1993. The defeat of this initiative and the Democrats' loss of the Congress in 1994 sent Clinton back to the center, a position that made many in the Democratic Party highly uneasy about his policies. At the same time, a leftist segment of the party believed that Clinton did not do enough on social programs, sold out the poor with welfare reform, pushed free trade too vigorously, and adopted the balanced budget mantra too thoroughly. As thinking about the 2000 nominating campaign began, it was an open question whether the New Democrat approach had taken firm root or whether Clinton represented a short-lived detour. The Democratic race, some believed, would be a test of that question, with one candidate or another making a serious challenge to the New Democratic position from the left.

But the Democratic Party cannot be understood simply in terms of ideological divisions. It is also very much a collection of large interests—principally labor, blacks, gays, feminists, and environmentalists—that possess an impressive degree of group cohesion and organization. While each interest shares ideological positions—all are on the left—each is also a distinct group to which appeals must be tailored. Between the ideological tendencies and the group interests, there is an intricate interplay that can never be fully predicted in advance.

In the end, the Democratic race failed to attract a traditional or trusted candidate from the left. Bill Bradley, who previously was situated in the party as a moderate, moved to the left of Al Gore upon his entrance into the race. But he failed to win the support one might have expected on ideological grounds alone. In part, this was because Gore himself moved quite far to the left, outflanking Bradley on some issues. More importantly, because of his years in the White House and the advantages of "incumbency," Gore had managed to wrap up much of the interest group support within the party. Bradley's voter base in the end was concentrated among that part of the party that was not as tied to organized interests, plus many independents. Bradley led a campaign in which he was forced to try to build up a new constituency in the party, one that was based on reform and that was not closely tied to the administration.

Republicans also split along a number of ideological dimensions in the 2000 primaries. In addition to the oft-remarked division between "conservatives" and "moderates," a division that turns on both social issues and fiscal policy, there was also an emerging division within the conservative camp between "limited government conservatives" and "national greatness conservatives." The limited government conservatives' main objective was the shrinking of federal power and resources, while national greatness conservatives, exemplified by William Kristol and David Brooks of the *Weekly Standard*, called for robust nationalism and a strong role for the federal government in certain areas. But overtaking any of these factional divisions was the desire, after two consecutive presidential defeats, to consider a fresh approach within the Republican Party. Because of this hunger for election, the vaguer theme of "compassionate conservatism," with aspects that appealed to conservatives as well as moderates, would shortly be thrown into the mix.

While Republicans as a party are less tied to large organized interests than Democrats, some groups do exert influence over the party. The Christian right, although perhaps less influential than it once was, was still an important force, enough so that many observers speculated that Governor Thomas Ridge of Pennsylvania was passed over for the vice presidential nomination because of the opposition of pro-life groups. And a few other groups, such as the National Rifle Association and its members, could be major players. But perhaps the most important organized "group" in the party in 2000 was the party itself. With Republicans controlling more than 30 governorships, it is possible that Republicans have more of a party structure or force than either the Democrats have or than the Republicans had themselves a few years ago. The 2000 contest was a test of whether that party structure could play an important, or even decisive, role in the outcome.

National mood

A final element affecting primary contests refers to moods and currents that run beyond or outside the usual ideological divisions in the nation. A single powerful mood or current—like outsiderism in 1992—can color a nomination race, and a candidate who can harness or capture that mood can boost his or her chances, perhaps even managing to seize control of the party.

The national mood that preceded the 2000 race was without a single dominant theme. Although Americans were highly satisfied with the state of the economy, they were also dissatisfied with the moral state of society. Bill Clinton was the recipient of a consistently high job approval rating and a consistently low personal approval rating. Similarly, satisfaction with material prosperity coexisted with shock at such events as the Columbine High School massacre. At the beginning of 1999, as the presidential nominating contests began to receive greater attention, Congress was temporarily discredited as a result of the impeachment, but President Clinton was equally disgraced (except, perhaps, in his own mind) for his behavior.

If any theme emerged, it was a concern over the condition of America's ethical compass and a reaction against the character of politics (though not the policies) of Washington. This mood benefited candidates perceived as Washington outsiders or self-styled straight talkers, while it harmed the perceived Washington insiders, whether linked too closely to Clinton or his congressional pursuers. Social conservatives ironically found themselves tainted, since they had been among the most fervent supporters of impeachment, at the very time that a part of their message was finding increasing resonance. Yet a space was open to pleas for some kind of "renewal" from outside. First Bill Bradley and then John McCain succeeded in appealing to this sentiment, though not with enough strength to win their parties' nominations. George Bush, while eschewing the campaign reform part of this mood, caught something of its ethical component, and this appeal would become an important element of his general election campaign.

Who Ran and Who Didn't

One of the most striking features of the 2000 nominating race was how many potentially strong candidates on both sides either decided not to run or started running and withdrew long before the first primary votes were cast. For the Democrats, by mid-1999 the race had resolved itself to a contest between Al Gore and former Senator Bill Bradley of New Jersey. The vice president was the son of former Tennessee Senator Albert Gore Sr., a liberal who had himself been considered for the 1956 Democratic vice presidential nomination. Growing up in Washington, D.C., Gore Jr. had been groomed by his parents for future office (some contemporary news accounts called him the "prince of Washington"). Before his two terms as vice president under Bill Clinton, Gore had served eight years in the U.S. House and another eight years in the U.S. Senate representing the state of Tennessee. He had also run unsuccessfully for the Democratic presidential nomination in 1988.

Gore had developed a reputation as a Democratic centrist. He voted for the Persian Gulf War in 1991, helped found the Democratic Leadership Council in the 1980s, and was the first candidate in 1988 to attack Massachusetts Governor Michael Dukakis, the ultimate Democratic nominee, for his furlough of convicted rapist Willie Horton (George Bush the elder later used the same issue to devastating effect). Gore also drew criticism, though, for environmental extremism (he had, for example, urged abolition of the internal combustion engine) and had clearly shifted to the left on a variety of other issues (like gun control and abortion) since his early congressional days. Earnest and wonkish, Gore was the object both of respect, for his grasp of issues, and of ridicule, for a wooden style. He could put people off with a certain intellectual arrogance and sanctimoniousness. Though sometimes uninspiring, Gore was a highly disciplined campaigner, and he had gained a reputation as a formidable opponent by having trounced both Ross Perot (in 1993) and Jack Kemp (in 1996) in public debates. Gore began the campaign season as the prohibitive favorite in the Democratic race.

After having spent months campaigning, Bill Bradley formally entered the race against Al Gore on September 8, 1999, emphasizing both a liberal program ("The economy soars, but some of us are left behind") and a promise to provide a "new kind of leadership" that was "more interested in leadership than in polls and politics" and that "puts people front and center—not the president."[8] Bradley had served as a senator from New Jersey from 1978 to 1996, before which he was noted for his basketball skills at Princeton, on the 1964 U.S. Olympic team, and for the New York Knickerbockers of the National Basketball Association. In the Senate, Bradley was widely considered a thoughtful, though sometimes intellectually aloof, member. He, too, claimed a somewhat centrist record. Though a conventional liberal on most issues, Bradley supported aid to the anticommunist Nicaraguan contras in the 1980s and took a lead role in forging the Tax Reform Act of 1986, which eliminated scores of deductions and reduced and simplified the income tax rates. Bradley had long been touted as presidential material, but he passed up entering the races in 1992 and 1996. In 2000, Bradley veered sharply to the left, proposing "big ideas" like a ban on handguns and a large and expensive federal health care program.

The two-man Democratic field stood in sharp contrast to the last time a vice president sought his party's nomination. In 1988, George H. W. Bush faced not one but five opponents—Jack Kemp, Bob Dole, Pete du Pont, Alexander Haig, and Pat Robertson. The elder Bush was seriously challenged from different directions, as each of these men had appeal inside of the party. The financial consequences of primary front-loading, in addition to a variety of political factors already noted, spelled the difference between five challengers to an incumbent vice president in 1988 and one in 2000. Numerous potential Democratic candidates considered a race against Gore, only to back out. House Minority Leader Richard Gephardt, the favorite of organized labor, left the race after the 1998 elections. Senators Paul Wellstone of Minnesota, Bob Kerrey of Nebraska, and John Kerry of Massachusetts all explored candidacy, as did perennial gadfly Jesse Jackson. For most, the financial hurdle was decisive—or at least it was the excuse they offered. Wellstone actually decried front-loading as an establishment conspiracy to make it impossible for insurgents to compete. Front-loading, he declared, was a "transparent" attempt by the Democratic establishment to "wire the whole thing."[9]

Gore and his campaign also deliberately sought to frighten away potential opponents by accumulating a large amount of money and dozens of early endorsements. He was assisted by the sense among many Democrats, during and immediately after impeachment, that to challenge Gore was akin to attacking the administration and Clinton himself. A *New York Times* analysis in April 1999 observed, "The parade of other Democrats who had planned to take on Mr. Gore has evaporated. . . . Never before in modern American politics, in a contest for an open White House, has the competition for a nomination been distilled to two people so early."[10]

For the Republicans, a potential field of at least thirteen was whittled down to six before the first real vote was ever cast. The six who survived to February 1, 2000, were George W. Bush, John McCain, Steve Forbes, Alan Keyes, Gary Bauer, and Orrin Hatch. George W. Bush was the son of former President George Bush and the incumbent governor of Texas. Bush was first elected in a 1994 upset over incumbent Democrat Ann Richards, and in 1998 he became the first Texas governor to be reelected to two consecutive four-year terms. Both before and especially after his 1998 reelection, Bush polled well nationally (no doubt at least in part because poll respondents thought he was his father). In some ways an accidental candidate—many speculated that his brother Jeb, who had narrowly lost the Florida governorship in 1994, had been the Bush heir who was "supposed to" run in 2000—Bush was nevertheless virtually coronated as the Republican front-runner by the media after the midterm elections of 1998, as a noncongressional Republican untainted by impeachment and a claimant to a new brand of "compassionate conservatism." He brought to the presidential campaign his father's contacts and some of his father's advisers, along with his own loyal team of strategists. That team included Karl Rove, Bush's chief political strategist in every one of his electoral races; Joe Allbaugh, Bush's 1994 campaign manager and gubernatorial chief of staff; and Karen Hughes, his communications director since 1994. These three comprised the "triumvirate" that would remain with Bush throughout the entire campaign and that would have the candidate's unwavering support. In truth, it is hard to recall any presidential campaign organization that had more stability and fewer intrigues or internal power struggles.

John McCain was the incumbent senior senator from Arizona. A maverick in the Senate, McCain had a generally conservative voting record but also sponsored measures like a 25-year, $500 billion tobacco tax and a campaign finance reform bill that would have banned independent "issue ads" and "soft money" contributions to the political parties. McCain was mightily assisted by his war record—as a navy pilot he had endured five and a half years as a North Vietnamese prisoner of war—and by a carefully cultivated image as a "straight talker."

Steve Forbes was a wealthy publisher who financed much of his own race. Forbes had run a strong campaign in 1996 and kept running for the four years until 2000. In the meantime, he made a concerted bid for the social conservatives he had largely ignored in 1996, broadening his economic appeal to include issues like abortion. Many in Bob Dole's campaign blamed Forbes's 1996 attack ads in Iowa and New Hampshire for fatally weakening Dole. Though that charge was exaggerated, it did seem possible, based on past experience, that Forbes might have the capacity to alter the course of the 2000 race.

Alan Keyes was a former deputy secretary of state, the only black in either field, and, like Forbes, had run in 1996. Noted for his rousing oratory, his appeal lay primarily with social conservatives. Possessing very little money and very little organization, Keyes used the presidential nominating contest as a platform for making a statement about the moral decline of American society.

Gary Bauer, like Keyes, pitched his campaign to social conservatives. A former domestic policy adviser to Ronald Reagan, and subsequently head of the Washington-based Family Research Council, Bauer claimed to be the only electable candidate of those appealing primarily to the religious right. Also like Keyes and Forbes, however, Bauer lacked experience in elected office.

Senator Orrin Hatch of Utah was the last of the six finalists to enter the fray (though McCain did not formally announce his candidacy until after Hatch). A four-term member of the Senate, Hatch chaired the Senate Judiciary Committee and carried the burden of close association with the impeachment trial. A solid conservative in most respects, he was nevertheless not fully trusted by conservatives owing to his famously close relationship with Massachusetts Senator Edward Kennedy, his willingness to approve liberal Clinton judicial appointments, and his Mormon faith, a problem with religious conservatives who, Hatch observed, "don't believe we're Christian."[11]

In shaping the 2000 Republican nominating race, however, those who did not run were as crucial as those who did. The list of noncandidates and protocandidates is lengthy and consisted of names of individuals who might have been viable or even formidable contestants: Lamar Alexander, former Tennessee governor and 1996 presidential candidate; Patrick Buchanan, a two-time candidate for the Republican nomination who had defeated Bob Dole in New Hampshire in 1996; Representative John Kasich of Ohio, the bright young chairman of the House Budget Committee; former Vice President Dan Quayle; Senator Bob Smith of New Hampshire; and Elizabeth Dole, Bob Dole's wife and former secretary of labor, secretary of transportation, and president of the American Red Cross. Finally, there was Senator John Ashcroft of Missouri who never entered, but who for a time cast a long shadow over the race until he announced his intention not to run in January 1999. Alone among the potential Republican field, Ashcroft might have unified social conservatives and reached out to the more economically oriented conservatives in the Republican Party. But concerned about the possible vulnerability of his Senate seat and facing the already formidable Bush campaign, he opted out of a presidential bid, making it inevitable that the social conservative vote would be significantly fragmented. Ashcroft's decision also ultimately had an effect on Bush's campaign—although Bush did not know it at the time—for it meant that Bush's strongest threat would emerge to his left rather than to his right.

A debate arose in 2000 about whether the lack of viable candidates associated with the "religious right," combined with the poor showing of social conservatives in the New Hampshire primary, represented the end of the religious right as a pivotal force in Republican presidential politics. Advocates of this view included William Kristol, who calculated the vote totals of the three surviving "movement conservatives" in New Hampshire (totaling about 20 percent) and concluded, "Leaderless, rudderless, and issueless, the conservative movement, which accomplished much over the past quarter-century, is finished."[12] On the other hand, it seemed just as reasonable to conclude that social conservatives, having passed their revolutionary phase, had simply been assimilated into the new (and altered) mainstream of the Republican Party. As Edwin Fuelner pointed out, "Each one of this year's GOP contenders, even the dropouts, has run as a self-proclaimed conservative. They may argue how conservative ideas should be applied to today's issues, but the heir to [liberal Republicans] Bill Scranton and Nelson Rockefeller is nowhere to be found."[13] Indeed, all 12 of the original field declared themselves pro-life in some degree, and campaign debates often revolved around whether particular candidates were really pro-life enough. Yet even if the latter interpretation were true—that social conservatives had matured as a force and had succeeded so thoroughly within the Republican Party that they could afford the luxury of participating in more "normal" politics—this development was still an unexpected and disorienting transformation in the Republican electoral environment.

In any event, like Napoleon's army retreating from Moscow, the field of Republican candidates that reached New Hampshire was only half as large as the field that had set out for it. The story of how that came about, and how Gore preemptively eliminated all but one of his Democratic opponents, is inextricably intertwined with the character of the "invisible primary" and its importance in a heavily front-loaded and compressed primary system.

The Invisible Primary

For at least a quarter of a century, analysts have stressed the significance of the so-called invisible primary, the period preceding the primary season when candidates and potential candidates compete for early positions and relative advantages.[14] Exactly when the invisible campaign ends and the visible one starts is, of course, a somewhat arbitrary judgment. For our purposes, we treat the transition to the "visible" campaign as beginning with the major events that led up to the Iowa caucuses or New Hampshire primary, which would mean the candidate debates in Iowa and New Hampshire in October and December.[15]

By almost all accounts, the invisible primary leading up to 2000 was more important than ever. As political scientist William G. Mayer argued, "With so many primaries and caucuses jammed together, the only kind of candidate who can run effectively—who can campaign in five or ten states every week, who can field effective organizations in each of those states, who can simply fill full delegate slates—is someone who is already well-known and well-financed."[16] Competition is carried out across a variety of venues:

- **Fund-raising:** Given the extraordinarily high "entry fee" established by the front-loaded system, early fund-raising is probably the number one test of candidate viability.
- **National poll results:** At early stages of the campaign, when most of the electorate is unfocused and lacks detailed information about the race, national polls are often reflective of little more than basic name recognition. Nevertheless, the credibility of candidates is often measured by their relative standing in the various polls concerning the party nomination races. Additionally, both analysts and party activists take cues on electability from surveys indicating how well one party's presidential aspirants poll against the other's.
- **National media attention:** Candidates compete vigorously for positive media attention, without which their supporters begin to lose heart and find themselves struggling against a downward spiral of failing and being ignored.
- **Endorsements:** While party organizations and officeholders wield less power than they did at earlier times in American history, the endorsements of major figures within the parties are still prized by candidates. Endorsements by interest groups and spokesmen for important voting blocs also carry weight. Good endorsements confer instant credibility, while lack of endorsements can be portrayed as evidence of weakness.

Additionally, in the Democratic Party, the endorsement of superdelegates (generally Democratic officeholders not initially committed to any candidates) can give a candidate a leg up on his opponents before any regular delegates are chosen anywhere.

- **Organization:** Media may be king of the current primary system, but candidates can still find it useful to develop strong campaign organizations in as many states as possible. This is especially true in early states like Iowa and New Hampshire, where "retail politics" still reigns, and in the dwindling number of caucus states, like Iowa. Furthermore, organization is often taken as a sign of both popular appeal and campaign savvy.
- **Straw polls:** While national polls are important, candidates also try to take advantage of the opportunities offered by the "straw polls" administered by state and auxiliary party organizations throughout the year or two prior to the election. In some ways a test of organization more than of popular support, straw polls can boost (or demolish) the credibility of presidential aspirants.

These components of the invisible primary interact with each other through the crucial nexus of the media. Fund-raising, for example, fuels good media coverage that can then fuel rising national poll results. But the reverse is also true: rising poll numbers provoke more, and more favorable, media exposure, which in turn makes it easier to raise money. Endorsements are likewise both a cause and a reflection of campaign strength. Organizational strength and straw polls have consequences insofar as they lead to positive media coverage, and that coverage may also have important secondary effects (especially in fund-raising). Together, since World War II, early fund-raising and high national polls in the year prior to the election have been amazingly accurate predictors of who will be the nominee.[17]

The year 2000 proved to be no exception. On the Republican side, George W. Bush not only vastly out-raised and outpolled all of his competitors, but he also decisively won almost every other battle of the invisible primary. Bush compiled an enormous campaign war chest, larger than any other candidate in either party since the adoption of the Federal Election Campaign Act amendments of 1974. Drawing lessons from difficulties faced by Bob Dole in 1996, Bush declined federal matching funds, thus freeing him from state-by-state and overall spending limits. By this step he was able to avert concentrated onslaughts by deep-pocketed rivals like Steve Forbes, who spent $4 million just to win the 1996 Arizona primary, and avoid ending the primary season broke and unable to respond to attacks from Al Gore.

Starting in early March 1999, Bush had raised $6 million by April, $36 million by July, and $70 million by December. John McCain, his closest monetary competitor, had by contrast raised only $6 million by July. As Lamar Alexander later pointed out, Bush's fund-raising success had two effects: it gave him more than ample funds to run a national campaign, and—even more importantly—it soaked up so many donors that other candidates found it difficult to find contributors. As Alexander put it, "The problem is not that Bush has raised too much, it's that nobody else can raise enough to compete."[18] Only Steve Forbes, who was able to draw on his personal fortune, could remain financially competitive with Bush. Of course, as McCain would later show, it was possible to be politically competitive without financially matching the front-runner.

Bush also handily won the battle of the national polls. From mid-1998, he led the Republican pack (as well as leading Gore in head-to-head matchups), and was never overtaken by his intraparty competitors. This advantage among Republicans only grew after the 1998 elections. Although it is easy to discount the meaning of these early polls—all the more so in this case since many poll respondents were confusing Bush with his father—a perception developed that Bush was ahead.[19] His advantage in money and polls was both the cause and the effect of positive media coverage he received until very late in the invisible primary season. As early as November 1998, many saw Bush not only as the Republican front-runner, but also as the only candidate who could save the GOP from its "discredited" congressional wing. Typical of this coverage was a November 16, 1998, *U.S. News & World Report* cover story that asked "Can Bush Save the GOP?"

Meanwhile, Bush racked up an impressive array of endorsements, centered especially on the Republican governors. After months of cultivation, Bush received the endorsement of the 31-member Republican Governors Association in November 1999, and he hoped to use their state organizations as a springboard to primary victories. Here in fact is a significant piece of the whole story of the 2000 nomination campaign. The Republican governors chose a captain from their ranks and never wavered in their support. Indeed, no other Republican candidate came close to Bush in terms of the number of high-level officeholders—governors, senators, and representatives—who supported him publicly. Before the primary voting began, for instance, Bush had obtained 36 endorsements from the 55 Republican senators, in contrast to 4 Senate endorsements won by John McCain, himself an incumbent Republican senator.

And in the Iowa straw poll of August 1999, the only straw poll to which the media paid extensive attention, Bush overwhelmed his opponents, gaining 30 percent to Forbes's 20 percent and Elizabeth Dole's 14 percent. Other candidates, including such well-known figures as Dan Quayle and Lamar Alexander, fared much worse. Critics charged that the Iowa straw poll was, as a gauge of public support, a farce. Indeed, it was originally conceived of by the Iowa Republican Party as a fund-raising device, charging participants $25 apiece to register their preferences. But since many commentators decided it was important, it was important—and the candidates knew it. Dole spent $200,000 campaigning for her third-place finish, while Bush spent $750,000 and Forbes spent twice that amount and took the unprecedented step of running television ads to promote himself. Bush and Forbes were both aided in their straw poll campaign by their refusal to accept federal matching funds. This allowed them to ignore a $1.2 million total spending limit in Iowa, a limit that the other candidates, who accepted public money, had to consider. The poor showings of Dan Quayle, Lamar Alexander, and John Kasich in the nonbinding straw poll literally knocked them out of the race, as their contributions dried up and their erstwhile supporters fled to more promising campaigns. Pat Buchanan's evident weakness (he came in fifth with 7 percent of the straw vote), after having finished a respectable second in Iowa's 1996 caucuses (with 23 percent of the vote), put him on the road to leaving the GOP altogether for the Reform Party. Even Elizabeth Dole, who finished third, was hurt and driven from the race by November. Anticipating his Iowa caucus strategy, McCain refused to participate at all, calling the straw vote a "sham." In the past, campaign analysts have spoken of Iowa playing a filtering role. It again performed that function in the 2000 presidential race, but not in the usual way. In a triumph of the virtual over the real, it was Iowa's straw poll, rather than the actual Iowa caucus, that played the main role in winnowing out the candidates.

Interestingly, Bush's invisible primary successes were obtained by a deliberately low-key and detached campaign run from the governor's mansion in Austin, Texas. Rather than launch a peripatetic campaign, Bush stayed in Austin for months, receiving influential visitors and relying on his national fund-raising network of "Pioneers." While there was little doubt that he would run, Bush spent most of 1999 coyly "considering his options." Compared by some to the front-porch campaigns of the late nineteenth century, Bush's strategy depended on a growing aura of invincibility that his own circle had carefully cultivated. As late as October 1999, Bush was attacked by the rest of the Republican field for declining to participate in the first New Hampshire joint appearance. Bush in fact was looking past the primaries to the general election, trying to capture the center ground of the electorate. In moves guaranteed to stir protest from conservatives, he first derided House Republicans for trying to "balance the budget on the backs of the poor" and then criticized Republicans again for excessive cultural pessimism. Likened by many observers to Bill Clinton's famous "triangulation" in 1996, Bush's positioning angered some in his party but resonated with the broader public.

While Bush's success in this period goes a long way to explaining his ultimate victory, the twists and turns of the invisible primary also help to explain why his victory was not as easy as some expected, and why it was John McCain who presented the greatest challenge. Just as media coverage first raised Bush to the status of front-runner, the media gradually fixed on McCain as its preferred underdog. John McCain was the favorite of the media, no doubt about it, and he worked assiduously to cultivate their support.

This process began in earnest during the NATO bombing campaign over Kosovo in March to June 1999, when McCain urged that the Clinton administration openly consider the introduction of ground troops rather than face the prospect of an interminable and indecisive air war. During this period, McCain was a frequent guest on television news shows and was by far the most prominent of the political figures demanding a policy that protected our national honor. To many, he looked to be more of the commander in chief than Clinton himself. Between February and June 1999, McCain's national name recognition increased by 10 percentage points, and he moved up to fourth place in New Hampshire, behind Bush, Dole, and Dan Quayle, in a June 1 Gallup poll. Pollster John Zogby declared, "McCain has set himself apart by seeming to stand for something and also by being ubiquitous. . . . He's gone from asterisk to first tier."[20]

In contrast, Bush's stance on Kosovo seemed indecisive. To columnist Lars-Erik Nelson, "Bush's bland statement of support for the troops, drafted only after hours of consultation with advisers, made it clear that he was out of his element."[21] To the *Wall Street Journal*, Bush's pronouncement was "so vague and tepid as to be almost Clintonian."[22] For the first time, analysts like William Schneider noted, "There's a big buzz about McCain and a lot of questions being raised about Bush."[23] However briefly, the episode also focused attention on foreign affairs and reminded Americans that the selection of a president is the selection of a commander in chief. That recollection clearly worked to McCain's favor.

Attention mounted for McCain throughout 1999. It focused in no small part on his bus tour aboard the "Straight Talk Express," where he consolidated his close relationship with members of the press. Also contributing to McCain's high visibility was his autobiography *Faith of Our Fathers*, which commentator Charles Krauthammer called "without a doubt the most important campaign book in recent American history." Krauthammer went on, "It is striking how many people bring the book for McCain to sign at rallies. It has become a totem," highlighting the way that McCain's war experience "sets him apart from other politicians, others of his generation, and other contenders for the presidency—most starkly from George W. Bush."[24] Indeed, McCain's 15-city book tour in September 1999—long after he determined to run but before he had officially announced—was a turning point in his campaign, as positive popular response clearly energized the protocandidate. At the same time, McCain's fund-raising picked up, and he consolidated his position as a (distant) second to Bush among all Republican aspirants. Wisely, McCain avoided the Iowa straw poll (as he later avoided the Iowa caucuses), so he, almost alone among Republican competitors, was not hurt by Bush's victory. As other Republicans dropped out, McCain moved to pick up their supporters, especially those of Elizabeth Dole.

When Bush stumbled a few times late in 1999, McCain was poised to benefit. The first crisis Bush faced was in the summer and fall, when he refused to answer questions about possible drug use in his past. McCain's "straight talk" theme drew voters who feared that Bush was another calculating, slick, and possibly dissolute Clinton. In the early fall, Bush's reluctance (contrasted with McCain's willingness) to criticize Pat Buchanan's book *A Republic, Not an Empire*, in which Buchanan argued that American intervention in Europe in World War II was unnecessary, worked to McCain's advantage. Later in the fall, when Bush was unable to answer a journalist's pop quiz about the names of obscure foreign leaders, McCain's Senate experience in foreign affairs contrasted favorably. Among the non-front-running Republican candidates, McCain alone had significant fund-raising success in the last half of 2000, as his total fund-raising grew from $6 million midway through the year to $15 million at the end.

As the Republican invisible primary gradually shaded into the real campaign for real delegates in real contests, there were six candidates remaining, but only one clear front-runner. All the other candidates had no choice but to attack Bush. Four of the five did so more or less from his right. This imbalance made Bush look like the centrist candidate, which suited his overall strategy quite well. But none of these four rightist candidates could plausibly be nominated—among other things, only Orrin Hatch had experience in elective office.[25] McCain was the fifth non-front-runner, an alternative to Bush but not yet clearly ideologically positioned. But he was gaining ground, and if he was not yet threatening Bush, he was steadily establishing himself as the main challenger. By the beginning of the election year, William Kristol could argue, "The story of the first half of '99 was obviously Bush and the second half is McCain. The question of 2000 is whether Bush's initial fund-raising advantage and huge lead in the polls hold up or does McCain's momentum overcome Bush? But the biggest story is that it's a genuinely competitive race. McCain has a real chance."[26]

On the Democratic side, there were two phases to the invisible primaries. Al Gore won the first phase so decisively in fund-raising, poll numbers, and endorsements that he preemptively drove all but one opponent from the field. As a measure of that strength, Gore had already locked up 500 of the 716 Democratic "superdelegates" by December 1999. He also won the crucial endorsement of the AFL-CIO in October and dominated the contest for the support of the constellation of interests that define the modern Democratic Party. But in a second phase, the one remaining opponent, Bill Bradley, gained so much ground that he seriously threatened Gore's hold on the Democratic nomination.

The difference between the first and second phases closely tracked evolving public attitudes about Bill Clinton and impeachment. As the months passed after Clinton's acquittal by the Senate, public sentiment gradually softened toward Congress and hardened toward Clinton. A new scandal erupted, centered on Chinese spying, and an Arkansas woman by the name of Juanita Broadderick produced a credible, though unprovable, allegation that Clinton had sexually assaulted her in 1978 (after the airing of the claim, *Newsweek* casually conceded, "Sounds like our man"). While Clinton retained a high job approval rating, voters increasingly told pollsters that they wanted an ethical change and that character loomed large in their presidential choice. By December 1999, some polls actually showed that a small plurality of Americans approved of the House impeachment, and commentators across party lines regularly spoke of "Clinton fatigue."[27]

It was no coincidence that this shift in opinion coincided with the ascent of Bill Bradley, whose demeanor and message promised a break from Clinton-Gore shadiness. For a time in late 1999, while Bush's stock was falling and McCain's had yet to reach its full height, Bill Bradley became the focal point of positive media attention. More than a few commentators touted his "authenticity" and spoke of his brilliance (he had been a Rhodes scholar in the 1960s). This burst of favorable publicity worked together with an impressive fund-raising capacity. By July 1999, Bradley had raised $11 million, and in the last half of 1999 he out-raised Gore considerably. By the end of 1999 he had raised about as much money as Gore overall and had more on hand. Bradley also received a few important (and surprising) endorsements, most notably one from New York Senator Daniel Patrick Moynihan, who argued, "Nothing is the matter with Mr. Gore except that he can't be elected president."

While national polls still showed Bradley trailing far behind Gore, he had narrowed that gap and actually overtaken Gore in state polls in New Hampshire and New York. Perhaps as importantly, Gore continued to trail Bush by double digits in head-to-head polls, keeping alive Bradley's argument that Gore was unelectable and that Democrats needed to look elsewhere for their nominee. Gore's weakness was displayed when he challenged Bradley in December to stop all television ads and engage in twice-weekly debates, tactics usually used by long-shot candidates and those running out of money. As the new year approached, a Gore adviser said of Bradley, "The momentum is in his corner."[28]

Gore responded to this unexpected threat with a major campaign shake-up. He moved his campaign headquarters from Washington, D.C., to Tennessee, in the process letting many of his big-salaried workers in Washington go, and brought veteran Democrat Tony Coehlo on board to be campaign manager. Some ridiculed this move, but it in fact acted as a needed stimulus to the Gore operation, which had grown complacent. Gore also hired literary feminist Naomi Wolf to provide image advice. For $500 a day, Wolf advised Gore to become more animated, wear earth tones, and play the part of the "alpha male."

Following that advice, Gore next went on the attack, defining Bradley as a quitter who had left the Senate in 1996 rather than stay to fight the Newt Gingrich–led Republican "revolution." Reminding Democratic voters that Senator Bradley had voted for the Reagan tax cuts in the 1980s, Gore simultaneously attacked Bradley for refusing to rule out tax increases in the future. Gore painted several Bradley policy proposals in ominous, though similarly contradictory, terms. For example, Bradley's health proposal was at once far too expensive and far too miserly for Medicare and Medicaid recipients. The thread of consistency that held Gore's project together was not substantive, but stylistic: Bradley would later describe the strategy as one of "a thousand promises, a thousand attacks" that was meant to put him on the defensive and allow Gore to dominate the campaign dialogue through sheer force of will.

Finally, Gore attempted to preempt Bradley's liberal challenge. He proposed gun licensing, a substantial expansion of health care and other federal spending programs, and an open acceptance of gays in the military (he was even forced to retract a statement that he would require appointments to the Joint Chiefs of Staff to scrap the "don't ask, don't tell" compromise of 1993). While moving significantly to his own left, Gore was careful to remain slightly to the right of Bradley overall, thus satisfying liberals without sacrificing too much his reputation as a centrist.

The Gore counterattack stanched the hemorrhage. But when the invisible primary ended, it was still an open question whether he or Bradley would ultimately win the prize. In January of 2000, Gore only managed to collect one-fourth his usual monthly fundraising average from 1999, and was out-raised by Bradley by more than a two to one margin.[29] Gore faced the prospect of losing in New Hampshire and not having another opportunity to redeem himself for over a month, during which time Bradley could spend money and more easily replenish his superior reserves in preparation for the next big round of primaries in early March. But Gore narrowly averted this fate, due largely to the third primary contest of 2000—an unexpected but decisive battle that crossed party lines. If one asks who ensured Al Gore's nomination, the paradoxical answer is not Al Gore himself. Rather, it is John McCain.

Notes

1. See William G. Mayer, "The Presidential Nominations," in *The Election of 1996*, ed. Gerald Pomper (Chatham, N.J.: Chatham House, 1997), pp. 23–24; Michael G. Hagen and William G. Mayer, "The Modern Politics of Presidential Selection: How Changing the Rules Really Did Change the Game," in *In Pursuit of the White House 2000: How We Choose Our Presidential Nominees*, ed. W. G. Mayer (Chatham, N.J.: Chatham House, 1999), pp. 37–38.

2. This tendency is even stronger on the Democratic side, which allots about one of every six delegate positions to "superdelegates"—ex officio delegates who are automatically seated due to the party or governmental offices they hold.

3. This issue is still a matter of dispute. It is arguable that it was not the rules that led to these men's defeat, but that neither ever really had the necessary support inside the party. However, the system still had many primaries between the beginning and end of the meaningful primary season, and still further front-loading might alter this.

4. There is a slight qualification to note. The national parties do not have direct power to prevent states from holding primaries; their leverage rather derives from their authority to seat delegates at the conventions, which they have exercised by rules that ban delegates chosen before a certain date. Normally, this threat is enough to prevent states from scheduling primaries of any sort before the permitted date. Nevertheless, two states in 2000—Delaware and Washington—went ahead and held Democratic "beauty contest" primaries, primaries in which voters express a preference for candidates but in which no delegates are selected, before March 1.

5. Serious intraparty challenges were mounted against Presidents Taft (1912), Truman (1948 and 1952), Johnson (1968), Ford (1976), Carter (1980), and Bush (1992). In only two of these seven cases (Carter and Bush) were midterm losses not higher than average. In four of the remaining cases, presidential party losses were higher than av-

erage in both the House and Senate; in 1950, Democratic losses were slightly lower than average in the House but higher than average in the Senate. Altogether, these seven instances include four cases in which the president ran a full-scale campaign for renomination against intraparty foes (1912, 1976, 1980, and 1992), two cases in which incumbent presidents had begun running renomination campaigns but were driven from the field at an early stage (1952 and 1968), and one case in which the incumbent president was renominated but faced two challengers from within his party who ran as third-party candidates in the general election (1948). In the seven cases taken together, the president's party lost an average of 37 House seats and 5 Senate seats, compared with an overall average from 1922 to 1998 of 32 House and 3 Senate seats.

6. *The Wirthlin Report*, December 1998.

7. Paul R. Abramson, John H. Aldrich, and David W. Rohde, *Change and Continuity in the 1996 and 1998 Elections* (Washington, D.C.: CQ Press, 1999), pp. 256–60.

8 Thomas B. Edsall, "From the Left, Bradley Enters the Race," *Washington Post*, September 9, 1999, p. A1.

9. "Primary Reform," *Boston Globe*, December 8, 1998, p. A2.

10. Richard L. Berke, "Bradley Takes Early Party Prize: He Goes One-on-One With Gore," *New York Times*, April 20, 1999, p. 1.

11. Orrin Hatch's news conference of January 26, 2000.

12. William Kristol, "The New Hampshire Upheaval," *Washington Post*, February 2, 2000, p. A21.

13. Edwin Fuelner, "We're Not Finished," *Washington Post*, February 12, 2000, p. A21. For similar responses to Kristol, see William F. Buckley, "Hope Yet for Conservative Movement?" *Houston Chronicle*, February 5, 2000, p. A36; William A. Rusher, "Is Conservatism in America 'Finished'?" *San Diego Union-Tribune*, February 18, 2000, p. B11.

14. See Arthur T. Hadley, *The Invisible Primary* (Englewood Cliffs, N.J.: Prentice-Hall, 1976), and the fine treatment of Emmet H. Buell Jr., "The Invisible Primary," in *In Pursuit of the White House 2000: How We Choose Our Presidential Nominees* ed. William G. Mayer (Chatham, N.J.: Chatham House, 1999).

15. One could consider the invisible primary as stretching right up to the date of the first actual contest in which delegates are at stake, but this is, in the end, unsatisfactory. It is clear that a gray area separates the invisible from the visible stages of the campaign, and the former conception does not take account of the campaigns for those first states which have a direct bearing on their outcome.

16. William G. Mayer, "Perspectives on the Current Presidential Selection Process," statement prepared for the Advisory Commission on the Presidential Nomination Process, Republican National Committee, November 22, 1999, *Nominating Future Presidents* (Washington, D.C.: RNC, May 2000), p. 114. For several supporting academic views, see more generally pp. 109–47.

17. William G. Mayer, "Forecasting Presidential Nominations," in *In Pursuit of the White House 2000: How We Choose Our Presidential Nominees*, ed. William G. Mayer (Chatham, N.J.: Chatham House, 1999).

18. Adam Clymer, "Standing on the Sidelines, Analyzing the Reasons Why," *New York Times*, January 18, 2000, p. A21. In this environment, Alexander and others (including Quayle) argued that competition required some very large contributions in order to allow one at least the chance to get into the campaign as a viable contender, but

such contributions were made impossible by the $1,000 maximum contribution limit imposed by federal election law.

19. See Adam Nagourney, "Wins of the Father Are Visited on the Son," *New York Times*, June 14, 1998, p. IV1.

20. Ronald Brownstein, "Crisis in Kosovo Gives McCain's Presidential Bid a Boost," *Los Angeles Times*, April 22, 1999, p. A8.

21. Lars-Erik Nelson, "Kosovo Shows McCain is Brains, Voice of GOP," *Arizona Republic*, April 7, 1999, p. B7.

22. *Wall Street Journal*. See also "Bush and the Art of Nothingness," *Buffalo News*, April 20, 1999, p. B2.

23. Linda Feldman, "War shifts outlook for 2000 race," *Christian Science Monitor*, April 15, 1999, p. 1.

24. Charles Krauthammer, "Profile in Courage," *Washington Post*, February 25, 2000, p. A23.

25. The lack of experience of these rivals clearly irked Hatch. Days before the Iowa caucuses, Hatch remarked to a reporter that "They have a right to run, but I believe you should be elected to something first." Dana Milbank, "Orrin Hatch, Running on Empty in Iowa," *Washington Post*, January 21, 2000, p. C1.

26. Finlay Lewis and Otto Kreisher, "Next Month Could Tell if McCain is real Threat to Bush," *San Diego Union-Tribune*, January 3, 2000, p. A1.

27. A CNN/USA Today/Gallup poll taken one year after the House impeachment decision showed that by a 50–49 percent margin, the public expressed support for that decision. At the time of the decision, the public disapproved by a 63–35 percent margin. Keating Holland, "A year after impeachment, public approval grows of House decision," December 16, 1999, http://www.cnn.com/1999/ALLPOLITICS/stories/12/16/impeach.poll/.

28. Susan B. Glasser, "A Bounce in Bucks for McCain, Bradley," *Washington Post*, December 30, 1999, p. A1.

29. George Archibald, "Campaign delays paying some bills," *Washington Times National Weekly Edition*, February 28–March 5, 2000, p. 1.

Chapter Three

The Party Nominations:
The Three-Way Race

As the "invisible" primary made the passage into the visible campaign of real caucuses and primaries, it gradually became apparent that one of the most important contests of the year would be between Bill Bradley and John McCain. Both had staked out positions as mavericks seeking to shake things up, Bradley with an emphasis on "big ideas" and McCain with an emphasis on campaign finance reform. Both claimed to offer a refreshing turn to idealism and "straight talk." Both were lauded for their "authenticity." And both tried to turn their undeniable status as underdogs to their advantage. The January 24 Iowa caucuses, which came after late surges by both McCain and Bradley, would be the first "real" test of the campaign season.

McCain's surge began in December, after Elizabeth Dole's withdrawal from the campaign. When Bush appeared to stumble in his first debate appearance on December 2, journalists redoubled their search for a viable challenger.[1] (Interestingly, commentators took more than a week to decide that Bush's performance was sub-par, having at first been satisfied that he had passed the minimum threshold of avoiding any major mistakes.) Key events in the Republican campaign in December also helped dictate the contours of the Bush-McCain race for the remainder of the primary season.

Another event in December that helped shape the contours of the Bush-McCain race was the unveiling of Bush's five-year, $483 billion tax cut plan. McCain saw an opening on Bush's left, and attacked him for supposed fiscal recklessness in terms reminiscent (as Bush would soon point out) of Clinton's attack on the failed congressional tax cut of 1999. This was also probably the decisive point at which a disillusioned media came to conclude that Bush actually was serious about the "conservative" half of compassionate conservatism. Media disenchantment with Bush at the end of the invisible primary was a crucial ingredient in McCain's subsequent surge. The tax issue also set both campaigns on the course that defined the rest of the primary contest. Ironically, Bush became the confirmed candidate of the right, while McCain appealed most strongly to independents and even Democrats.

The Republican debates leading up to Iowa undeniably helped to shape the race. As was expected, given Bush's status as front-runner, the debates that began on December 2 were a match of all against one.[2] With the exception of McCain, the "all" tilted heavily to the right, making issues like abortion and religion the major topics of discussion. The tone of the debates might have left Bush thinking that his major competition remained to his right. As it turned out, this was incorrect, as there seemed to be an inverse relationship between the influence exerted on the debate topics by outspoken social conservatives and the support those candidates subsequently received in the primaries. Bush managed to deflect attacks — and indeed made great headway in consolidating his previously tenuous hold on the Christian right — when he answered a question about which historical thinker had influenced him the most with "Jesus Christ" because, as Bush said, "He changed my heart." His answer forced the social conservative candidates, who named more traditional political philosophers, to scramble to amend their answers in response. In spite of their effort, Bush seized the initiative to win the crucial social conservative constituency, and he did it in a way that minimized emphasis on divisive issues. As one journalist pointed out, "Bush is pioneering a more personal religious style in his courtship of evangelical votes. Rather than agreeing to a checklist of religious right issues such as abortion and gay rights, Bush seeks to connect to his fellow born-again Christians 'from the heart' as he was to say."[3] But Bush's answers provided an opening for McCain, who was perceived as the only "secular" candidate in a religiously dominated field.

McCain ran no real campaign in Iowa, conceding the caucuses as he had conceded the earlier Iowa straw poll.[4] Despite McCain's surge in some polls, Bush won Iowa over Steve Forbes 41 to 30 percent, with McCain getting only 5 percent. With his second-place showing, Forbes claimed to be confirmed as Bush's main threat to the right, a result that could have meant trouble for Bush. Though McCain and his supporters might have secretly harbored some disappointment at his weak showing, they could plausibly claim that it meant nothing, since he had not been engaged. McCain adviser Dan Schnur justified their strategy by saying, "You've got such a compressed calendar that it's going to be difficult for almost any candidate to fight everywhere. If you're smart you pick your spots."[5] Bush, for his part, believed he received a boost from Iowa, and could take encouragement from the lack of a spontaneous groundswell for McCain. But given Forbes's stronger than expected showing (and abundant resources) and the continuing appeal of McCain in New Hampshire, Bush was faced with the dangerous prospect of defending himself against attacks on both his left and right flanks. Republican pollster Linda Divall described New Hampshire as "a test for Bush to see if he can fight a two-front war."[6]

In the simpler, two-man Democratic race, Bill Bradley's surge came in the fall of 1999, several months earlier than McCain's. As he steadily gained on Gore, Bradley made a critical strategic decision. Having pulled ahead in the New Hampshire polls, he chose to contest Iowa as well, where he still trailed Gore by a large margin. Bradley ran an expensive television ad campaign and spent nearly three days in Iowa for every two days he spent in New Hampshire (by contrast, Gore divided his time more evenly).[7] At the same time he downplayed his effort by having his advisers intimate that it would be a moral victory if he outperformed Edward Kennedy's 31 percent showing against Jimmy Carter in 1980.

In this early campaign, Bradley was undoubtedly damaged by Gore's aggressive campaigning, to which he often failed to respond. In their precaucus debates, Gore was both energetic and caustic as he blistered Bradley for supporting education vouchers and threatening Medicare and Medicaid. Bradley's plan would, Gore charged, "shred the social safety net." [8] Worse for Bradley in Iowa, the vice president claimed Bradley had not supported disaster assistance after floods in 1993. As it turned out, Bradley had voted for a large package of disaster relief, but had opposed an additional increment—as had the Clinton administration itself until the last possible moment. Faced with this rather bald-faced misrepresentation, Bradley failed to answer effectively, leaving many viewers with the impression that Gore's charges were true. In contrast to the studious Bradley, Gore also anticipated his combative general election campaign theme, saying, "For 23 years, I have fought for working families, for working men and women."[9]

Starting in mid-December, Bradley was also slowed down by a recurring heart condition that took him off the campaign trail for several days. What hurt him more than the lost time was the appearance of not being forthright with the public, as he failed for some time to acknowledge or explain his condition and withheld his relevant medical records. As McCain would later discover in the aftermath of the Michigan primary, candidates who base their appeals on "authenticity" and candor have much to lose from perceptions of dishonesty and evasion.

Bradley met his self-proclaimed vote percentage target on caucus day in Iowa, but just barely, winning only 35 percent of the vote to Gore's 63 percent. But Bradley's target did not necessarily correspond with others' expectations, who suspected that he had set it artificially low. Unlike McCain, who could argue that the Iowa results were meaningless because he had not campaigned there, Bradley had campaigned enough in Iowa to acquire a stake in the results. At the same time, Bradley's neglect of New Hampshire put him in jeopardy there. It might have been the case, however, that unlike McCain, Bradley had no choice but to contest Iowa. As one Bradley strategist lamented, "In a two-man race, the press would never let you skip Iowa."[10] Plus, Bradley had a sufficient reserve of resources that he could not claim poverty as a reason to choose between a full-scale campaign in Iowa and one in New Hampshire.

What, then, in the end, was the significance of Iowa? For Republicans, the caucuses exposed the weakness of most of the candidates to Bush's right. Of course the straw poll taken the previous summer, in August 1999, had already significantly winnowed down the field, so only one candidate, Orrin Hatch, left soon after losing the Iowa caucuses. For Democrats, the conclusion is more complicated. A Bradley win, or even a stronger showing, could have put him over the top in New Hampshire. But it is not at all clear that his wide defeat hurt him, as he won a majority among New Hampshire voters who made their choice in the week following the Iowa caucuses. Gore's win in Iowa also came at a heavy price. His tactics in the run-up to the caucuses angered Bradley, who finally came out swinging in the last week of the New Hampshire campaign, focusing on the vice president's lack of trustworthiness—a theme that would dog Gore through (and even after) election day. Bradley, on the other hand, spent precious time and money in Iowa—money that he later needed to deal with Gore's resurgence in New Hampshire. All in all, David Broder contended that Bradley's Iowa miscalculation meant Gore was "in the driver's seat now."[11]

The Iowa results illuminated the challenge facing Bradley's campaign and the reasons why winning the Bradley-McCain contest was so vital to Bradley's chances. Exit polls indicated that Gore had done exceptionally well among self-identified Democrats, union households, elderly voters, and voters with a favorable opinion of Bill Clinton. Bradley did best among the youngest voters, upper-income voters, Internet users, and non-union households, and actually beat Gore among independents, 42 to 39 percent. Among the small group of voters who gave Bill Clinton failing marks for job performance, Bradley also won (62 to 25), and he held his own (45 to 45) among the much larger group—the four of nine Democratic caucus attendees—who had an unfavorable opinion of Clinton *personally*.[12] In short, if Bradley was going to beat Gore, it was clear he would have to do it on the strength of independents, nonorganizational reform Democrats put off by the Clinton-Gore scandals, and the youngish, affluent, wired, and polit-ically unattached denizens of the "new economy." It was precisely this group—as difficult to mobilize as it was important—that became the object of competition between Bradley and McCain. The Iowa caucuses also made it clear that Bradley would have to become more aggressive. He lost 67 to 30 percent among Iowans who followed the debates "very closely" but only 45 to 42 among those who had followed them "not closely"—a result un-doubtedly tied to the greater interest of strong partisans in political events, but also probably connected to Bradley's weak debate performance.

Leaving Iowa aside, New Hampshire seemed a good target for both Bradley and McCain. The state had a historical tradition of boosting un-derdogs, held an open primary with a large population of independent vot-ers, and promised enormous positive media attention for an upset win. Bradley and McCain even took the step, highly unusual for primary can-didates of different parties, of holding a joint appearance in New Hamp-shire in mid-December to discuss campaign finance reform. They had be-come aware of their common interest in promoting change and hoped that the joint appearance would legitimize scattered press speculation of a pro-reform, all-underdog, McCain-Bradley contest in November. They did not yet seem aware, however, that they were also engaged in a zero-sum strug-gle with each other, despite the anecdotal evidence presented by the media in the fall of 1999 of New Hampshire voters torn between the two men.[13]

By December 1999, some polls in New Hampshire showed Bradley pulling in front of Gore and had McCain surpassing Bush. McCain pro-ceeded to hammer Bush as the representative of a corrupt status quo, ar-guing that Bush's tax plan would favor the rich at the expense of Social Se-curity and Medicare. Bush stepped up his appearances in New Hampshire, but otherwise adhered to the front-runner's strategy of remaining as far above the fray as possible. His advisers expressed confidence that their man's slippage was the result of his personal inattention to the state rather than McCain's appeal.

Gore took a very different approach, aggressively challenging Bradley on a variety of issues, as he did in Iowa. Gore apparently regained the lead. In this race, for weeks, it was the challenger Bradley who appeared aloof. In the last days of the campaign, Bradley finally took off the gloves, ques-tioning Gore's honesty. Bradley called the Clinton-Gore 1996 fund-raising scandal "disgraceful," and asked Gore in a televised debate, "If we can't trust what you say when you campaign, how are we supposed to trust you when you are president?" Bradley also pressed Gore on abortion, forcing him to disavow a statement he had made in the 1980s acknowledging the potential life of the unborn child. In the end, while Bradley outspent Gore in New Hampshire, Gore out-organized Bradley, claiming to have contacted over 300,000 households either in person or by telephone.[14] Both Bradley and McCain fought hard for the independent voters and weak partisans who could vote in either primary. Going into the final weekend, no one could say who would win.

On election day in New Hampshire, McCain pulled away from Bush by a larger margin than anyone had thought possible, garnering 49 percent of the vote to Bush's 31 percent. He did it by beating the Texas governor 62 percent to 19 percent among self-identified independents, who made up two-fifths of the electorate in the Republican primary.[15] The level of non-GOP turnout was no doubt aided by election day registration of young independent voters. The Arizona Senator also built a fairly broad ideological coalition in New Hampshire, a feat he had difficulty repeating elsewhere. McCain won handily the support of those who had voted for Pat Buchanan in 1996, won more narrowly among Bob Dole's 1996 voters, and beat Bush three to one among Steve Forbes's voters from four years before (though Forbes, who was still running in 2000, won the most votes from that grouping). McCain won all ideological groups except those identifying themselves as "very conservative" and even polled a small plurality among "born again"/evangelical voters. McCain also prevailed with voters who said they most wanted a candidate who "stands up for what he believes in," "is a strong and decisive leader," and "cares about the average American." These candidate qualities were as salient as any issue; McCain's trademark stand on campaign finance reform was identified as the most important issue by only 9 percent (though campaign finance probably improved McCain's position on the dimensions of leadership and integrity).[16] Among Republicans, the two ran very close.[17]

Bradley, on the other hand, lost New Hampshire to Gore by the narrow margin of 50 percent to 46 percent. While self-identified independents represented 40 percent of the Democratic primary electorate, Bradley won only 56 percent to 41 percent among them, while losing Democrats by 18 percentage points, 59 percent to 41 percent.[18] Bradley lost among all ideological groups except the "very liberal," but he again won the anti-Clinton vote, the Internet-user vote, the nonunion vote, and the vote of those with college degrees and high incomes. Though his margin shrank considerably, Gore essentially maintained the same coalition that had propelled him to victory in Iowa.

In the end, McCain and Bradley were competing for, and attracting, the same vote in New Hampshire. Both did best among independents. Both won among voters who were willing to consider voting for the Reform Party (McCain by 48 to 21, Bradley by 55 to 41) and lost among those who were not. Finally, of the one in six Republican voters who had considered voting in the Democratic primary for Bradley, McCain won 72 percent; of the one in three Democratic voters who had considered voting in the Republican primary for McCain, Bradley won 57 percent. But from this point on, the parallels ceased. McCain's campaign began a run that took the Arizona senator to the threshold of the Republican nomination. Bradley's campaign began a slide that took the former New Jersey senator into near oblivion. There were several explanations for this outcome.

Bush's unexpected collapse in New Hampshire may have been at least partially due to a last-minute appearance by his father that backfired. At a Bush campaign rally the Saturday before the primary, the former president attempted to stir support for his son, saying, "This boy, this son of ours, will not let you down." Broadcast all over New Hampshire (and the nation), the remarks by Bush the elder accentuated Bush the younger's alleged immaturity and reminded voters of the charge that Governor Bush had made his way in life feeding from the silver spoon of his father. Additionally, one of George W. Bush's greatest challenges among Republican primary voters was to convince them that he was *not* his father, a man many of them blamed for running the Reagan legacy into the ground with his 1990 tax increase and his often directionless administration.[19]

Bradley's defeat can be attributed to his unwillingness to respond to Gore's aggressive tactics until very late in the contest. Had his counterattack against Gore started even one week earlier, he might well have won, as he only needed a 2 percentage point shift from Gore to himself. Indeed, exit polls indicated that Bradley had actually won by a significant margin among voters who had decided whom to support sometime in the last week of the campaign.[20] Bradley lost, then, partly because he was not tough enough early on, despite his status as an ex-jock. In the end, it was Gore who seemed to have the athlete's proverbial "fire in the belly." Also, Bradley's heart problem (and seeming lack of candor surrounding it) may have swayed enough voters to cost him New Hampshire. According to exit polls, one-fifth of the Democratic primary electorate was concerned about Bradley's health, and of those, more than four-fifths voted for Gore.

The most important factor leading to both Bradley's defeat by Gore and the size of McCain's triumph over Bush, however, was McCain's decisive victory over Bradley among independents and weak partisans. The miracles of opinion polling allow us to reconstruct the estimated vote totals of all of the races in New Hampshire, including the interparty primary between McCain and Bradley that was never actually held (see table 3.1). For Bradley, simply not enough independents voted in the Democratic primary, and of those who did, not enough voted for him. By examining the

Table 3.1.   The Three Races in New Hampshire

A. Republican Primary

Actual Republican Primary

All Voters			Only Republican Self-Identifiers		
Candidate	Vote Total	Percent	Candidate	Vote Total	Percent
McCain	115,490	49	Bush	51,056	41
Bush	72,262	31	McCain	47,319	38
Forbes	30,197	13	Others	26,151	21
Keyes	15,196	6			
Bauer	1,656	1			
Others	155	1			

B. Democratic Primary

Actual Democratic Primary

All Voters			Only Democratic Self-Identifiers		
Candidate	Vote Total	Percent	Candidate	Vote Total	Percent
Gore	76,681	52	Gore	48,461	59
Bradley	69,993	47	Bradley	33,676	41

C. "Reform" Primary

Votes for McCain and Bradley among Independents and Cross-Party Voters

Candidate	Vote Total	Percent
McCain	67,056	67
Bradley	32,855	33

voting turnout and the results in the Republican and Democratic primaries, and then extrapolating from exit poll data, it appears that about 38,000 more independents voted in the Republican primary than in the Democratic primary. Moreover, McCain won something on the order of 26,000 more votes from independents than did Bradley, all while Bradley lost to Gore by fewer than 7,000 votes. Finally, more than twice as many Democrats voted in the Republican primary (most of them for McCain) than did Republicans in the Democratic primary.

McCain's victory in that contest was the result of several factors. First, McCain was a more dynamic candidate than Bradley, with a more compelling personal story. Somehow relaxed and passionate at the same time, with a reputation for raunchy humor, McCain appeared to many voters as more approachable than the professorial and understated Bradley. The Rhodes scholar simply could not compete with the war hero who had once refused early release from the "Hanoi Hilton" because other prisoners had been there longer.

Second, and just as important, the media not only soured on Bradley, but became even more enamored with McCain. By mid-January, commentators focused on Bradley's lack of engagement, the diminishing appeal of his old-time liberal message, and sometimes his alleged pomposity. Media reports called him, among other things, "curt and uncommunicative," "sarcastic and condescending," "aloof," "vaguely disdainful," and "holier than thou."[21] McCain, on the other hand, became the undisputed darling of the media, a position made possible by his personality and the virtually unprecedented access to the candidate offered to media correspondents. As one major newsmagazine reported, "It was McCain's inspiration to reverse the popular wisdom that candidates had to be protected and insulated from the press. Instead, he gave the press total access for 18 hours a day on his 'Straight Talk Express' bus."[22] As Joe Klein of *Newsweek* put it, Bradley "has the opposite-of-John McCain effect, because he is so removed from us." To Klein, the souring of the media on Bradley "has been brewing for a long time."[23] McCain also became a frequent subject of the satirical news program "The Daily Show," poking fun at himself and playing along with the "correspondents." Widely watched among younger voters, McCain used this unconventional forum to demonstrate a sense of humor and a connection to popular culture, both of which Bradley seemed to lack.

Finally, some Democratic consultants argued that Bradley's early surge had been fueled largely by Republican-leaning independents. Once McCain emerged as a viable contender, those voters naturally gravitated toward him.[24] Indeed, evidence indicates that McCain, who was much closer to the ideological center than Bradley, was also more attractive to weak Democrats than Bradley was to weak Republicans.[25] By constructing a chart placing each of the four major contenders on a scale of ideology and reformism, we can see how McCain was better positioned to win the reform vote than was Bradley.

McCain's victory over Bradley was not just the decisive event of the New Hampshire primary, but also one of the decisive events of the whole primary season. The downward spiral suffered by Bradley proved impossible for him to escape, due not only to McCain's political momentum but

Table 3.2. Position of Major Candidates

		Ideology		
		Left	Center	Right
Reform	Pro-Reform	Bradley	McCain	
	Not Major Issue	Gore		Bush

also to the ban on Democratic, but not Republican, delegate selection for the remainder of the month of February. After the New Hampshire primary on February 1, there was no meaningful Democratic contest until March 7. By contrast, Republicans held at least five high-profile primaries during that period, primaries that monopolized public attention and media coverage and allowed McCain to consolidate his hold on independent voters. In the New Hampshire Democratic primary, fully one-third of voters had considered voting for McCain in the Republican primary instead of Bradley or Gore in the Democratic contest, but had finally decided against it. Now that Bradley had lost and was out of the spotlight, similarly ambivalent voters in future states were free to flock to the Arizonan.

Unnoticed amid the McCain hoopla, there was a second winner in New Hampshire: George W. Bush. To be sure, he could ill afford very many more such victories. Nevertheless, while he lost a crucial battle against McCain, Bush won an equally important battle against Forbes (who had received the coveted endorsement of the *Manchester Union-Leader*), holding him to a mere 13 percent. The Bush campaign had correctly identified Forbes as its greatest threat on the right from an early date; Forbes had been the target of some of Bush's initial New Hampshire television ads, which reminded voters of the slash-and-burn campaign run by Forbes against Dole in 1996. The ads served a dual purpose, inoculating Bush against similar Forbes attacks and increasing Forbes's negatives. Within a few days, Bush beat Forbes again in Delaware (along with McCain), getting 51 percent to the publisher's 20 percent and driving him from the race. By winning decisively against Forbes, Bush ended the specter of the "two-front war" and made it possible to consolidate his hold on the Republican right.[26] In the end, this early consolidation was a key to Bush's success.

The February 19 Republican primary in South Carolina was the next major test of strength. After New Hampshire took its inevitable toll on the weaker candidates, only Bush, McCain, and Alan Keyes remained. For all practical purposes, the nomination contest had narrowed to a two-man race. That race, as former Reagan speechwriter Peggy Noonan argued, pitted the "boss's son" Bush—the safe, establishment choice—against the "flyboy" McCain, who captured the imagination of primary voters but whose success may have been built on "less a crusade than a crush." Noonan pinpointed the ambivalence of Republicans: Was McCain "the opposite of Mr. Clinton," war hero, peppery, and honest, or was he really "Clinton II," a "strange and self-promoting egotist, one who is unpredictable, inconsistent, and vain?" Did the Washington establishment dislike McCain so much because he was "so much his own man" or "so much a flawed man?"[27]

Bush strategists had long viewed South Carolina as the proverbial "fire-wall," a state where Bush could stop McCain's momentum in the event of an upset in New Hampshire. South Carolina, in contrast to New Hampshire, was well disposed to the Bush family, dating back to the 1988 and 1992 primaries that gave a significant boost to the elder Bush. Moreover, the party establishment in South Carolina traditionally exerted significantly more influence than in New Hampshire. In 1996, for instance, Bob Dole had relied on South Carolina as a "firewall" against the surging Buchanan campaign. Nevertheless, after his New Hampshire surprise, McCain cut deeply and immediately into Bush's South Carolina lead, overcoming a 25 percentage point deficit almost overnight. McCain also narrowed Bush's lead in national polls. After Iowa, Bush was in front 65 to 16, after New Hampshire 56 to 34.

Many analysts also noted the potential for McCain to do well among South Carolina's numerous military personnel and veterans. What's more, South Carolina, like New Hampshire, had an open primary, allowing McCain to heavily target non-Republican voters. McCain announced that his goal was "to bring about a new Republican Party" and pleaded for the votes of "Republicans, Democrats, libertarians, and vegetarians." Utilizing the Internet, McCain raised one million dollars within three days, and he acquired the endorsement of social conservative Gary Bauer.

In contrast to the chummy atmosphere of New Hampshire, both Bush and McCain went on the attack. The bitterly fought campaign featured negative ads on both sides, including a McCain ad that compared Bush to Bill Clinton. Both candidates were also caught up in a local controversy regarding the flying of the Confederate battle flag over the South Carolina state capitol. While Bush said that this was a matter for South Carolinians to decide, McCain gave conflicting answers that seemed to belie his image of candor.

Shedding his prior placidity, Bush counterattacked McCain's charges with a ferocity resembling Gore's war on Bradley. Indeed, there were more than a few analysts who detected a whiff of panic in the Bush camp. Long the assumed front-runner, Bush suddenly and unexpectedly had his back against a wall. Tactically, Bush opened up and borrowed heavily from McCain's town meeting format. As Bush later explained it, "I felt there had been something of a disconnect between me and the voters, so I went face to face with as many voters as I could."[28] Emphasizing his belief in limited government, Bush offered himself as "the conservative candidate," using the word "conservative" seven times in one short speech the day after New Hampshire. Bush also received the endorsement of Steve Forbes and stepped up accusations that McCain's tax cut plan was Clintonesquely small.[29] Independent groups supporting Bush also attacked McCain for alleged ambiguity on abortion, stemming at least partly from an interview in which McCain refused to say that he would discourage his daughter from obtaining an abortion. The South Carolina Right to Life Committee organized a "get out the vote" drive for Bush, and Pat Robertson launched a campaign of automated telephone messages accusing former New Hampshire Senator Warren Rudman, whom McCain had mentioned as possible attorney general material, of anti-Christian bigotry.

Most significantly, Bush reconfigured his message, though not quite in the way that was claimed by analysts who later decried a drastic shift to the right. Bush did emphasize more conventional Republican issues like limited government, but what changed most was that "compassionate conservatism," which seemed to stir few voters in New Hampshire, was dropped in favor of the slogan "a reformer with results." Acknowledging his opponent's reformist appeal, Bush contrasted his own record of education and tort reform in Texas with McCain's cozy relationship with interests regulated by the McCain-chaired Senate Commerce Committee. As E. J. Dionne later pointed out, Bush reconceptualized reform as a deeper moral revival, in contrast to the merely political reform advanced by McCain.[30] This attempt by Bush to claim the mantle of the "true" reformer was scorned by an outraged McCain, but not entirely by South Carolina's voters. By election day, more voters thought Bush was a "real reformer," and they were more likely to say that McCain's, rather than Bush's, campaign attacks had been unfair.[31] In the end, McCain, the optimist and "anti-politician," probably suffered disproportionately from using typical political tactics.

Pollsters on primary eve declared the race too close to call, but Bush won by a comfortable margin, 53 percent to 42 percent. Approximately two of every five voters were non-Republicans, a figure comparable to (and possibly surpassing) that in New Hampshire. While Democrats went for McCain at a rate of 79 percent, they represented only one-tenth of the electorate. Independents were about one-third of the primary voters and went 60 percent for McCain, though his 43-point margin over Bush in New Hampshire was shaved to 26 points in South Carolina. The biggest difference, however, was that where McCain ran neck and neck for Republicans on February 1, he lost self-identified Republicans by a margin of 69 to 26 percent on February 19.

Bush's change in strategy and tactics had two particularly important consequences. First, as was widely noted, he strengthened his appeal among religious conservatives (a task that was aided by the removal from the race of most of the social conservative candidates). In New Hampshire,

Bush held a mere 10 percentage point advantage over McCain among voters who identified themselves as members of the religious right. In South Carolina, that margin ballooned to 44 percentage points. Second, Bush expanded his appeal to include the moderately conservative. In New Hampshire, he had won only among "very conservative" voters and voters who favored making abortion "always illegal." In South Carolina, Bush again won these groups handily (by margins of about three to two), but he also won among the "somewhat conservative" ideological identifiers and among those who believed abortion should be legal in only "few" cases.[32]

In both instances, the moderately conservative position represented the largest grouping in the electorate, significantly outnumbering the category of most conservative. Bush's ability to control the moderately conservative vote was thus decisive.[33] This shift among moderate conservatives was the result of McCain's leftward moves (at least rhetorically), the withdrawal of Steve Forbes from the race (which left an opening for Bush to build a broader conservative coalition), and Bush's own emphasis on his conservativism. In New Hampshire, his relatively nonideological campaign meant that only those who were linked to conservative organizations and those most amenable to Bush's personal discussion of faith were likely to have gotten the word that he was a conservative candidate. In South Carolina, his emphasis on conservative rhetoric quickly established him as the remaining viable candidate from that wing of the party, in contrast to McCain. After these decisive results in South Carolina, numerous election analysts instantly declared the Republican race essentially over. In their view, Bush, like Dole four years earlier, had retaken control and would not lose it again. That view lasted exactly four days.

On February 22, Michigan and Arizona held their Republican primaries. Arizona was assumed to favor McCain, although he had trailed in polls there a year earlier and Arizona's Republican governor had endorsed Bush. Michigan was believed to be a Bush state, in no small part because Governor John Engler and his reputedly strong organization solidly backed the Texan. Indeed, a *Detroit News* poll taken January 7–14 showed Bush beating McCain in Michigan 51 percent to 17 percent. In the whirlwind post–South Carolina campaign in Michigan, McCain struck back, accusing Bush for the first time of being an unelectable captive of Pat Robertson and the religious right. To support his charge, McCain pointed to Bush's campaign visit to Bob Jones University in South Carolina. Bob Jones University was notorious (at least among the small percentage of Americans who had ever heard of it) for its official policy banning interracial dating and for the rabidly anti-Catholic views of its founder. McCain seized on Bush's university speech, an innocuous call for limited government, for its failure to condemn the dating policy. (Ironically, the policy was implemented in 1953 as the result of a lawsuit brought against the university by a disapproving Asian couple whose student son had almost married a Caucasian girl.) Ultimately—that is, after the Michigan primary—Bush felt compelled to make multiple apologies and even sent a lengthy letter disavowing any anti-Catholic sentiment to Cardinal O'Connor of New York.

By this point in the campaign, it was clear that a certain level of mutual personal hostility had crept into the Republican race, just as it had done earlier in the Democratic race. Weeks and months before, during the debates that led up to the first primaries, Bush and McCain had struck a positive, even friendly, note. In certain respects, they had a shared problem: Bush, as the front-runner, and McCain, as the man rapidly becoming the one significant challenger to the front-runner, were both frequent targets of the rest of the aspirants. But this comity began to crumble in the last stages of New Hampshire when McCain launched the first negative ads against Bush, collapsed in South Carolina with Bush's counterattack, and finally vanished altogether in Michigan.

Given both the high stakes and the brief turnaround time between South Carolina and Michigan, both of the candidates and their campaigns were driven to the point of exhaustion. In a sense, McCain's campaign was more agile. As a smaller operation with a more spontaneous (many said disorganized) style, it was able to turn around quickly, adjust, and fling itself once more into the fray. While that spontaneity proved costly later in the campaign, in Michigan it gave McCain the advantage.

Appealing directly to independents and Democrats, McCain won as decisively in Michigan as he had lost in South Carolina. In one sense, his victory—won after his campaign's epitaph was widely read in South Carolina—gave his campaign much-needed new life. Exit polls showed he had regained control of the "reform" issue, and proved once again his strong appeal to "swing" voters.[34] Nevertheless, McCain's win flashed warning signs to his campaign. The core of his support came from Democrats and independents, who together made up 52 percent of Michigan primary voters. Of these groups, McCain won two-thirds of independents and four-fifths of Democrats, all while receiving less than a third of the votes of Republicans. McCain was the first candidate in Michigan history to win a Republican primary while receiving more than half of his votes from non-Republicans. It was emblematic of McCain's Michigan coalition that he was most strongly favored by those who were not affected at all by Governor Engler's endorsement of Bush, and by those whom it affected "a great deal." In other words, McCain's support came from those with weak, or no, party ties, who did not care about the party establishment, and from those with strong Democratic ties, for whom Engler's endorsement of Bush was a strong reason to vote for McCain. For his part, Engler caustically remarked, "John McCain isn't party-building. He's party-borrowing." The unusually high turnout of independents and Democrats, who represented 35 and 17 percent of the Republican primary electorate respectively, masked the continuation of Bush's South Carolina coalition. In Michigan, like South Carolina, Bush soundly beat McCain among the "somewhat conservative" voters and those supportive of legal abortion only in a few cases, while at the same time carrying the religious right 67 percent to 27 percent.

McCain's dual victories in Michigan and in Arizona (where he won two-thirds of the vote) gave him a lead over Bush in delegates won and renewed his confidence. Polls showed him surging into a very competitive position in the March 7 New York and California primaries. McCain's fund-raising again spurted, while Bush's pre-primary war chest of $70 million had dwindled to $20 million, leaving him with not much more cash on hand than McCain. In the 24 hours after Michigan, McCain demonstrated his fund-raising momentum by raising another $250,000 over the Internet.[35] Bush—so recently saved from disaster—was facing it again. He now appeared somewhat uncertain, even dazed.

The last contests before March 7 Super Tuesday came on February 29, when North Dakota, Virginia, and Washington held Republican primaries. North Dakota was for Republicans only, while Virginia and Washington were open (although in Washington, only the votes of Republicans counted toward delegate selection, and then for only about a third of the delegates—a caucus in March would choose the rest). After McCain's victories in Michigan and Arizona, Bush's lead in Virginia was cut in half.[36] At first McCain heeded the warnings from Michigan: to win a Republican nomination, you must win Republican votes. His strength among crossover voters was a double-edged sword. On one hand, that strength caused Bush to lose the image he had long cultivated of being the one Republican candidate who could best reach out and broaden the party's base. But on the other hand, Republican Party activists who feared that McCain was "hijacking" their nominating process with the help of their political enemies increasingly resented McCain's successes with nonparty members.

Coming out of Michigan, McCain emphasized his conservative Republican credentials. "I am a proud Reagan conservative," McCain repeatedly intoned, as he tried to make a conservative case for campaign finance reform (it would make it harder for special interests to lobby for higher spending) and smaller tax cuts (which would make it easier to pay off the national debt). He acquired the near-endorsement of conservative cultural guru William Bennett, who said, "It is pretty clear that John McCain is a better bet for winning the Presidency for the Republicans than George Bush."[37] McCain campaigned hard as the Republican best equipped to "beat Al Gore like a drum," and as the only Republican able to fully exploit Gore's fund-raising scandals. This argument was only bolstered by new national polls that suddenly showed him leading Gore by a wider margin than Bush in a general election matchup.

McCain then succumbed to the fatal temptation to play to his strength, instead of confronting his weaknesses. After barely beginning the arduous task of winning the trust of Republican conservatives, McCain launched into a tirade against much of the leadership of the social conservative movement in America. Lumping together Bob Jones, Pat Robertson, and Jerry Falwell, whose theologies and idiosyncrasies are quite distinct, McCain attacked them as "agents of intolerance," compared them to Al Sharpton and Louis Farrakhan, and assailed the influence of the religious right in Republican politics. "We are the party of Ronald Reagan," McCain said, "not Pat Robertson." The very next day he expanded on this theme, calling Falwell and Robertson "evil."

Though McCain belatedly apologized and made a distinction between the leaders and their grassroots followers, the damage was done. However well his comments may have been received on National Public Radio and at the Harvard Faculty Club, they clearly backfired in Virginia and Washington, two states with large blocs of conservative Christians. Bush immediately pounced, accusing McCain of being a divider and "playing the religious card." Ronald Reagan, Bush said, "didn't point fingers. He never played to people's religious fears like Senator McCain has shamelessly done."[38] Gary Bauer, who had endorsed McCain in South Carolina, called on him to apologize, while William Bennett, who had touted him only a few days before, said the Arizonan was guilty of "rhetorical overkill not appropriate for a man running for president of the United States." Bennett elaborated, "I don't know what's going on . . . I'm not a psychiatrist."[39] McCain's remarks were particularly damaging when combined with the revelation days earlier that the "straight-talking" McCain had lied when he earlier denied that his campaign had orchestrated a phone campaign prior to the Michigan primary accusing Bush of anti-Catholic bigotry.

When the voting in North Dakota, Virginia, and Washington was over, McCain lost in the open Virginia primary 53 to 44, in the closed North Dakota primary 76 to 19, and by a 19-point margin in the Republicans-only vote that determined national convention delegates from Washington. Even more damaging to McCain, Bush eventually also squeaked by to win in the nonpartisan "blanket primary" in Washington, where Democrats and independents could also vote. Unfortunately for McCain, it was not clear how close the symbolic blanket primary truly was (0.17 percent separated the two in the final vote tally) until long after the national media had indicated a wider Bush win on the basis of early returns. While McCain still won among non-Republican voters in Virginia, his Republican vote collapsed completely. Only a week before the primary, McCain was losing to Bush among Virginia Republicans 50 percent to 24 percent.[40] On election day the, split was 69 to 28. Self-described religious conservatives voted for Bush by a whopping margin of 66 percentage points in Virginia (80 percent for Bush versus 14 percent for McCain), but once again Bush's coalition of moderate conservative and very conservative self-identifiers held firm.

McCain's defeat in these three primaries was caused in great part by the reaction of religious conservatives against McCain's anti-Christian conservative outbursts. But there also might have been at least three other, subtler, consequences of McCain's statements. First, many Republicans not affiliated with the religious right might well have thought he was recklessly threatening party unity, even if they agreed with portions of his argument. Second, questions about McCain's mercurial temperament and unsound judgment, first raised in late 1999 as he began his campaign in earnest, resurfaced. Finally, for the first time in the Republican presidential race, a significant gender gap developed, with McCain doing significantly worse among women than among men. This was perhaps caused by women's oft-hypothesized aversion to confrontational political strategies.

Analysts offered a range of explanations for McCain's behavior. This could be a tactical ploy, they said, inoculating him against a probable loss in Virginia by playing to voters in the more liberal venues of California, New York, and Ohio, with the assumption that he could win back social conservatives by November if he won the Republican nomination. McCain might also have sought to lay the groundwork for a new Republican Party shorn of its social conservative wing, others posited. Or, more pessimistically, some said he simply succumbed to his "fabled temper" over the role Pat Robertson and others played in his South Carolina loss.[41] In any event, with these losses McCain's momentum was gone, his message unglued, and the Republican vote he needed—and that seemed, at least on the surface, to be within his grasp only a few days before—was rapidly receding. In retrospect, John McCain's quest for the Republican nomination for the presidency ended when the polls closed in Virginia and Washington on the evening of February 29.

But an open question remains. Was this finality a fresh truth, or was it instead a recognition of a reality that had existed since South Carolina? On one hand, Michigan had given McCain a tangible boost. While it was difficult to quantify, there was a definite sense among many Republicans that they were open to McCain and were waiting, and perhaps even hoping, for him to close the sale. In this view, that the sale did not happen was largely of McCain's own doing. Charles Krauthammer, for one, argued that, based on his record, "there is no reason McCain should not be splitting the religious right with Bush."[42] Political scientist Mark J. Rozell similarly argued that McCain "simply cannot wrest the nomination from Bush unless he somehow convinces enough of the Christian social conservatives that he is their best candidate. . . . His record makes him credible in that regard. But his rhetoric in the campaign has not. McCain almost seemed to be going out of his way to alienate the most conservative GOP activists—a group he could easily have appealed to."[43]

On the other hand, despite the subsequent oscillations of the campaign, Bush assembled in South Carolina an enduring center-right conservative coalition that appeared in every other primary and caucus state. It was difficult to imagine that, over time, he would not win the nomination of the nation's center-right conservative party. Given this underlying structure of the campaign—a structure many commentators did not recognize due to their incomplete interpretation of South Carolina—McCain's decision to lash out against the religious right might have been more strategically justified than was widely understood. In this view, his only (and, despite Michigan, rapidly dwindling) hope was to drive a wedge between the very conservative and the somewhat conservative parts of the Republican primary electorate. In other words, he had to restore the division among conservatives that characterized the results in New Hampshire. If this is true, he gambled and lost, but only as the result of a calculation that convinced him he had little choice.

During this entire nearly month-long period, almost all attention was focused on the heated and constantly shifting Republican race. Bill Bradley had only two small electoral opportunities to work his way back into the news: Delaware's nonbinding presidential preference vote on February 5, and Washington's nonbinding presidential preference vote on February 29. Delaware received little attention from Democrats or Republicans—McCain avoided campaigning there entirely—so in one sense Bush's win and Bradley's defeat were not very consequential (indeed, subsequent news reports routinely failed to even include Bush's

Delaware win in their tallies). In another sense, though, Bradley was not in a position to be satisfied with avoiding public relations disasters; he needed wins before March 7.

Consequently, Bradley chose to concentrate on the February 29 Washington primary, even though no delegates were at stake, to try to regain some momentum and puncture the increasing aura of invincibility surrounding Gore. Finally recognizing the mortal danger posed by McCain, Bradley went on the attack in Washington against the Arizona Republican, whom Bradley accused of environmental laxity. Despite five full days of hard campaigning, an extraordinary time commitment heavily criticized by some political consultants who questioned why he was not in New York or California, Bradley lost by 68 to 31 among Washington Democrats, and among all voters by a slightly narrower margin of 65 to 35. Furthermore, for the first time, Bradley and McCain were locked in a death grip. As in New Hampshire, McCain cost Bradley dearly, trouncing him among unaffiliated voters by a margin of three to one. Bradley, however, might have won enough unaffiliated votes to deprive McCain of a much-needed victory in the beauty contest.[44] Having staked everything on Washington, Bradley's defeat left him on the edge of extinction.

Aside from the Delaware and Washington votes, Bradley had only a handful of moments in the spotlight. At one point, he caused a small stir by suggesting on ABC's *This Week* that an independent counsel should have been appointed to investigate Al Gore's fund-raising shenanigans. On February 21, Bradley sought to seize the initiative in New York and nationwide by attacking Gore as too conservative in a televised debate held in the venerable Apollo Theater in Harlem. But both candidates vied to be "leftier than thou" on matters including affirmative action, racial profiling, gun control, health care, and obeisance to Al Sharpton (who was given the honor of asking the first question). Bradley landed few clean blows and even took some unfair blows from Gore, who charged before the mostly black audience that "racial profiling" of blacks by the police "practically began" in Bradley's New Jersey.[45] Otherwise, Bradley was a nonentity for five weeks, a fatal situation for an underdog—and a somewhat surprising situation for a man who had come within a whisker of beating an incumbent vice president in New Hampshire and who still retained vast financial resources.

As media scholar Kathleen Hall Jamieson remarked in mid-February, "The press is functioning as if the Bradley-Gore race is over. Bradley has been effectively closed out of the news since New Hampshire."[46] Eric Hauser, Bradley's press secretary, observed in frustration, "We almost won New Hampshire. We needed attention and, given the normal rules of politics, earned it with the New Hampshire performance." On a lighter note, an unnamed network reporter covering the Bradley campaign was overheard complaining in a telephone call to his wife, "I'm in a vacuum—it's a waste of time. They [the networks] don't have any interest at all. We're going to have to come back with some naked pictures or something to get on TV." Bradley himself, in a rare moment of levity, proclaimed, "I need an event. I should hold up a bank."[47]

On March 7, the Republican and Democratic races fully converged again. Republicans held primaries or caucuses in 14 states, and the Democrats in 16 states, including delegate-rich California, New York, and Ohio. At stake were 528 of the 1,034 Republican delegates needed to win nomination (51%), and 959 of the 2,170 delegates needed for the Democratic nomination (44%). While everyone understood how desperate Bradley's position had become, McCain's was more ambiguous. Prior to February 29, both New York and California seemed within McCain's reach. At the very least, McCain's strategists believed he might win the nonpartisan California preference primary (the so-called blanket primary, such as the one used in Washington State) even if he lost the Republicans-only delegate selection primary. This convoluted system had arisen because of a conflict between California law and party directives. California's primary had a single ballot for all voters, listing all candidates, and therefore allowing any voter to vote for any one candidate, regardless of party. Because of the single ballot, the results are tallied and expressed for the whole candidate field, not divided per party. But the rules of the Republican and Democratic national parties prohibit such voting methods, thus potentially invalidating California's delegates. This conflict was resolved in 2000 when a second, simultaneous, primary was established for delegate selection. California accomplished this by setting up three different balloting options: one for only Republicans to vote for Republican candidates, one for only Democrats to vote for Democratic candidates, and a third for any voter to vote for any candidate. McCain strategists hoped that they could retain some momentum, even if they lost the party delegate selection, if they could claim their candidate to be the most popular *total* Republican vote-getter among all California voters. (Some even speculated that under such circumstances McCain might challenge the legitimacy of the California delegation at the Republican National Convention.)

In the battle for California and New York, where a court challenge had made it easier for McCain delegates to appear on the primary ballot, the Republican race reached its crescendo in early March. McCain grew increasingly shrill, while an independent group supporting Bush bought ads attacking McCain for, among other things, his environmental record and opposing funding for breast cancer research. When it became known that the ads were paid for by Sam and Charles Wyly, wealthy Texans who had long supported Bush, McCain thundered, "Where's the outrage?" Nevertheless, McCain's 16 percentage point lead over Bush among New York Republican Catholics evaporated in the growing backlash against McCain's inflammatory religious remarks.[48] On election day, Bush won big, carrying New York with little difficulty, beating McCain in both the blanket and delegate primaries in California, winning the big open primary in Ohio, and prevailing in nine of fourteen primaries overall.[49]

If the Republican race concluded with a bang, the Democratic race ended with a whimper. A debate held the week before the vote was amazingly conciliatory, as if both candidates knew the game was up. A few days before March 7, Bradley spoke like a defeated candidate, referring to his campaign in the past tense. On election day, he clearly was a defeated candidate: Al Gore swept every one of the 16 Democratic contests, most by huge margins. Two days later, Bradley announced the formal end of his campaign, and McCain declared that he was "suspending" his. The nomination race was over, before 31 states had selected delegates.[50]

Explaining the Results

In the end, there were several reasons why Al Gore pulled ahead of Bill Bradley. Gore turned out to have a demonstrably stronger base within the Democratic Party than Bradley. His vice presidential incumbency was a major factor in his ability to woo blacks and organized labor, two mainstays of the party. Bradley found Gore's hold on black voters particularly frustrating, since he himself had made racial issues a key part of his campaign. In this, Gore seems to have benefited from his ties to Bill Clinton, who was called by Toni Morrison "the first black president." Gore was also aided by Clinton in another way: while Clinton's "legacy" will be debated for years to come, the primaries showed that the president had largely succeeded in changing the center of gravity within the Democratic Party, at least for the time being. Bradley's old-line liberalism, which had a great appeal to Democrats in the 1980s, seems to have been passé in 2000. Clinton made Democrats comfortable with incrementalism on health care, gun control, and many other issues. Gore also proved to be a much stronger and more tactically adept campaigner than Bradley, especially after his makeover in the fall of 1999. Bradley's responses to Gore were often too little and too late. His key mistakes included shifting resources from New Hampshire to Iowa and, depending on which analyst one believes, either targeting Washington State too late to be effective (that is to say, not putting in enough effort there) or targeting it at all (putting in too much effort).

Above all, though, Gore beat Bradley because McCain beat Bradley first. Had that not occurred, Bradley might easily have won New Hampshire and left Al Gore struggling for five weeks. As columnist George Will commented, "[A]t most, one candidate in any given year can mount a strong campaign for a presidential nomination by relying to a significant extent on independents, and on members of the other party who are only lightly attached to it. . . . This year, either Bradley or McCain could win the contest for this free floating constituency. McCain did."[51] In the view of Senator Paul Wellstone, Bradley's first supporter in the Senate, Bradley's collapse in February had much to do with the fact that "Bill has not yet been able to do what McCain has been able to do: show that this is an insurgent campaign with a galvanizing message."[52] Or as an unnamed White House adviser so aptly put it, "You can't start a fire without oxygen, and John McCain is sucking it all up."[53] In the view of several commentators, Bradley made the fundamental error of not recognizing early on that his and McCain's interests were in conflict. As E. J. Dionne put it, "The first month of primaries were not primaries at all but a state-by-state general election in which the candidates in both parties were competing for many of the same votes."[54]

Just as Bradley lost to Gore because he first lost to McCain, McCain came much closer than expected to Bush because he had first beaten Bradley as the standard-bearer for "change," "authenticity," and "straight talking." The importance of that contest also indicated that there was a stronger undercurrent of dissatisfaction in the electorate than many analysts had previously detected. The appeal of "outsiderism" was much less dominant in 2000 than it had been in 1992 and 1994—the year of Pat Buchanan, Ross Perot, Bill Clinton, and massive congressional turnover— but it was almost certainly a more powerful force than in 1996. However, it was also a different shade of outsiderism than seen in 1992, less hostile and alienated. Rather, it took the form of candidates within the establishment (who could argue that Bill Bradley and John McCain, the chairman of the Senate Commerce Committee, were not part of the establishment?) who claimed to be able to revamp that establishment from within. Nevertheless, both McCain's and Bradley's rhetoric, but especially McCain's, often veered into the Manichaeanism of the outsider. For example, McCain sometimes fashioned himself as a political Luke Skywalker of *Star Wars* fame, saying, "I feel like Luke Skywalker in the Death Star," and brandishing a toy light saber on stage after being introduced to the strains of

John Williams's famous score.[55] It is also interesting to note that McCain shared a certain affinity with Ross Perot's faith in the power of apolitical "experts" to solve national problems. Indeed, his attachment to campaign finance reform was seen by skeptics as a related attempt to remove politics from politics.

Also, as the Democratic Party had changed since 1992 in ways that favored Gore, so changes in the Republican Party in 2000 created divisions that made it difficult for Bush or any other front-runner to gain nomination by consensus. McCain drew close to Bush by tapping both moderates and "national greatness" conservatives. McCain also gave George W. Bush a race because of the media's and some of the public's sudden disenchantment with Bush: many began to perceive him as possessing too little intellect and perhaps too much conservatism. What's more, since McCain did better among independents and Democrats than among Republicans of any stripe, the rules of primaries were a crucial factor in his drive for the nomination. Where Democratic rules probably favored whoever won New Hampshire, the Republican primary schedule, with so many early open primaries, clearly favored McCain.

Just as Gore out-campaigned Bradley, McCain closed the gap with Bush by ably executing a well-conceived campaign, at least until late February. McCain also made the most of free media, thus nullifying much of Bush's early financial advantage. Bush, for his part, also helped McCain by playing a sort of political "prevent defense" until late in the campaign season, during which time he seemed more concerned with avoiding mistakes than in fighting aggressively for the nomination. (Bush's tendency to "sit on a lead" recurred in the general election campaign, once after the Democratic Convention and once in the last week before election day, and nearly cost him the presidency.) McCain also pioneered the use of new campaign technologies, signing up thousands of volunteers and receiving unprecedented financial contributions over the Internet. By Super Tuesday on March 7, McCain had garnered $5.6 million via his Web site, three times as much as Bill Bradley, five times as much as Al Gore, and eight times as much as George W. Bush. He had also recruited at least 2,000 volunteers through the Internet in Michigan, 16,000 in California, and undoubtedly thousands more around the rest of the country.[56]

In the end, Bush beat back McCain's strong challenge because the Texan himself improved as a candidate throughout the primary season. By the debates in late February and early March, Bush had become more comfortable, more assertive, and more capable. His campaign, highly scripted in the beginning, had become much more tactically adaptable. Furthermore, observers had long noted the contrast between

Bush's meticulousness on issues and McCain's tendency to, as one analyst put it, "wing it." As the primary season rolled on, that contrast became more apparent to voters. Bush had a national organization and a fund-raising network that McCain could not match. When the going got tough, Bush was able to fall back on reserves that McCain never possessed.

Even though the Republican Party was divided, conservatives continued to outweigh moderates or liberals, and limited-government conservatives outweighed "national greatness" conservatives. Given the firestorm on the right that followed Bush's October 1999 attacks on the Republican Congress and on conservative icons like Robert Bork, it was not inevitable that Bush would become the candidate of the limited-government conservatives. (Bork had responded that Bush "intends to reach the White House over the dead bodies of conservatives.") Bush therefore owed McCain a debt of gratitude, for attacking him from the left and thus defining the race in a way that aligned Bush with the strongest element of the Republican Party. It was Bush's ability to meld together the "very conservative" and "somewhat conservative" ideological identifiers, starting in South Carolina—and McCain's inability to disrupt that coalition—that guaranteed Bush's victory.

Having failed to appeal to the party's dominant wing on philosophical grounds, McCain also failed (though he might have come close in succeeding) in making the one argument that could have brought conservatives over in spite of their distrust: that he alone could beat Gore. McCain emphasized this argument after New Hampshire and won over (for a time) some key conservatives like Bill Bennett, but he never convinced a majority of primary voters. Throughout the primary season, exit polls showed Bush beating McCain on the question of who was most likely to win in November, even in states like New Hampshire and Michigan that McCain won.

While McCain was clearly a more colorful character than Bush, Bush was better liked than McCain by the end of the primary campaign. There were constant rumblings, especially from other senators and Arizona's governor, about McCain's alleged temper and inability to work with others. Bush, in contrast, portrayed a "good ol' boy" likability and self-effacing persona. In a sense, just as in the general election campaign against Gore, voters' judgments about Bush's likability were arguably really about temperament. In any event, focus groups organized by *U.S. News & World Report* and MSNBC indicated that Bush wore well, while McCain—especially at the end of the race—appeared whiny.[57] *New York Times* columnist Maureen Dowd complained that, by the end, "The Arizona senator wasn't running a campaign so much as an auto-da-fe, with himself as the martyr in the flames. . . . Even in an America that worships victimhood, you can't run for president as a victim."[58] In short, McCain imploded at a critical stage in late February. He became angry and unfocused, waging a counterproductive war against elements of his party that he needed to pacify and seeming to confirm the whispering campaign that had followed him for months. Despite all of Bush's advantages, McCain defeated himself.

Observers could draw a number of lessons from the role of the invisible primary in the Republican race. On one hand, in the end, Bush's huge advantage in fund-raising, endorsements, and national poll results carried the day. On the other hand, these massive advantages that were accumulated during the invisible primary quickly evaporated. While predictions of a Bush victory eventually held true, the results easily could have turned out otherwise. At more than one juncture, Bush's campaign seemed like a huge army with every advantage, yet one still about to crumble anyway. If social scientists are tempted to use 2000 to prove that the final outcome of a race is strictly predictable on the basis of the invisible primary, politicians could take heart in knowing that nothing in 2000 was inevitable.

The Aftermath of the Primaries

Immediately after the March 7 coup de grâce administered by Gore and Bush, a flood of commentary appeared arguing that Gore had gained the most from the primary season. In this view, Bush was hurt by swinging wildly to the right, while Gore had managed to hew more closely to the center. As longtime political correspondent R. W. Apple put it, Bush "emerged from the campaign a weaker candidate than he began it, scuffed by the attacks of his rival . . . and with a party dangerously split between conservatives and moderates." Gore, on the other hand, "emerged as a stronger, more vivid campaigner, and stands at the head of a much more unified party."[59] There was some evidence for this view. Most notably, Bush's lead in national polls shrank from double digits six months earlier to only a few points, often within the poll's margin of error. From late 1999 to the aftermath of the South Carolina primary, Bush's national negative ratings grew by half, from 20 percent to 30 percent, to about equal his positive ratings.[60] Some state-level polls showed a clear primary effect, as well. In Michigan, for example, Bush's lead over Gore evaporated at the time of the Republican primary, with his greatest slippage occurring among women and Catholics, two groups specifically targeted by McCain.

There were reasons, however, to question that Bush had lost so much ground. It was obvious that Gore and Bush had *both* taken advantage of the primaries to hone their messages and campaigning skills, so that they were both stronger candidates than before. As for Bush's alleged deathbed ideological conversion in South Carolina, in fact his movement to the right was more one of appearance than substance. Indeed, critics were unable to identify a single policy position of Bush's that was reversed during the primary season. At most, he shifted his *emphasis* to more traditional Republican issues. If he became the candidate of the right, it was mostly because he started as moderately conservative and the right moved toward him, not because he moved toward the right. In any event, Bush's adoption by conservatives, who mistrusted him even as late as the fall of 1999, gave him a stronger position within his party and more room to maneuver in the general election campaign. Likewise, the Republican split, while real enough, was overstated. McCain, after all, had never won a majority of Republicans in any big primary, and his Republican share of the vote actually declined throughout the primary season. As one Republican wag asked, pointing to Bush's overwhelming support among Republicans and McCain's strength among independents and Democrats, "What split?" So far as one can determine from the exit polls, McCain's supporters, without regard to party, liked him because of his character and his general theme of reform, not primarily because of his stand on issues. Campaign finance reform was never ranked the most important presidential campaign by more than 10 percent of Republican primary voters.

It is true enough that Gore's nomination victory was far easier than Bush's. But the primary results also sent some warning signs to the vice president. First was his razor-thin margin in New Hampshire. Next was the way McCain appealed across party lines to a large number of Democrats and independents—an indication that Gore did not have a strong hold on that crucial constituency. In a similar vein, Democratic primary turnout was lower than Republican turnout, which was partially the result of a more intense Republican race, but also potentially an indicator of a lack of excitement among Democratic voters. News stories also regularly appeared assailing Gore's veracity, reinforcing the negative message Bradley had left with voters.[61] Also troubling was that, from the beginning, Gore lacked a clear idea of how to manage his relationship with Bill Clinton. After keeping his distance for months, he began associating himself more closely with Clinton (by, for example, running ads touting the Clinton-Gore economic record) in the days before the Iowa and New Hampshire contests.[62] But finally, and perhaps most ominous for Gore, even after Bush's bruising nomination fight, when pundits declared Gore to have been advantaged by the primary season, Bush still held on to a narrow lead in most national polls.

Al Gore had actually done what Bush was inaccurately accused of doing: shifting his ideology in a way that made November victory more difficult. In contrast to Bush's consistency on a variety of issues throughout the primary season, Gore became beholden to the AFL-CIO and even cozied up to the racial demagogue Al Sharpton. Gore was temporarily rescued from criticisms for his leftist shift only because his opponent, Bill Bradley, consistently attacked him for his centrist past, never for his current leftward move. But there was no reason to believe that Bush would give Gore a free pass or that public perceptions could not be altered once voters began focusing more clearly on the race.[63] Because of this, moderate Democrats like Louisiana Senator John Breaux and Democratic Leadership Council Chair Al From began to express concerns that it was Gore who was the more ideologically exposed of the two major party candidates. From conceded, "I fear that Gore will not be able to win the vital center by pushing Bush to the right with a negative campaign. He will need to affirmatively occupy the center himself."[64]

Bush's declining lead during and after the primaries was probably as much the result of a setting in of political reality than of damage to Bush. There was little reason to believe that a Bush-Gore race was going to be an easy one. Bush's large leads of 1998–99 may have been a reflection of public disgust with scandal, a nebulous desire for change, or even nostalgia for Bush's father. Once combat truly began, it was inevitable that the race would narrow considerably. Whatever his weaknesses, Gore was riding the wave of a booming economy and was a disciplined campaigner. Whatever his strengths, Bush was still an unknown quantity, and many voters were certain to leave him when hard issues had to be discussed. The political balance in America was so tight—the politics of the Perfect Tie had long been observable, signified by the extremely close partisan division of Congress—that anything but a highly competitive presidential election was unlikely. What some analysts missed was that if Bush was overestimated when he led Gore by 15 percentage points in the Gallup polls, he was also underestimated after the primaries when his lead had shrunk to a more natural level.

The primaries sent a mixed message that both candidates strained to decipher. Overall turnout in the meaningful primaries increased considerably. The message seemed to be this: Voters were uneasy with the status quo, tired of politics as usual, but reluctant to rock the boat too much in good times. Measured reform was preferable, though reform of *what* remained a question. Voters were tired of the unrelenting political calculations of the

Clinton era and searched for someone they could trust. Issues were important, but so too was character. Outsiderism à la 1992 was gone, but a milder outsiderism was still in evidence. The McCain vote loomed large and was potentially decisive to both candidates. If that reading was correct, neither major party nominee had quite found the formula for November. If anything, though, Bush rather than Gore seemed to have the inside track.

Notes

1. Bush had declined to participate in the three earlier debates.

2. See David S. Broder, "Bush Faces Barrage in New Hampshire Debate," *Washington Post*, December 3, 1999, p. A1; Hevin Merida, "Hitting a Man While He's Up," *Washington Post*, December 3, 1999, p. C1. Merida referred to the first debate, held December 2, as "an evening of 'Get-the-Governor.'"

3. Hanna Rosin, "Bush's 'Christ Moment' is Put to Political Test by Christians," *Washington Post*, December 16, 1999, p. A14.

4. Analysts speculated that McCain avoided Iowa largely because his outspoken opposition to federal ethanol subsidies made success highly unlikely.

5. Dan Balz, "McCain Hears New Hampshire; GOP Presidential Hopeful Tries to Make Inroads on Bus Tour," *Washington Post*, September 2, 1999, p. A4.

6. David S. Broder, "A Two-Front Fight is Looming for Bush," *Washington Post*, January 25, 2000, p. A1.

7. Mike Allen and Ceci Connolly, "Bradley Divides His Time," *Washington Post*, January 20, 2000, p. A6.

8. Dan Balz and Ceci Connolly, "Gore Asserts Rival Would Need Hike for 'Flawed' Health Plan," *Washington Post*, December 6, 1999, p. A1.

9. Dan Balz, "Candidates Accomplished Their Mission in Democratic Debate," *Washington Post*, December 18, 1999, p. A8.

10. David S. Broder, "Bradley's Expensive Detour," *Washington Post*, January 26, 2000, p. A23.

11. Broder, "Bradley's Expensive Detour."

12. "Dem. & GOP Caucuses: Iowa: Entrance Polls," http://www.cnn.com/ELECTION/2000/primaries/IA/poll.html.

13. For example, see Marc Sandalow, "Voters at Ease With Laid-Back McCain," *San Francisco Chronicle*, December 4, 1999, p. A2; Melinda Henneberger, "Bobbing Up in the Polls, McCain is Feeling Buoyant," *New York Times*, October 30, 1999, p. A11.

14. Allen and Connolly, "Bradley Divides His Time."

15. "GOP Primary: New Hampshire; Exit Poll: Republicans." http://www.cnn.com/ELECTION/2000/primaries/NH/poll.rep.html McCain also won a 78–13 margin among self-identified Democrats, but they only made up 4 percent of the primary electorate. By a slightly different measure—voter registration, rather than self-identification—McCain did about as well among independents and actually won Republicans 44–35. All further voter statistics from New Hampshire are found in this source.

16. VNS Exit Polls, *New York Times*, February 2–3, 2000.

17. McCain claimed a modest victory on the basis of his 44–35 advantage among registered Republicans, though in response Bush could point to his own narrow 41–38 victory among self-identified Republicans.

18. Voter News Service, "Dem. Primary: New Hampshire; Exit Poll: Democrats," http://www.cnn.com/ELECTION/2000/primaries/NH/poll.dem.html

19. Exit polls showed that Bush actually won among voters who called the effect of Bush's father very or somewhat important, but it is still possible that the sudden interjection of Bush *pere* into the race had a less conscious negative effect on some voters.

20. VNS Exit Polls, *New York Times*, February 2–3, 2000.

21. See Howard Kurtz, "Bill Bradley No Longer So Lofty in Media Eyes," *Washington Post*, January 19, 2000, p. C1. Also Mike Allen, "In Iowa, Bradley's Style Leaves Some Cold," *Washington Post*, January 13, 2000, p. A1.

22. Kenneth T. Walsh and Roger Simon, "Bush turns the tide," *U.S. News & World Report*, February 28, 2000, p. 25.

23. Kurtz, "Bill Bradley No Longer So Lofty in Media Eyes."

24. Kenneth T. Walsh, "Meanwhile, on the Democratic side," *U.S. News & World Report*, March 6, 2000, p. 20.

25. Michael G. Hagen, Richard Johnston, and Kathleen Hall Jamieson, "Crossover Voting in the 2000 Primary Season: Results From a Longitudinal Study," paper presented to the Annual Meeting of the American Political Science Association, Washington, D.C., August 30–September 3, 2000.

26. Bush did not win the "two-front war" in New Hampshire itself but he achieved the next best thing, what the Pentagon now declares to be U.S. strategy in the two-war scenario: "hold and win." While holding on against McCain to fight another day, he ended resistance on the second front. Thus freed, he was able to redeploy his resources and turn his full attention to McCain in future primaries.

27. Peggy Noonan, "The Flyboy vs. the Boss's Son," *Wall Street Journal*, February 9, 2000, p. A26.

28. Walsh and Simon, "Bush turns the tide," p. 22.

29. Dave Boyer, "Bush says he's the real conservative," *Washington Times National Weekly Edition*, February 7–13, 2000, p. 8.

30. E. J. Dionne Jr., "What McCain Started," *Washington Post*, December 29, 2000, p. A33.

31. Voter News Service, "GOP Primary: South Carolina; Exit Poll: Republicans," http://www.cnn.com/ELECTION/2000/primaries/SC/poll.rep.html.

32. Of course, these are self-identifications, and it is possible that they vary from one place to another. Someone who considers himself somewhat conservative in South Carolina might, with the very same opinions, consider himself very conservative in New Hampshire. However, as we will see, the pattern established in South Carolina held firm for the rest of the primary season in both northern and southern states.

33. On the ideological scale, the "somewhat conservative" outweighed the "very conservative" by 37–24; Bush won that group by a 59–37 margin. On abortion, those believing it should be legal in "few cases" outweighed those who believed it should "never" be legal, and Bush won them by a 58–37 margin.

34. Voter News Service, "GOP Primary: Michigan; Exit Poll: Republicans," http://www.cnn.com/ELECTION/2000/primaries/MI/poll.rep.html.

35. "Bush loses fund-raising momentum; McCain gains," *Denver Rocky Mountain News*, February 24, 2000, p. 33A.

36. John Aloysius Farrell, "Bush Courts Virginia voters as poll shows lead over McCain shrinking," *Boston Globe*, February 26, 2000.

37. Ronald Brownstein and T. Christian Miller, "Bennett, Conservative Bulwark, Likes McCain," *Los Angeles Times*, February 25, 2000, p. A27.

38. Ron Fournier, "McCain derides Robertson," *Denver Rocky Mountain News*, February 29, 2000, p. 2A.

39. David Von Drehle, "Trying to Erase 'Evil,'" *Washington Post*, March 2, 2000, p. A7.

40. Farrell, *Boston Globe*, February 26, 2000.

41. See Michael Kelly, "The Christian Right: Past Its Prime," *Washington Post*, March 1, 2000, p. A17; Robert D. Novak, "Dissing the Christian Right," *Washington Post*, March 2, 2000, p. A19.

42. Charles Krauthammer, *Washington Post*, March 3, 2000, p. A29.

43. Mark J. Rozell, "Or Influential as Ever?" *Washington Post*, March 1, 2000, p. A17.

44. Though McCain won 139,000 more unaffiliated votes than Bradley did, Bradley lost by almost 148,000 to Gore, so McCain's success was not decisive. On the other hand, while Bradley won only 69,000 unaffiliated votes, McCain lost the "beauty contest" to Bush by fewer than 2,500 votes.

45. Ceci Connolly and Mike Allen, "Gore and Bradley Woo Minorities, Attack Records in Harlem Debate," *Washington Post*, February 22, 2000, p. A1.

46. Tom Hamburger, "Bradley supporters bemoan slide since N.H.," *Denver Rocky Mountain News*, February 20, 2000, p. 59A.

47. Dana Milbank, "The Man in the Gray Flannel Campaign," *Washington Post*, February 23, 2000, p. C1.

48. Ralph Z. Hallow, "Religion gambit draws quick backlash," *Washington Times National Weekly Edition*, March 6–12, 2000, p. 10.

49. As in Washington, though McCain handily beat Bradley in the "cross-party vote," Bradley—by merely remaining in the race—may have cost McCain a shot at winning California's nonbinding "beauty contest." Bradley's votes totaled nearly twice the size of McCain's margin of defeat in that portion of the primary. On the other hand, by this point in the race, Bradley may have been such an exhausted and shrunken force that his vote total represented his basic hard core of support, not easily transferable to McCain.

50. Robert D. Loevy, "Relevance and Irrelevance in State Presidential Primaries and Caucuses," paper presented to the Western Political Science Association meeting, San Jose, California, March 2000.

51. George Will, "Seven lessons from Bradley's fall," *Denver Rocky Mountain News*, March 5, 2000, p. 4B.

52. Hamburger, "Bradley supporters bemoan slide since N.H."

53. Walsh, "Meanwhile, on the Democratic side," p. 20.

54. E. J. Dionne Jr., "Bradley: On the Beaten Track," *Washington Post*, March 3, 2000, p. A29. See also Barton Gellman, Dale Russakoff, and Mike Allen, "Where Did Bradley Go Wrong?" *Washington Post*, March 4, 2000, p. A1.

55. David Von Drehle, "Campaign Diary; McCain Seeks Favor as Happy Warrior," *Washington Post*, January 31, 2000.

56. Jeff Glasser, "Virtual campaign pays off," *U.S. News & World Report*, March 6, 2000, p. 22.

57. Kenneth T. Walsh, "A bloody battle," *U.S. News & World Report*, March 13, 2000, pp. 16–18.

58. Maureen Dowd, "McCain falls victim to victimhood," *Denver Rocky Mountain News*, March 9, 2000, p. 49A.

59. R. W. Apple Jr., "As primary dust settles, victors seen in new light," *Denver Rocky Mountain News*, March 8, 2000, p. 2.

60. Walsh and Simon, "Bush turns the tide," p. 23

61. See Seelye and Broder, *New York Times*, February 19, 2000.

62. Charles Babington and Ceci Connolly, "Gore's Comfort Zone Now Close to Clinton," *Washington Post*, January 26, 2000, p. A1.

63. See David Broder, "Bush challenges Gore for control of the 'vital center,'" *Denver Post*, March 22, 2000, p. 7B; Michael Barone, "Eight More Months," *U.S. News & World Report*, March 20, 2000, p. 34.

64. Michael Kranish, "Party Moderates Fear Gore May Lose the Middle Ground," *Boston Globe*, May 5, 2000, p. A1.

Chapter Four

The Interregnum:
The Four Faces of Al Gore

The nearly six-month period between March and August, during which the two candidates have been chosen but not yet officially nominated, is the most recent addition to the modern presidential campaign. Only a decade ago, candidates competed for their nominations well into the spring, and most Americans did not think of the final presidential race as actually beginning until after the party conventions met in late summer. But with the front-loaded primary system that is now in place, the contest for the presidency in some sense now begins in March. This new phase has altered the character of the presidential campaign by allowing an entirely new layer of impressions about the candidates to develop before the start of the fall contest. Previously, the voters' last and most vivid memory of the candidates was of their performance in the primaries. Now, it is of their performance during this new part of the campaign.

Commentators are still struggling to develop a working vocabulary to deal with this period. Major media sources agonized over how to refer to the candidates before arriving at the pompous title of "presumptive party nominees." More importantly, the period itself has no commonly accepted name. We once suggested the Latinate term "interregnum," which is generally used to designate the interlude between two kingly reigns, but so far it has had few takers. Another possibility, which has the merit of paralleling the division of the nomination campaign into its phases of the "invisible" and the "real" primary, is the "invisible campaign." Like its namesake, though, it is a bit of a misnomer, as the candidates' activities during this period—much like their activities before the primaries—hardly pass unnoticed.

The interregnum or the invisible campaign—we will use both terms—is without doubt the least well understood phase of the presidential race.

Commentators and political practitioners alike are still trying to figure out how it fits into an overall campaign strategy. The events of the first full interregnum, in 1996 led many to draw the conclusion that this period is decisive to the outcome of the election. In that year, President Clinton leaped on Republican nominee Bob Dole in March and April, just as Dole was catching his breath from an unexpectedly difficult primary challenge from Pat Buchanan, Steve Forbes, and Lamar Alexander. Using the public funds Clinton saved from the primary period (when he faced no opposition), and with additional moneys he raised from the infamous White House coffees and sleepovers, the Democrats launched an ad blitz, linking Bob Dole with House Speaker Newt Gingrich, hardly the most popular man in America at the time. The Republican nominee, who did not respond in ads until two months later, never fully recovered. As a result, the 1996 campaign, as many tell the story, was virtually over before the party conventions. In the colorful language of Bob Dole's press secretary in 1996, "They destroyed our fighters on the ground."[1]

But a single case can hardly establish a general rule, and the basic strategic questions about this period still remain. What might it mean to "win" the interregnum? And how much does "victory" in this period really matter? No one, after all, enters a presidential race just to win the interregnum!

Campaign professionals insist that performance during the interregnum should be judged according to how it sets the stage for the fall campaign, rather than by its effect on candidate preference polls in the spring and early summer. Stanley Greenberg, Al Gore's chief pollster in 2000, contended that the test for this period should be the strength of the "building blocks" that are laid down. Electoral analyst Thomas Mann agreed, urging observers to focus on the "broader forces that shape the race but don't really settle in to be measured in the polls until the end of summer."[2] But given the uncertainty that characterizes political campaigns, commentators naturally gravitate to the "objective" or, at any rate, quantitative measure of poll standings. And despite what professionals may say, they too keep a close watch on the polls. They realize that even if the polls may be changeable, they still influence the flow of money and the strength of organizational commitment candidates receive. These in turn can translate into "real" gains over the long term.

Ceding to the vulgar practice of employing poll standings as a point of departure, George W. Bush can be declared the winner of the 2000 interregnum (see table 4.1). Bush won both in an absolute sense (he finished with a higher score than Al Gore) and in a relative sense (he gained ground on Gore from where they began in March), although his largest margin of advantage in this period came not at the end, but rather partway through.

Table 4.1.   Gallup Poll Results at the Beginning, Middle, and End of the
2000 Interregnum

March 30–April 2, 2000		*June 23–35*		*July 25–26, 2000**	
Bush:	46%	Bush:	52%	Bush:	50%
Gore:	45%	Gore:	39%	Gore:	39%
Other:	1%	Other:	1%	Other:	6%
Unsure:	8%	Unsure:	8%	Unsure:	5%

Source: Gallup.com.
* Note: This poll was taken two days after Bush named Dick Cheney as his running mate.

Bush's victory in the polls was confirmed by most observers' qualitative assessments. These held that Al Gore had not run a particularly effective campaign and that Bush had at a minimum made his candidacy more viable. Yet at the end of the interregnum, it is much harder to say whether Bush was actually in a better position than Gore heading into the general election. In 1996, Bill Clinton not only led in the interregnum polls, but he also held an advantage in the fundamentals known to influence the outcome of elections. Clinton at the end of this interregnum faced a cakewalk, running downhill all the way. In 2000, however, the winner of the interregnum did not have these fundamentals working in his favor. They favored Gore rather than Bush. So in 2000, George W. Bush, even though he was ahead at the end of this period, was still most likely running uphill.

The reader at this point is sure to wonder about all the attention devoted here to the invisible campaign. After all, as everyone knows, George W. Bush did not win the election simply because he won the interregnum, for no sooner did the real campaign begin than he fell behind Al Gore and remained there for more than a month. What then was the significance of Bush's interregnum "victory"? It appears that it was a necessary, though not sufficient, cause of George W. Bush's election. As the candidate running uphill, Bush needed a victory in the invisible campaign to put himself in a position to win. If he had fallen short in this period, victory in November would probably have been beyond his reach.

The Great Analogy: 1988 and 2000

Political commentators rely on three approaches for understanding presidential campaigns. First, they refer to basic models that codify important factors from past campaigns in order to indicate or predict which candidate "should" win the election. Setting aside the obsession some analysts display for purely mechanical prediction, these models rest on the perfectly

commonsense rationale that the condition of the country—as indicated by
various measures of how well the country is doing under the current party
holding the White House—should have a powerful effect on which candidate wins the election. Second, commentators look for specific campaigns
from the past that resemble or parallel the current one, on the grounds that
these cases will be able to shed some light on how the current campaign
will unfold. Finally, commentators take a direct look at the immediate case
in front of them, analyzing the mood of the country and assessing how well
the candidates are performing. Any intelligent study of political campaigns
will judiciously employ all three of these approaches. Each has certain
strengths and weaknesses, and all of them combined provide the greatest
degree of perspective.

Our focus for the moment is on the second approach of searching for
parallel historical cases. This is a common way of discussing not only electoral campaigns, but major events in foreign and domestic policy decisions
as well. The underlying idea is that there is a cause-and-effect pattern in
human affairs. If a major event happens one way at one time, it will most
likely happen again, given similar circumstances. Alternatively, it says that
a study of past events will at least bring to the surface tendencies held in
common during comparable times. Of course, through the study of the
past, human beings often hope to take steps that will either alter or fortify
past results. It is for this reason that campaign advisers, like military analysts, devote so much time to analyzing past campaigns.

Quite often, disagreements exist about which historical cases parallel
the case in study. But in 2000, only one case was widely referred to: the
1988 campaign between George H. W. Bush and Michael Dukakis. Not
only was this campaign recent, but its parallels to the conditions of 2000
were almost uncanny. In both cases, one of the candidates was an incumbent vice president in the prime of his career with a long and impressive
résumé, who, after making an earlier, unsuccessful run for the presidency
on his own, settled in to serving under a two-term president presiding over
a nation enjoying peace and prosperity. Their opponents were both popular governors serving their second term, who had recently won reelection
by impressive margins. Neither governor had held national office before,
nor could either claim much experience in the conduct of foreign policy.[3]
Finally, both were trying to modernize their parties by steering them away
from the more ideological stances associated with their parties' congressional wing, which held the majority in both houses.

So close are the similarities that it is possible to recycle much of the coverage of the 1988 campaign and use it to describe parts of the 2000 campaign.
In fact, probably the greatest obstacle in referring to the 1988 campaign to

describe the 2000 campaign was not in the analogy, but rather in keeping the names straight. One had to remember that the Democrat Al Gore was the counterpart to the Republican George Bush (father), while the Republican Governor George W. Bush (son) was the counterpart to the Democratic Governor Michael S. Dukakis. (It did simplify matters a bit, however, that Dukakis's father had never been vice president.) As for the candidates' intentions in looking at this historical model, Gore hoped that the race would turn out like 1988, while George W. Bush was seeking just the opposite. Al wanted to be like George, but George surely did not want to be like Mike.

The 1988 campaign was used not just by commentators, but also by practitioners from both campaigns in planning their strategies. In the script line of 1988, Governor Dukakis (=George W. Bush) led Vice President Bush (=Al Gore) in the polls by a significant margin throughout the summer. That lead collapsed during the incumbent party's (Vice President Bush's) convention, after which Bush pulled ahead with a lead of his own that he never thereafter lost. Three factors are credited with explaining this reversal in 1988. First, the Republican Convention in 1988 provided the opportunity for Vice President Bush to step out from the shadow of the incumbent president (Ronald Reagan) and become his own man, while at the same time highlighting the administration's accomplishments. Second, as the election approached, voters began to focus on the true condition of the country, and their assessment of these "fundamentals" clearly favored Bush, the incumbent party's candidate. Finally, Bush undertook an aggressive campaign against Michael Dukakis, labeling him a strong liberal and attacking his record as governor in Massachusetts. Dukakis failed to responded effectively, preferring "sitzkrieg" to blitzkrieg.

In the planning from Al Gore's side, a literal application of the lessons of 1988 might imply that no change in his fortune could be possible until after the Democratic Convention. He would have to be patient and "wait" for history to play itself out—(which, as it turned out, was exactly what happened, as Gore pulled ahead only after his convention). Yet the study of past examples inclines those of an activist bent, like Al Gore, to try to speed things up. Gore has never been one to bide his time—in the fashion, say, of General Kutuzov in *War and Peace*. He has instead sought to shape events and "force the spring."[4] Gore adopted a more proactive approach to the interregnum for another reason, as well. The new, longer interregnum period in 2000 meant that the election calendars differed between 1988 and 2000. Gore's team therefore concluded that he could not wait until the conventions to make his move, lest he wait too long.

The view in Al Gore's camp was that the real campaign should begin in earnest in March. As an indication of just how earnest, Gore sent an e-mail message Gore to Bush on March 15, and then promptly released it to the press, in which he congratulated Bush on securing his party's nomination and challenged him to "agree to a regular series of debates on the major issues facing the country" that would begin "within two weeks." "Get back to me," Gore concluded.[5] Bush politely declined, although not by the medium of e-mail. While the press was still referring to Al Gore as "the presumptive nominee," this presumption was not about to hold him back in any way. Nor did it deter George W. Bush. Within one week of their nomination victories, a national television ad-war between the two candidates was already under way.[6]

The Stages of the Interregnum

In Hindu theology, the god Siva is known for its manifestations in radically different forms, appearing alternatively as the Destroyer, the Redeemer, and the Creator. Al Gore achieved a similar reputation for himself in the pantheon of American politics during the interregnum, successively assuming the different shapes of the Reformer (March and April), the Attacker (May), the Affirmer (June), and finally, the Populist (July). Adopting this Gore-centered schema of periodization is not a mere construction, but rather reflects stages that were all but publicly proclaimed by the Gore campaign itself, when it sought to call attention to the "new looks" of its candidate. Such a tactic, one should add, is not unusual today when a campaign is trailing. If a candidate is in a downward spiral, campaign managers may calculate that they have no alternative but to "reintroduce" their candidate in a new incarnation.

Whatever benefit may derive from this tactic, it obviously opens the door to criticisms of inconsistency and opportunism. Al Gore's campaign endured just such criticisms during the interregnum period, not only from the Bush camp, but also from the press. This left a negative impression that Gore had great difficulty erasing. Who or what was the real Al Gore? Or, even more, was there one? Meanwhile, the Bush campaign, which enjoyed the luxury of pulling ahead during this interregnum period, was able to follow the steady plan of presenting George W. Bush as a "new kind of Republican." Bush was merely trying to return to the message that he had planned to promote before being sidetracked by the Republican primary campaign, when he found himself forced to track farther to the right to defeat John McCain. Bush's campaign did, of course, evolve over the course of the summer. But in contrast to the abrupt changes in Gore's campaign, its different phases resembled the seamless gear shifts of a supertanker slowly gathering speed. By the time of the Republican Convention in August, the Bush campaign had won a reputation for constancy and steadiness that stood in striking contrast to the changing campaign of Al Gore. The Bush campaign did not really hit troubled waters until September.

Al Gore the Reformer (March and April)

Immediately after the nomination races were decided in March, Gore and Bush found themselves locked in a tight race. In one respect, this position marked a dramatic improvement for Al Gore, who had trailed George W. Bush considerably in polls taken before the beginning of the primary season. Inconsequential as such early polls may be, Bill Bradley had frequently referred to Bush's lead over Gore as one of the reasons to select him as the Democratic Party's nominee. By pulling even with Bush in March, Gore was in his best position since the race began. It is no wonder that he felt poised to take off and grab control of the race.

But there was a major complication. Gore's rise was not due so much to an increase in his own strength as it was to a decline in Bush's appeal following his divisive primary battle against John McCain. Despite his defeat John McCain emerged from the race as the golden boy, with growing support among independent voters and continuing adulation from the press. As Bush was competing for some of McCain's support, so too was Al Gore. Gore's strategy under these conditions was to try to fill the vacuum of a reform center in American politics that had been occupied by Bradley and McCain. Hence, his first incarnation as Gore the Reformer.

For Gore to make campaign reform a central theme of his campaign, when he himself was embroiled in campaign finance irregularities stemming from the 1996 campaign, demanded both bravado and a capacity for self-abasement. Gore lacked neither of these qualities. During his primary race with Bill Bradley, Gore had concluded that where he was personally vulnerable, his best defense was an aggressive offense. The only difference between the primary and the interregnum was that instead of waiting for the attack, Gore launched a preemptive strike. On practically the first day of the interregnum, he granted an interview with the *New York Times* in which he claimed that "like John McCain, I took from my personal experience a deeper commitment to the battle for campaign finance reform."[7] He went on to observe that Bush's avoidance of this issue was symptomatic of his whole political position, charging, "[Bush] has been writing it [campaign reform] off from the very start, but it is intricately linked to this Bush risky tax scheme, which would devastate funding for education and environment and health care. It is closely linked to Bush's record of creating the worst pollution in America, in the state of Texas."[8]

Gore continued his reform theme later in the month in a major address at Marquette University. Conceding that he was perhaps "an imperfect messenger for this cause," he unveiled a new plan for eliminating soft money and financing American elections with a new public–private endowment fund.[9] Gore was not to be deterred by criticisms from the Bush camp that he "lacked credibility" on this issue. Instead, he sought to identify himself with John McCain. Even observers highly sympathetic to Al Gore could not help but remark on the heavy-handedness of his effort. Gore, as always, was the champion of constant repetition, the hammer who tried to nail his message into the anvil of public thinking. As *Washington Post* columnist E. J. Dionne remarked: "The Vice President can hardly speak 10 sentences these days . . . without including warm and flattering references to the man who once promised to 'beat Al Gore like a drum.' The next thing you know, Vice President Al Gore will file papers requesting that his name be listed on this fall's ballots as John McGore."[10]

For George W. Bush, the strategy immediately following his Republican primary victories—and indeed for the whole interregnum—was to return to themes that he had developed before his primary battle. Bush's idea, like Al Gore's, involved capturing the center. His efforts, however, did not focus on campaign finance reform, but rather on reforms in many substantive policy areas, such as education and Social Security. Bush's position was designed to show that he was "a new kind of Republican" and to put symbolic distance between himself and the congressional wing of the Republican Party, which, at least in the public mind, was identified overwhelmingly with a negative or "less government" approach. In March and April, Bush announced a literacy program and pledged $3 billion for teacher recruitment, training, and tax breaks. Tellingly, the first post-primary political advertisement that Bush released was a spot on education in which he claimed that national reading and math scores had stagnated under the Clinton-Gore administration, and that as president, he would "challenge the status quo" in education.

Bush's focus on education was part of a more general strategy that revealed the core of his entire campaign. He wanted to try to take on, and therefore neutralize, Gore's advantage on many traditionally Democratic issues. Bush would, of course, advance Republican positions on some of the more traditional party issues, most notably tax cuts. But the Bush campaign also assumed that a substantial part of the 2000 election would be fought on territory that Democrats had traditionally emphasized. This position was no doubt born in part out of the realization that these were the issues of greatest concern to many Americans. Still, this conclusion was not a new one. It had been the operating premise for

Bush, and many other Republican governors, for five years. Bush was aware, as Fred Barnes noted, that "the hardy perennial wedge issues of Republican campaigns—crime, welfare, balancing the budget"—were no longer paramount, and that he had to come to grips with four Democratic issues prominent on the 2000 agenda: education, Social Security, health care, and the environment.[11]

Political campaigns are not, however, just about "ideology" and issue positions. They are three-dimensional affairs that also make appeals to the general mood of the country and to the public's assessment of the candidates' personal qualities. Bush sought to link these last two dimensions. The mood to which he appealed was that of a desire to change the moral climate surrounding the presidency and to restore the dignity that was once attached to the office. Although Bush did not speak directly of President Clinton's impeachment and the actions causing it, he did refer regularly to a corrupt political climate and offered his candidacy as a way of purging the nation of this malady. This theme struck a major chord with his audiences. At this point in the campaign, Bush's focus of attention and criticism were centered as much on Bill Clinton as on Al Gore. The two were still bound together as incumbents of the same administration, and there was enough in Gore's own propensity for opportunistic and insincere statements and actions, dating from his primary campaign against Bill Bradley and before, to allow their character problems to meld together.

It is generally far easier to articulate one's own issue positions than it is to define the image and character of one's opponent. Conducting a frontal attack against the other candidate is a hazardous enterprise that can easily backfire, especially in a climate in which engaging in negative campaigning is being treated as a venial sin. Creating a negative image obviously succeeds best when the opposition candidate actually behaves in a way that confirms the charges and when the media play up these qualities on their own. The media in matters of candidate character often set the agenda and enjoy the status, unlike the two opposition campaigns, of being the neutral "umpire."

One of the most interesting aspects of the 2000 campaign was the degree to which nearly everyone—the two campaigns, the working journalists, and the commentators—settled on a single negative image for each candidate early on. In Bush's case, it was that of an intellectual lightweight, a person lacking not only the experience but also the intelligence to be president. This image was often referred to, however unfairly to its namesake, as the "Quayle factor." While foes would concede that Bush might be an amiable fellow—in itself a way of condemning him under the guise of faint praise—they labeled him an "empty suit" who lacked the "heft" to be president. The

Gore campaign encouraged this view, sometimes implicitly, at other times more directly. By contrast, the positive picture that the Gore campaign wished to provide was of their candidate as a serious person of great experience and intellect. They acknowledged that Gore was not particularly "exciting"—a criticism that is not much of a liability—but said that this only showed he was serious, prepared, and competent.[12]

In Al Gore's case, the negative image—which grew up in the press and was promoted by the Bush campaign—was that of an opportunistic politician willing to say or do anything, from exaggeration to outright distortion, to advance his career. This dimension of insincerity was expanded to include the accusation of Gore lacking a political and personal core to guide his decisions. It was thus an image of someone always changing who he was and what he espoused for political expediency. By contrast, the positive picture that the Bush campaign sought to portray of their candidate was that of a person possessing an inner comfort, who knew who he was and what he wanted. It was an image of steadiness, calmness, and sincerity.

Whether the qualities stressed in these two images were the only ones needing attention is a theoretical question worthy of analysis.[13] But from a practical political standpoint, it became clear early on that these two negative images—and practically only these two—would be the standards employed to judge and assess the candidates. The concentration on these images took hold no doubt in part because they had a firm basis in reality. For example, George W. Bush had hardly distinguished himself in his early debates during the Republican contest, while Al Gore had been accused over and over again by Bill Bradley of opportunism. It also appealed to a desire in the journalistic community for a kind of symmetry in discussing the liabilities of the two candidates, allowing commentators to switch in a seemingly evenhanded fashion from the treatment of the faults of one candidate to the faults of the other. Literally thousands of news articles and stories appeared in which these two unfavorable images were repeated and discussed, nearly to the point that they became stereotypes that were impossible to challenge or replace.

As a result, each candidate was placed, as it were, on national probation, the terms of which were known to both the public and the candidates. Each man had a clear "assignment": do everything possible not to confirm the negative stereotype. Only then could they avoid violating the terms of their probation. Neither candidate during the campaign succeeded entirely in walking the straight and narrow. But Al Gore in the end fell victim to his negative stereotype to a far greater degree than did George W. Bush. And therein lay a substantial part of the explanation for the outcome not just of the interregnum but of the final election as well.

It was on this score that Al Gore suffered the single greatest setback of the period. It came in his response to the Elian Gonzalez affair, which, incidentally, turned out to be perhaps the only real-world event that intruded itself in an important way into the 2000 campaign.[14] Elian Gonzalez, a six-year-old Cuban boy who had been miraculously rescued at sea during an escape effort in which his mother drowned, captured the nation's attention for over a month. He was in the care of his Cuban relatives in Miami, who wanted to keep him in America and begin a process of adjudicating his status by Florida state courts. The Clinton administration, however, determined that this matter was under the jurisdiction of the federal immigration service and that Elian should be returned to his father in Cuba. Most Democrats backed the president, while many Republicans lent support to the Miami relatives. Al Gore's campaign made a decision to break with the Clinton administration—perhaps more than he actually intended to—by calling for a resolution of the issue in the state courts. Gore lost, it seems, on all sides. He surely lost among those within his own party who backed the president and who expected loyalty in this instance. But more importantly, he lost among the large mass of Americans who regarded his position as an opportunistic attempt to win votes in the Cuban community and therefore demonstrative of a willingness to say or do anything to get elected—the stereotypical flaw in his character. Gore's image suffered, and his own campaign manager, Tony Coelho, later admitted that "it was probably one of our biggest mistakes."[15] Gore's statement of support did not sway votes in the Cuban community either, where George W. Bush reportedly won an estimated 60,000 more Cuban American votes than Bob Dole in 1996.

In the end, Al Gore's incarnation as the "reformer" fell flat. While finance reform was mentioned during the fall campaign, it never became a driving electoral issue. In fact, it had not been the greatest source of John McCain's appeals in the primaries either, as it was never listed among the top concerns of more than 10 percent of respondents, even in states that McCain won.[16] Gore evidently mistook public enthusiasm for McCain's image of sincerity and integrity for support of his reform positions, and by Gore's sudden and halfhearted embrace of Elian Gonzalez's cause he may have hurt himself with his courtship of precisely the segment of the electorate most concerned with sincerity.

Al Gore the Attacker (May)

A month and a half into the interregnum, Al Gore had not only failed to pull out in front of Bush, but he actually began to slip behind him. To use the word "panic" to describe the feelings in the Gore campaign would be far too strong (although some did in fact use it). "Frustration" would probably be more accurate. The following lead from a front-page story in the *New York Times* sums up the situation well:

> Two months after Al Gore triumphantly claimed enough delegates for the Democratic presidential nomination, his campaign is struggling to reorient itself toward the general election, and many of the vice president's closest advisers concede that Gov. George W. Bush of Texas has outmaneuvered them in appealing to moderate voters. Several senior Gore advisers interviewed at the campaign headquarters here and elsewhere in the country acknowledged that . . . the campaign had drifted and lost focus since the primaries [and that] Mr. Bush's move to placate moderates after his sharp turn to the right in the primaries was more swift and successful than they expected.[17]

Beginning in early May, Al Gore therefore decided to change course. Instead of Al Gore the Reformer, he became Al Gore the Attacker. The new strategy was based on two considerations: First, it followed—albeit earlier in the campaign season—the plan of 1988, when George Bush strongly attacked Michael Dukakis. The strategy of attacking Governor Bush came to be referred to in the press by the neologism of "dukakisizing" one's opponent. The plan here was to speed up the timetable of 1988, doing to Governor Bush in May what Vice President Bush had done to Michael Dukakis in September. Susan Estrich, who managed Mr. Dukakis's campaign in 1988, now offered her advice to the Gore campaign in 2000, touting her personal experience: "If you become viewed as a risk, as Michael Dukakis was in 1988, it is a very tough road to get back from; if Al Gore can raise questions about Bush, Bush may never get off the ground. So Gore will just keep doing it."[18] Second, Gore strategists recalled their recent experience early in the primary battle with Bill Bradley, when Gore turned the race in his favor through the use of tough attacks. Human instinct is always to revert to what has worked well in the past. Perhaps too, as *Wall Street Journal* columnist Paul Gigot argued, this was also the style most natural to Gore. Gigot recalled how "The vice president's campaign against Bill Bradley was floundering, until he turned into Terminator 3. . . . Attack politics is what Al Gore does best. Empathy (Bill Clinton) and optimism (Ronald Reagan) aren't his forte."[19]

Geneticists may debate about whether the emergence of Gore the Attacker was a product of nurture or nature, but whatever the cause, there was no mistaking the transformation. In his new role, Gore became relentless. In almost every speech he delivered in May, he called Bush's experience and his readiness for the presidency into question. He attacked an array of Governor Bush's policy proposals as "risky," "reckless," and "irresponsible," and described Bush's foreign policy outlook as reflecting a "Cold War mentality." "Risky" became Gore's operative term, which he repeated as a mantra, as George Will parodied in a column that received widespread attention: "Al Gore thinks it is risky. The antecedent of the pronoun 'it' could be anything (school choice, tax cuts, entitlement reforms, the internal combustion engine, repeal of the designated hitter rule) that George W. Bush favors."[20] Bush, too, adopted a very effective version of this parody in his acceptance speech at the Republican Convention in Philadelphia.

Also evident during this period was the media-induced effect that contributes to the downward spiral of a campaign. Recognized by almost all students of the media, this effect works in the following way. A candidate is observed to be doing poorly, which becomes a "fact" that necessitates news stories to explain *why* this is so. The "conclusions" then become the focus of more news coverage and commentary, which lead to more intense scrutiny of the candidate. This increased scrutiny inevitably uncovers more flaws, thus making matters worse. This effect continues for some time, until at least the purely media-generated part of the explanation finally exhausts itself, if it does not destroy the candidate first. The cycle is then complete, and the afflicted candidate can only hope that his opponent will be treated with the same attention. These templates have been aptly labeled by Thomas Patterson as "losing ground" narratives, and they form, along with their opposite ("bandwagon narratives"), two of the most important frameworks for media interpretations of political campaigns.[21]

On Bush's side of the campaign, this was the period that was most devoted to setting out much of the substance of his agenda. He did so in a series of formal speeches on such topics as Social Security, tax reform, and foreign affairs. The speech on foreign affairs, delivered on May 23, was also part of a process designed to combat perceptions of Bush's inexperience in a realm where Americans wish to be reassured of their candidates' competence and judgment. This speech, which was attended by foreign policy experts from four Republican administrations, received generally respectful reviews from the serious journalistic community.

In addition to delivering these speeches, Bush also embraced a strategy of making small, symbolic gestures that straddled the line between Republican and Democratic issues. In May, he proposed spending to help people buy long-term care insurance and offered a "silver scholarship" program under which senior citizens could volunteer as tutors in after-school programs in exchange for $1,000 educational scholarships funded by the federal government. Seniors who volunteered at least 500 hours a year would be eligible for the scholarships, which they then could pass on to their children, grandchildren, or other children in need. These moves by Bush to co-opt the middle and become a "different kind of Republican" naturally invited comparisons to Clinton and his famed "triangulation" strategy, designed by Dick Morris for 1996. Richard Lowry of the *National Review* observed that "since the primaries, the Bush campaign has been playing a version of the Dick Morris gambit that worked so well for Clinton: offering small-scale proposals that aren't so important as policy but that make symbolic statements about a candidate's character."[22]

Attempts to define one's opponent's negative image, as previously noted, work best when the media, rather than the campaign itself, execute the job. This fact accounts for the inordinate effort and energy that campaigns devote to trying to launder their message through respected media sources or pressure them to cover the other candidate in a certain way. It is even more fortuitous, of course, when journalists decide to pounce on a candidate on their own initiative. In any case, the media's concentration on the difficulties of the vicepresident's campaign in this period was doing for the Bush campaign what it could not possibly have done on its own. Bush meanwhile could allow himself to take the high road, limiting his criticisms of Gore to occasional asides that Gore was a person who had "trouble with the truth," repeating Bill Bradley's question in his New Hampshire debate with Gore: "Why should we believe you would tell the truth as president if you don't tell the truth as a candidate?"

Al Gore the Affirmer (June)

By the middle of May it became clear that the manifestation of Gore as the Attacker was not working. An in-depth poll conducted in the late spring by CBS and the *New York Times* cataloged the difficulties the Gore campaign was facing. Not only did Bush enjoy a healthy 8-point margin over Gore in the head-to-head matchup, but Bush was also the favorite among three groups that voted Democratic in 1996: Catholics, independents, and northeasterners. Bush not only held a 50 percent to 36 percent advantage among men, as he was expected to do, but he also was slightly favored by women, 44 percent to 42 percent. Results like these made even some in Gore's own party openly critical of his campaign. As Bush was laying out a broad agenda on the issues, consolidating his base, and reaching out to independent voters, Gore had not yet settled on a consistent campaign theme. He was seen to be not so much drifting as thrashing about, simply responding negatively to Bush's initiatives.[23] While Gore remained on the attack, Bush remained on the offensive.

Yet one thing that Al Gore had learned quite well from his struggle for the nomination against Bill Bradley was to be flexible in his campaign tactics. That is, if things are not working, it is best to take one's loss, cash out, and try something else. A clear problem Gore faced, however, was the number of times he shifted strategies. This not only opened the door to taunts from the other side, but also played into the negative stereotype of Gore being without a genuine core. Still, Gore's pragmatism told him that he would do better to endure the criticisms he sustained by reinventing himself rather than to permanently wed his campaign to an approach that was failing.

Consequently, at the end of May Gore inaugurated the new strategy of Al Gore the Affirmer, who would deliver a kinder and gentler, or at any rate a more positive and upbeat, message. As explained by E. J. Dionne, "In the coming weeks Gore plans to answer his critics by going positive, policy heavy and autobiographical."[24] On May 25 Gore kicked off a series of speeches on his "family agenda," announcing a proposal to increase funding for after-school programs, and delivering speeches on mental health care funding, cancer, and the responsibility of fathers. "The light touch," one reporter remarked, "is a marked departure for the candidate who, for weeks, has hammered Bush as smug, arrogant, reckless and irresponsible."[25] The most striking change came in Gore's restraint in banishing the word "Bush" from his vocabulary and never mentioning his opponent by name. His silence on this point was deafening.

Consistent with the content of his new theme, Gore also tried to display a more consensual leadership style. The point was to celebrate the general condition of the nation from which all had benefited. Gore set out to claim credit for the strong economy of the Clinton-Gore years and to assert that continued prosperity was possible only with a Democratic president at the nation's helm. On June 13 he embarked on a "progress and prosperity" tour intended to highlight the economic successes of the past eight years. Deeply concerned that voters were not crediting the Clinton-Gore administration for the good economy, Gore sought to drive home the connection between the two, while suggesting that a Republican president would threaten the country's prosperity.[26] This strategy also brought Gore closer to President Clinton, although Gore hoped that by framing the presidential race as a contest over which candidate could better run the economy, he would deflect attention from a focus on character.[27]

Gore's strategy during this phase was no doubt the plan many expected would be at the center of the Gore campaign. For one thing, it fit with the moderate philosophy of the Democratic Leadership Council (DLC). Gore was often connected with this wing of the Democratic

Party, and Bill Clinton had successfully run on its principles, despite occasional wanderings. The progress and prosperity tour promised an administration that would bring benefits to all. It would assist not just labor unions and the working classes but also, and perhaps especially, elements of the newer knowledge sector of the middle and upper middle classes that had gained so much during the Clinton presidency. This too was DLC politics: the new sectors of the economy were the ones that the DLC had identified as being the key to the success and future growth of the Democratic Party.

More importantly, the peace and prosperity strategy adopted the classic successful incumbent-style campaign, based on the famous "Are you better off now than you were (four or) eight years ago?" test. Gore's appeal was reminiscent of the Reagan campaign of 1984 and the Clinton campaign of 1996. The logic of such a campaign accords with the theory of voting behavior known as "retrospective voting." This theory holds that voters, in making their decisions, look back on the performance of the person (or party) in office and then ask how the incumbent (or incumbent party) has done. If the incumbent (or the incumbent party) is judged to have done well, voters will tend to give him (it) their vote, either as a reward for good service or, more likely, because of the calculation that the same people and policies will continue to produce positive results in the future. The logic here supplies—rather obviously it would seem—the basis for how to run a campaign: the job of a candidate running as a successful incumbent is to drive home to the electorate arguments about how well things have gone and how well they are likely to continue to go under the same person or party.

But whether this "obvious" conclusion on how to run a campaign is borne out in fact is not so clear. While retrospective voting may indeed provide the reason why many vote as they do, it does not necessarily follow that voters want candidates to make a defense of their or their party's record their central campaign theme. Also, there is some question that this model applies to a candidate who is himself not the incumbent, but rather the vice president of the incumbent party. What's more, this strategy could link the vice president too closely to the president, thus preventing him from appearing to be his "own man." Returning to the election of 1988, we see there is little doubt that George Bush benefited from the logic of retrospective voting, but his campaign also encompassed other issues, with retrospection far from being the most prominent.

This period saw a shake-up in Gore's campaign staff with the resignation of campaign manager Tony Coelho, who had been brought in to save Gore's floundering nomination campaign against Bradley. Although his resignation occurred for reasons of failing health, it came at a time when Gore was contemplating an organizational change. The truth was that Gore was never personally very close to Coelho, who was faulted in particular for Gore's strategy in the Elian Gonzalez case. Coelho was also under fire for ethical problems of his own. Columnist Marjorie Williams put it this way: "Gore's biggest liability is that he is seen as a political opportunist, who will say anything to get elected. The last person whose advice he needs is, well, a political opportunist who thinks his candidate should say anything to get elected."[28] But Gore handled the shake-up in the best way, avoiding any semblance of crisis. There was no waiting period and no time given for speculation. Commerce Secretary William Daley, who resigned from the Cabinet to fill Coelho's position, immediately replaced Coelho. Labor was not entirely pleased with a commerce secretary who had fought so hard for trade with China, but the choice was generally applauded and gave Gore a manager with a good deal of experience and visibility.

At this time Bush was making modest proposals on a variety of topics, including federal aid for use of high technology and Internet in the schools ($400 million), for programs to ease transportation problems for disabled workers ($145 million), and for a plan to help lower-income parents pay for after-school activities ($400 million). He also sought to reach out to traditionally Democratic constituencies, speaking out again in a speech to the United Latin American Citizens on the need to revamp the Immigration and Naturalization Service. The basic plan of presenting compassionate conservatism was working well, and Bush saw no reason to do anything other than to remain on the course that had been charted the previous year.

Al Gore the Populist (July)

The consensual strategy of Al Gore the Affirmer brought neither improvement in the polls nor joy to the candidate, who seemed to chaff under the restrictions of referring only gently to his "opponent." The end of this period was probably the lowest point of the Gore campaign during the interregnum. Gore's position suffered not only from a continuing erosion in the center, where Bush seemed to be making inroads, but also from a new and unexpected challenge: the emergence of a nemesis on the left in the person of Ralph Nader. Contrary to all the expectations of the previous year, when it had been widely believed that a third party, in the form of a Reform Party headed by Patrick Buchanan, would harm the Republicans, it was now the Democrats who faced the greater danger. The Buchanan campaign was going nowhere, while the Greens under Nader were beginning to pick up considerable support. Gore was faced with the dilemma of squelching a challenge from the left, while at the same time trying to vie for votes from the center.

Gore therefore risked yet another shift in strategy at the end of June, changing from Al Gore the Affirmer to Al Gore the Populist. Instead of basing his candidacy on taking credit for the status quo, he turned to speaking to the frustrations that many had *with* the status quo. He then blamed these frustrations on powerful forces in society, which he linked to George W. Bush and the Republican Party in Congress. During a swing through Ohio, Illinois, and Pennsylvania in early July, Gore depicted Bush as the candidate of special interests, of oil and pharmaceutical companies, while claiming that he represented the "mainstream majority." He highlighted the increasing cost of prescription drugs, accused drug companies of "price-gouging" and "special interest schemes" to keep drug prices high, and proposed a prescription drug plan.[29] He drew a connection between Bush and "big oil" companies, blaming them for the rising gasoline prices, especially in the Midwest. Gore then turned his sights on the Republican Congress as the captive of special interests—big oil, big drug companies, big insurance companies, and health maintenance organizations—and attacked it for failing to pass legislation raising the minimum wage, protecting the environment, making drugs cheaper for the elderly, and strengthening gun control laws.[30]

This new strategy sought to energize the Democrats' following by dividing the country and creating the feeling of a "we" oppressed by the "they." In classic populist style, Gore said he was "fighting for" certain groups against the forces of oppression. It was a Gore who now sounded as much like a challenger as an incumbent. The campaign took on a tone more like the Democratic campaign of 1984, harkening back to the traditional Democratic appeal of dividing classes, than it did the retrospective election of 1996. The Bush campaign naturally attacked this new strategy, mocking Gore's new approach as "Al Gore Version 7.0: The Class Warfare Warrior."[31]

Gore's shift toward populism coincided with his choice of Stan Greenberg to be one of his chief advisers. Greenberg believed that the key element in the electorate for Gore was not the new rich, but rather the working and middle classes.[32] He had written about just this point in his 1995 book *Middle Class Dreams*, in which he studied voters in Macomb County, Michigan, home to many of the Reagan Democrats. Two years later, in conjunction with Harvard sociologist Theda Skocpol, Greenberg elevated this electoral analysis to an "ideological" level in a major attack on the flabby centrism favored by the Democratic Leadership Council. Greenberg accused the leaders of the 1990s DLC of apostasy, "distancing themselves from the very Democratic Party that they helped to transform." New Democrats' concern for the pioneers in the "knowledge" industry "hardly speaks to the experience of most working men and women in the late twentieth century United States." Greenberg then called on Americans to "heed the populist call to stand with the majority of working Americans."[33]

Gore's reliance on Greenberg marked what would arguably become the turning point of not just the interregnum but of his presidential campaign as a whole. Although Gore was not interested in the theoretical polemics taking place between Greenberg and the DLC, he was interested in a strategy and approach that could breathe life and energy into his campaign. The decision to side with Greenberg meant a return to the style of appeal and the rhetoric of the "old" Democratic Party. It meant a more confrontational and divisional tone, and it clearly seemed to be a call for vastly more government, whatever the actual details of his plans might be.

Many commentators thought that this was only going to be a temporary phase, designed to last only until the Democratic Convention, after which Gore would return to a more consensual campaign. They doubted that Gore would long continue with his populist appeal, because, while it held the advantages of energizing strong Democrats and allowed for a separation from Bill Clinton, it also held the disadvantages of frightening off parts of the center and of the "new rich," who might find Gore's rhetoric too antibusiness. Gore clearly hoped to have it both ways. He sought the support of economic winners who benefited from the status quo but also those who were not so content. This strategy had the potential inconsistency of trying to take credit for the booming economy on the one hand, while attacking many of the institutions responsible for that prosperity on the other.[34]

Whatever the long-term strategy, the populist theme was the first of the many versions of Al Gore that improved his standing and traction in the campaign. It also appealed to Gore's instincts as a campaigner. As he picked up a bit in the polls, Gore decided to carry this populist message into the convention and make it the centerpiece of his acceptance speech. This decision was fateful. From that point on, try as he might—and toward the end he did try a bit—Gore could not escape being identified as an Old Democrat. Gore's adoption of a populist theme at the end of the interregnum energized his base and guaranteed a competitive election, but it also locked him into a strategy that fixed a ceiling on his performance. It contributed to the geographical split in the electorate that endangered not only Gore's prospects of winning the electoral vote, but also perhaps the Democrats' chances of regaining control of the U.S. House of Representatives.

Bush's strategy during this period of the interregnum could hardly have been more different. He continued to depict himself as a "different kind of Republican" by reaching out to traditionally Democratic groups, including minorities. On July 5 he met with members of the National Council of La Raza, one of the nation's largest and most influential Hispanic groups, and introduced his half-Hispanic nephew, George P. Bush, who was on his way to becoming a heart-stopper for many younger female voters. Both the Republican National Committee and the Bush campaign also released ads in both English and Spanish that targeted Latino voters.

On July 10 Bush delivered a speech to the NAACP convention, an event that Bob Dole had shunned in 1996. Bush was accorded a polite reception from the delegates, and he promised to "enhance social programs and cultural expectations to boost private homeownership, public education and health care for the poor."[35] Even though many conventioneers criticized the speech for failing to cover special topics of interest such as the death penalty, Supreme Court nominees, and affirmative action, the fact that Bush showed up still counted as an effort on his part to be more inclusive.[36] Indeed, his appearance was designed to send a message to moderate and swing white voters, in addition to African Americans. This aspect of the campaign also presaged the "script" of the party convention in Philadelphia, where a large percentage of the speakers were either Hispanic or African American.[37]

Another way in which the Texas governor sought to appeal to independent and moderate voters was by devoting several weeks in July to speaking about social welfare measures for low-income and struggling Americans. He called for measures to promote adoption, held a discussion about how churches provide services, offered a proposal to help low-income parents pay for after-school activities, and pledged to spend more money to promote responsible fatherhood.

When the Gore campaign was lurching, the Bush camp tried to look even more like the very essence of steadiness and professionalism. The picture was even keel, and the ship kept pushing ahead, moving steadily toward the convention in Philadelphia. The Bush team, having faced and overcome its primary election defeats at the hands of John McCain, had regrouped and set sail for its final destination, all the while maintaining the same captain and crew. This was the famous Bush quality of "loyalty," which, to this point, seemed to bring him only success.

There have now been two experiences with the new "interregnum" period in our electoral process: 1996 and 2000. In 1996, Bill Clinton won the interregnum and then went on to win the general election. In his case, there was no "break" between the two periods. The trends that began in April—trends that favored Bill Clinton—simply continued through until November. There is little question that Clinton was helped by his interregnum campaign, but this was a race that favored him in the fundamentals of victory. He did not need the interregnum to win the presidency.

In 2000, the winner of the interregnum (George W. Bush) also won the presidential election. But the similarity between the two cases ends there. Bush's victory was not the final or decisive cause leading to the election outcome. In contrast to 1996, there was a clear "break" between the interregnum and final election campaigns, as Bush fell behind Al Gore after the party conventions and remained so for over a month. Gore's lead in August and September, furthermore, represented more than a short-term convention "bounce" or "glow" that was destined to wear off. The election at this point became Gore's to lose, and he managed to lose it.

The fact that Bush lost his lead after the interregnum therefore raises again the question of the value, if any, of winning that race. Bush's victory at this stage, it would appear, was a necessary, though certainly not sufficient, step for his final election victory. As the candidate running uphill in 2000, Bush needed to establish credibility and steadily gain ground with the American populace. Perhaps more importantly, Gore harmed himself during this period and was in a worse position at its end than at its beginning. To return to the comparison to the 1988 campaign, we note that George Bush (father) was behind Michael Dukakis when the conventions met, but Bush really had done nothing before the conventions to harm his candidacy. (In fact there was as yet still no full-length interregnum campaign in effect.) The last important impressions of George Bush came from his own primary contest that year, and of course from his performance as vice president. What the interregnum campaign has brought to American politics—and here we return to its precise addition to the American presidential campaign—is a major event between the primaries and the final election campaign. This period allows the candidates to size each other up and to stake out ground on new issues that they think will become important during the fall campaign. Without this phase, Gore might have been more vulnerable on the tax issue (where he developed an alternative to Bush's plan), and Bush more vulnerable on the health care issue (where he promised a prescription drug plan for elders). The effect can be to bring the candidates closer together. More importantly, the interregnum serves to etch a new stratum of memory into the electorate's mind that replaces (or pushes farther into the background) the impressions made during the primaries. Under certain triggering circumstances, these memories can be brought back to the surface during the fall campaign.

This is exactly what occurred in 2000. While trying, perhaps too hard, to do himself good in the interregnum campaign, Gore added to negative judgments about his personal qualities of opportunism and insincerity. Although he was able to cover these impressions with his reintroduction at the Democratic Convention, he made a critical error during his first televised debate with George W. Bush. The negative image of the interregnum period then returned, like the resurgence of a repressed memory. This change was the event that turned the election to Bush.

Notes

1. Peter Marks, "The 2000 Campaign: The New Offensive; Bush TV Ad Attacks Gore, Who Swiftly Answers Back," *New York Times*, March 18, 2000, A9.
2. Dan Balz, "The Story So Far: Outmaneuvered by Bush, Gore Faces Questions," *Washington Post*, May 28, 2000, A1.
3. Edward M. Rogers Jr., "Bush Won't Be a Dukakis," *New York Times*, August 16, 2000, A27.
4. The only barely memorable line of Bill Clinton's first inaugural
5. Staff, Gore, Bush Trade E-Mail Barbs Over Funds Challenge On Soft Money Draws Rebuff," *Boston Globe*, March 16, 2000, A20.
6. The introduction of the advertisement, less than two months into the primary election season, indicated how swiftly Mr. Bush and Mr. Gore were moving to full-throttle general election campaign. The early attack and response is in part a function of the lessons learned in previous contests, when candidacies suffered after the opposition succeeded early in a campaign in defining a rival in unsympathetic terms in the minds of many voters. Peter Marks, "The 2000 Campaign: The New Offensive; Bush TV Ad Attacks Gore, Who Swiftly Answers Back," *New York Times*, March 18, 2000, A9.
7. McCain was implicated in the "Keating Five" campaign funding and influence scandal of the late 1980s.
8. Staff, "Excerpts From a Talk With the Vice President," *New York Times*, March 12, 2000, A38.
9. Walter Shapiro, "For Whatever Reason, Al Gore Reforms," *USA Today*, March 29, 2000, A10.
10. E. J. Dionne Jr., "Following McCain's Lead," *Washington Post*, March 24, 2000, A23.
11. Fred Barnes, "Bush's Democratic Issue Strategy; How Bush plans to neutralize Al Gore's trump cards," *Weekly Standard*, April 3, 2000, 14.
12. This point follows the line of analysis developed by Larry Sabato in *Feeding Frenzy* (New York: Free Press, 1993), where he refers to "sub-texts" or "between-the-lines character sketches" that can "guide and set the tone for press coverage," p. 47.
13. A few others, such as Bush's playboy past, had been brought up earlier, only to fall by the wayside as the interregnum got under way.
14. Certain notable events did not affect the campaign: no special prosecutor was appointed to look into Al Gore's campaign finance problems, and the special prosecutor found no basis for proceeding against the Clintons in Whitewater. During the fall

campaign there was a brief crisis in the Mideast, which may have had the paradoxical effect of slightly helping the Bush candidacy, due to the selection of Dick Cheney as Bush's running mate.

15. Richard L. Berke, "Gore's Campaign Struggling To Regain Primary Energy," *New York Times*, May 15, 2000, A1.

16. According to Voter News Service exit polls, 9 percent of New Hampshire primary voters and 8 percent of Michigan primary voters rated campaign finance reform the "most important issue."

17. Richard L. Berke, "Gore's Campaign Struggling To Regain Primary Energy," *New York Times*, May 15, 2000, A1.

18. James Dao, "Giving Bush the Bradley Treatment," *New York Times*, May 5, 2000, A1.

19. Paul Gigot, "Potomac Watch: Gore Runs Against Creature From The Black Lagoon," *Wall Street Journal*, May 4, 2000, A16.

20. George Will, "Gore the Hysteric," *Washington Post*, May 21, 2000, B7.

21. Thomas Patterson, *Out of Order* (New York: Knopf, 1993), p. 119.

22. Richard Lowry, "Slow and Steady, But will it win W. the race?" *National Review*, July 3, 2000.

23. Dan Balz, "For Candidates, Are Patterns Set?" *Washington Post*, May 28, 2000, A1.

24. E. J. Dionne, "Meet Upbeat Al," *Washington Post*, May 30, 2000, A19.

25. Sandra Sobieraj, "Gore Leaves Bush Attacks to Others," *Los Angeles Times*, May 31, 2000.

26. Ron Faucheux, "Gore Campaign Needs to Make Connections," *Congressional Quarterly*, June 17, 2000.

27. Bob Davis and Jackie Calmes, "Gore Calls Bush's Economic Plan Irresponsible," *Wall Street Journal*, April 26, 2000, A4.

28. Marjorie Williams, "The Coelho Question," *Washington Post*, May 19, 2000, A31.

29. Alison Mitchell, "Gore Links Drug Industry and G.O.P to High Costs," *New York Times*, July 4, 2000, A11.

30. Katharine Q. Seelye, "Gore Tries Linking Bush With a 'Do-Nothing' Congress," *New York Times*, July 11, 2000, A21.

31. "Perspective," *Baltimore Sun*, July 23, 2000, 5C.

32. John F. Harris and Ceci Connolly, "Shaking Off the Clinton Strategy, Too: With Populist Push, Gore Looks Toward a Different Group of Swing Voters," *Washington Post*, August 24, 2000, A1.

33. Stanley Greenberg and Theda Skocpol, *The New Majority* (New Haven: Yale University Press, 1997), pp. 11, 12, and 16.

34. Kate O'Beirne, "Inside Politics," CNN, July 11, 2000.

35. Steve Miller, "Bush tells NAACP his way to boost opportunity," *Washington Times*, July 11, 2000.

36. Alison Mitchell, "Courting Civil Rights Group, Bush Gets a Polite Reception," *New York Times*, July 11, 2000, A1.

37. Jack W. Germond and Jules Witcover, "Is That Bush or Clinton?" *National Journal*, July 8, 2000. According to Jack Germond and Jules Witcover, Bush's strategy was "to write a new definition of the Republican Party, much as candidate Clinton did when he declared himself 'a different kind of Democrat' in 1992."

Chapter Five

The Final Election Campaign: Roller Coaster

The 2000 presidential election occupies a highly respectable place, perhaps even the seat of honor, among an elite group of close presidential elections. Historically, close elections have been defined in several ways: by the difference between the candidates in the national popular vote, by their difference in the electoral vote, and by the difference in popular votes that would actually have changed the election outcome. The last conception, generally taken to be the truest measure of closeness, is best illustrated by the "classic" close contest of 1884 between the Democrat Grover Cleveland and the Republican James Blaine, in which a swing of a mere 534 votes in the state of New York would have changed that state's electoral votes and given the presidency to Blaine. Historians even locate a specific cause for Blaine's defeat: his appearance at a late October rally in New York City, where an overly zealous supporter labeled the Democrats the party of "Rum, Romanism, and Rebellion." Needless to say, Irish American voters were not pleased.

Step aside 1884. From now on, the new classic case of the close contest will be the 2000 election (see table 5.1). Forgetting all the dimpled *thises* and hanging *thats*, and consulting the official ("certified") total, a swing of just 269 votes from Bush to Gore in Florida would have given Al Gore the presidency. Furthermore, even if Florida had gone safely to Al Gore, the election of 2000 would still have ranked among the closest in American history. Modest swings from Gore to Bush of 183 votes in New Mexico, 2,854 votes in Wisconsin, and either 2,072 votes in Iowa or 3,383 votes in Oregon would have resulted in an electoral vote tie, while those same changes in just Wisconsin, Iowa, and Oregon would have given the presidency back to Bush.

Table 5.1.   Five Closest Presidential Elections

Election and Candidates	Number of Electoral Vote Changes Required to Change Election Winner	Minimum Vote Shift Necessary to Change Critical Number of Electoral Votes	Popular and Electoral Vote Shift States
2000: Bush-Gore	3	269	Florida
1876: Hayes-Tilden	1	445	South Carolina*
1884: Cleveland-Blaine	19	524	New York
1916: Wilson-Hughes	12	1,711	California
1976: Carter-Ford	29	9,246	Hawaii, Ohio

Adapted from: James E. Campbell, *The American Campaign: U.S. Presidential Campaigns and the National Vote* (College Station: Texas A&M University Press, 2000).
*Popular vote totals from South Carolina were in dispute.

One reason for dwelling on these tiny swings is to make the obvious point that the actual campaign—meaning here what candidates say and do and how they decide to deploy their resources—clearly made a difference in the 2000 election. Readers may find it a bit odd that in the study of elections today, a strong tendency can be found in many quarters to discount the effect of campaigns. The general argument, which we have encountered earlier, is that election results can be predicted within a fairly close range from the prevailing conditions in the nation, without any need to consider campaigns. But even these analysts concede that in close elections, the campaign can make a difference.[1]

Close election campaigns in the past, it seems, tend to follow a pattern similar to that of a long-distance footrace. One candidate is in the lead for most of the contest, until another makes a single "run" at him near the end, either overcoming him or falling just short. With its ups and downs and frequent lead changes, the 2000 campaign was different. The graph line for the campaign resembles less a marathon than a roller-coaster ride (see figure 5.1). Certainly the experience of being on a roller-coaster ride comes closest to capturing how the candidates must have felt during the campaign.

The rises and dips of support are generated by shifts in the "soft" or swayable segment of the electorate, consisting of those still deciding for whom to vote or even whether to vote at all. Identifying this segment is tricky, in part because many people do not always consider themselves to be swayable until the moment they actually sway.[2] Much of the evidence

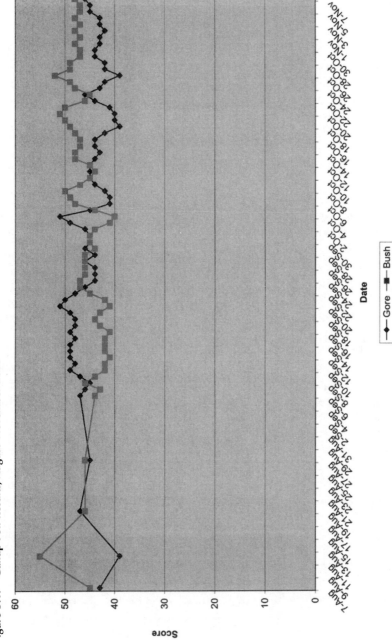

Figure 5.1. Gallup Poll Results, August–November 2000

suggests that a portion of the woman's vote—perhaps different subgroups of women—accounted most for volatility. This was certainly the view of the campaigns, as shown by the assiduous efforts made by both candidates to court the woman's vote. Because of the closeness of the race, the decisions of swayable voters were of course decisive in 2000, but it is not clear that their number was exceptionally large. By some accounts it was about the same as in 1996.[3] Shifting poll figures can also reflect changes in the voting enthusiasm of the candidates' core supporters. It is well known that candidates who make too concerted an effort to win swing voters (the "undecideds") with Milquetoast appeals, or who otherwise fail to meet the expectations of their supposed committed voters, can depress turnout among their "base," a portion of which is far more sensitive to turning out to vote than many suppose.

Understanding the conflicting sentiments of the undecided voters in 2000 is not very difficult. While both candidates were generally acceptable or satisfactory to these voters, neither presented a commanding presence. Political analyst Charles Cook described the undecided's dilemma in the following refrain, heard a thousand times over the course of the campaign: "Once undecided voters begin to settle on either Bush or Gore, they begin wondering whether they've made the right decision. An undecided voter leaning toward Gore might begin shifting to Bush if the news of the day is that Gore is playing loose with the truth. If the news focus shifts toward the Texas governor's thin reservoir of expertise on key issues and his lack of intellectual curiosity, an undecided voter leaning toward Bush might edge back to Gore. The swing voters see good and bad qualities in both candidates."[4]

The target of inquiry in studying voters depends very much on the political analyst's interest. Some focus on all voters, while others concentrate on swayable voters. In the first case, each voter's preference is worth as much as another's, just as in a close basketball game: a basket made early in the first half is worth just as much as a basket made right near the end. Scholars here are interested in *election outcomes*, which are important for analyzing the general strength of the parties. But in the other sense, the decisions of swayable voters, like the last-minute baskets, count more in explaining what caused the outcome (if causality is understood as the last important event in a chain that alters the outcome). Scholars who are interested primarily in *campaigns* are much more likely to concentrate on the swayable voters, as these are the people up for grabs at the point where deliberate acts of persuasion might have changed a decision.

The final election campaign falls into four periods. The first period, which is really ground zero, began near the end of the interregnum period with George Bush's selection of Richard Cheney as his running mate and continued up until just before the Democratic Convention. George Bush started this period in the lead, and, with the standard bounce from his convention, pulled ahead to his largest margin since January, before the primaries. The second period began with the Lieberman vice presidential selection and the Democratic Convention and continued until the start of the presidential debates at the beginning of October. Normally, campaign analysts skip the convention period, allowing the respective popularity "bounces" of the two conventions to work their way through the electorate, and then pick up their study again a week or ten days after the conventions are over. But in 2000, following the pattern of George Bush in 1988, Gore bounced up at his convention and then did not come down for an extended period, indicating that a new norm, with Gore slightly ahead, had set in. The third phase was Bush's recovery and overtaking of Gore beginning in late September, and continuing with the debates starting on October 3. If Gore's lead in the previous period is considered "real," then this period marks the decisive turning point of the campaign, with the debates being the last events that explain the ultimate outcome. Finally, the fourth phase (and some analysts dispute if there really was one) was the movement in the polls in favor of Gore during the last week of the campaign. Gore went from being slightly behind in national support before November 7 to being the narrow winner of the national popular vote on election day. As a result of all of these changes, as election day drew closer, more and more, rather than fewer and fewer, states appeared in the "undecided" column—a marked shift from the patterns of previous elections.

Completing the Tickets and Starting the Race: Vice Presidential Selection in 2000

George Bush's selection of Dick Cheney as his vice presidential running mate marked the start of the final election campaign. The choice of a running mate is conditioned by where the major party candidates stand in the race at the time they make their decision, both objectively and in their own estimation. George Bush was ahead in the polls in July; and even if he and his team believed (as they always insisted) that the race would be close, they did not feel themselves behind or under a compulsion to take a risk. Bush chose the candidate he wanted, without being pushed. Gore's situation was quite different. Behind in the polls, he was under pressure to shake things up. Would Joe Lieberman have been his choice if he had been in command of the race? No one can ever know. But once he made his choice, there was an immediate feeling that it was the right one. The risks or downside of selecting a Jewish running mate never openly manifested themselves. After the huge initial spate of commentary about selecting the first practicing Jew to run on a national ticket, the only public figure to keep belaboring the point during the campaign was Joe Lieberman himself.[5] Gore reaped many benefits from a decision that looked bold, but that turned out to be completely safe.

Political scientists, viewing matters at a distance, often argue that the choice of a vice presidential running mate counts for "very little" in affecting the final election results, though recent history suggests that poor vice presidential choices hurt more than good ones help.[6] But many in the media, hungry for news in the lean months of early summer, insist that it counts a great deal, positively as well as negatively.[7] In full awareness that in a close race what seems very little can mean a lot, it seems prudent to stress the potential importance of the vice presidential choice. Furthermore, as with so many other factors in a political campaign, clear and direct effects are not easily separated from subtle and indirect ones. Joe Lieberman's strong code of ethics could not compensate completely for Gore's lapses in campaign finance or obscure his strong support of President Clinton during the impeachment crisis, but his selection certainly contributed greatly to Gore's break with Clinton at the Democratic Convention. Likewise, Dick Cheney's distinguished record of service could not really compensate for Bush's inexperience in foreign affairs, but Cheney's performance by the end still provided important reassurance to the nation and confirmed Bush's good sense in selecting so able a partner.[8]

As far as there were political calculations in these choices, they were surely not conventional geographical ones. If his choice was to be based on geography, Bush would have chosen from among other vice presidential finalists from key states or constituencies, such as Governor Tom Ridge of Pennsylvania or Frank Keating of Oklahoma. Ridge, popular in his state, might have helped Bush in Pennsylvania, as Keating, a Catholic, might have among Catholic voters in the industrial Midwest. Likewise, picking a geographically advantageous vice president for Gore might have meant choosing Senator Evan Bayh of Indiana, John Edwards of North Carolina, or Bob Graham of Florida. By contrast, Lieberman came from Connecticut, whose eight electoral votes were already a safe bet for Gore, while Cheney came from Wyoming, a state holding three electoral votes in confirmed "Bush country." In the end, both candidates chose individuals who balanced the perceived weaknesses in their own personal qualities and helped them nationally across the board. Bush's selection of Cheney added a dimension of gravitas, while Gore's choice provided a moral prophylactic, helping Gore to separate himself from Clinton by running along-side the first Democratic senator to strongly criticize Clinton's conduct during the Lewinsky scandal.

There were nevertheless differences in what the two choices brought in a political sense. Lieberman's selection, many believed, added to Gore's base. His appeal to Jewish voters helped put Florida in play for Al Gore, while his centrist or New Democratic views offered an opening to moderate voters, balancing Gore's own move to the left as a populist. In fact, the only appreciable opposition to the Lieberman selection came from some on the left in the Democratic Party, who sought reassurances that Lieberman's centrist positions on such issues as school vouchers, affirmative action, and privatization of part of Social Security would not become part of the Democratic campaign or a Gore administration. For his part, Cheney shored up Bush's support among conservatives, though Bush perhaps did not need much additional reinforcement from that quarter. Since Cheney did not "add" anything further electorally, more than a few wondered why Bush had not, like Ronald Reagan in 1980, taken a bold step and chosen his chief rival John McCain, who might have brought another dimension (along with perhaps a ton of troubles) to the ticket. The best answer might be to look beyond November 7: While Cheney may not have come with his own loyal constituency, he was a man who would help Bush govern.

The public and pundits reacted favorably to both choices, although the pundits generally thought Gore's was better strategically. No Democrat, they concluded, could have helped the ticket more than Joe Lieberman, while few made the same claim about Cheney. In addition, Cheney got off to a bit of a rough start, not being entirely prepared for the scrutiny of his congressional voting record from 20 years before. The system used to select and prepare vice presidential nominees did not function in Cheney's case, because Cheney, who was the one charged by Bush to vet the potential choices, himself became Bush's choice. Later in the campaign, on the eve of the vice presidential debate, political analyst Bill Schneider assessed the situation as follows: "Joe Lieberman seems to be helping Al Gore more than Dick Cheney is helping George W. Bush. Lieberman helps Gore reach out to the center; Cheney does not. Lieberman helps Gore break his ties to Bill Clinton; Cheney looks like Bush's father's choice. Lieberman makes Gore look more inclusive; two Texas oil men on the ticket does not exactly expand the GOP base."[9]

But as the campaign continued, the net advantage Lieberman held over Cheney, if there ever really was one, diminished. Lieberman's choice inevitably lost its novelty and excitement as time went on, and Lieberman jettisoned many of his centrist positions to attain greater consistency with

Gore. For Cheney, the turning point coincided with (and contributed to) the turning point for the entire campaign. It came in the vice presidential debate in early October, at the time of a flare-up in the Mideast between Israel and the Palestinians. Both candidates did very well in that debate—so much so that many newspapers editorialized that both tickets would have done better to reverse the positions of the candidates—but Cheney's performance was superb. Partially because of his great experience in foreign affairs at a moment of great international tension, an ABC News poll of debate viewers found that Cheney had "won" the debate by a 42–23 percent margin. By the end of the race it was clear that Cheney, far from being a drag on the campaign, had become a real asset. And in the postelection campaign—and no one should be under any illusion that there was not an important public campaign in that period—Cheney emerged as the most trusted and mature figure of all the candidates, helping to keep public opinion in Bush's favor.

The net impact on the vote resulting from the choice of a vice presidential candidate can never be known in detail. All one can do is state certain general facts from which rough inferences may be drawn. Lieberman did not (as some feared) hurt Al Gore with the left of his Democratic base, as Gore ran very strongly among these voters. How much Lieberman helped with moderates is difficult to say, but many argued that he was an attractive choice for many suburban voters in some of the battleground states. Al Gore had very little cross-partisan appeal, and Joe Lieberman certainly could not solve this problem for him. Within the religious community, religious leaders, including many on the Christian right, applauded the Lieberman selection and his defense of the place of religion in the public square. But there is no evidence that this approval translated into popular votes. On the contrary, it is clear—without making any unseemly charges—that Joe Lieberman's appeal was chiefly in the urban sector, not in small-town America. As in physics, where every action provokes an opposite reaction, so in politics every mobilization tends to create a countermobilization. The Gore-Lieberman ticket, in some measure because of Joe Lieberman, played best in urban and suburban areas, while it lost ground in small-town and rural America. This shift in the voting patterns of urban and nonurban voters was one of the most striking and important developments in the 2000 election. As for Bush's pick of Cheney, it clearly did not draw in a new constituency. Bush lacked the decisive breakthrough in one of the demographic groups that could have given him a state like Pennsylvania or Michigan. But along with his overall appeal, Cheney might have helped Bush nail down just the small-town and solid heartland vote that gave Bush victories in states like Arkansas, Tennessee, and Missouri.

In their choice of running mates, as in so many other decisions made during the campaign, there was a hare-and-tortoise quality to the candidates' behavior. Gore, the hare, was continually shifting, jumping about, and taking risks—no doubt in part because, being behind, he had to. Gore's maneuvers and tactics were sometimes well conceived and often brought him an immediate advantage. By contrast, Bush pushed slowly and methodically ahead, continually opting for the steady over the theatrical. So pronounced was this approach that over time his persistence itself became noteworthy. There was a certain boldness to his blandness and a daring to his steadiness. The choice of Richard Cheney, Mr. Bland and Steady, was emblematic of the entire Bush campaign.

Phase One: George Bush Widens His Lead

Days after Bush's selection of Cheney, Republicans formally launched their fall campaign with their national convention. National party conventions have historically served the major purposes of choosing the presidential nominee and the vice presidential nominee and deciding on the platform and party rules. They have served a host of minor purposes as well, including an assembling of party figures from across the nation to build party enthusiasm and establish personal ties. Today, of course, the conventions no longer perform any of the major functions in a robust sense. This fact now regularly brings forth on the eve of conventions a spate of lamentations from feature writers, who, in fits of peevishness or nostalgia, seem to think that these functions themselves have vanished from American political life. The reality, of course, is that they are now performed at another time and in another way. The choice of presidential nominees takes place in the primaries in February and March, often supplying all the suspense now missing from the conventions, as in the case of the dramatic contest between Bush and McCain. The discussion of the issues, which decides the platforms, now takes place in the debates during the primaries in December and January. It might, of course, be argued that these functions would better be performed at the convention, but no one has yet presented a sensible case for why they should be done twice.

In the old days, there was a rule of party discipline that was fairly widely respected, except in cases of the most intense conflict. It was simply that after all the fights and disputes of the party convention, party members should leave their battles behind and come together to support the nominee and the platform. What has been evolving in our times, slowly, is a similar rule, only with the time of application coming after the verdict of the primaries, rather than after the convention. For a good part of the past two decades, it is true, candidates who were defeated in the primaries proceeded as if they had a right to carry on their struggle and, if not sufficiently mollified by the nominee, to bring their complaints onto the floor of the convention and to deliver an uncensored convention speech. But it has become increasingly clear that putting this disunity on public display harms both the nominee and the party. The realization has thus dawned that, if a party wishes to win, its defeated candidates must limit their protests and be reasonably good soldiers. By and large, both John McCain and Bill Bradley did this, although Bradley took longer than McCain to meet with his party's winner.

The changed character of today's national party conventions is easily expressed in the formula that the convention, once the prelude to the campaign, is now part of the campaign. And as part of the campaign—indeed an important part—it must obey the campaign's logic, which is to do whatever helps the candidate to win. The role of the convention has been summed up clearly by Robert Healy, who ran more than a few Democratic Conventions: "Conventions are framing devices, mechanisms that help frame the presidential choice. They have one principal task: positioning the presidential candidate for the fall election."

If it is an error—a mistaking of form over function—to compare the party conventions today to the party conventions of the nineteenth century, to what then should they be compared? The answer, it seems, is to the official campaign biographies of that epoch, which could be penned by such luminaries as Nathaniel Hawthorne and George Bancroft.[10] These commissioned biographies sought to present the party and candidate in a favorable light for a mass audience, which is exactly what the "authors" of the convention try to do today. It is undoubtedly true that convention authors face a more complex and daunting task. The biographer works with the simple and pliable medium of pen and paper, whereas the convention authors must deal with a multidimensional event that includes audio, visual, musical, and textual elements. On occasion, too, their material can be recalcitrant and resist their complete control. Should a Bill Clinton, for example, choose to strut through a maze of tunnels for three minutes before making a triumphant entrance into the arena, what convention author is going to prevent him from doing so? Clearly, however, the ideal of the modern convention authors—and the end point toward which developments are moving—is for the candidate's campaign organization to fully script the affair, reading and approving, if not actually writing, every word of every speech. The Republican Convention of 2000 came the closest of any convention thus far to realizing this ideal. One oddity of the convention, on which many remarked at the time, was a speech delivered by the once famous movie star Bo Derek. No one could quite figure out the reason for this appearance, unless it was to remind people that the convention was a Perfect 10.

There is a clear irony to this "development" of the convention. The more controlled and scripted the convention becomes, the less likely it is to survive as a vital institution. No human arrangement that is so contrived and lacking in spontaneity can be expected for long to hold the public's interest. A number of "serious" observers have raised this concern as a theoretical matter, but it has not troubled the practitioners. Their task is to produce the perfect convention, even if it means destroying the convention in the process. This is essentially what happened to the commissioned campaign biography as an important genre. Practitioners must, however, take account of some nascent signs of decline, as these have already become a part of the practical reality with which they must contend. As the convention authors have gone to greater and greater lengths to present a media-perfect image of their candidate, there has been a corresponding precipitous drop both in the viewing audience and in the prime-time programming slots allotted the conventions by the traditional major broadcast networks, although part of the slack has been taken up by PBS and the cable channels CNN and C-Span. Convention authors have responded by trying to inject some excitement, but balloons, rock groups, and professional wrestlers can only add so much.

For all the attacks made today on the party conventions, there does seem to be a need at some point for the candidate and party to have the unvarnished opportunity to present themselves just as they wish, without the disdainful remarks of too many precocious commentators. (By their complaints in recent years the parties have forced the mainline television anchors to be a bit more measured than they used to be, even as the cable commentators with their throngs of "panelists" have had a field day criticizing the conventions.) There is also surely a need for the candidates' acceptance speeches, which today set the main themes of the campaign and have taken the place of the platform as the main statement of the party's principles. The speech could no doubt be delivered in studio, with a false background and dubbed cheers, but the face-to-face encounter brings an important human element into the process and produces an emotional impact on the large number of partisans in attendance. For all their fluff, it is remarkable how much of the essential message of the conventions registers with voters. No one watches the conventions, but everyone ends up with a pretty clear idea of what they were all about.[11]

Returning to the Republican convention, each evening had a central "theme," with an accompanying "message" delivered by that night's carefully chosen speakers. Monday night was "Opportunity with a Purpose: Leave No Child Behind," with the message "Governor Bush's proposals for improving education and expanding health care are examples of his vow to 'leave no child behind' and ensure access to quality care for all Americans." Tuesday night was "Strength and Security with a Purpose: Safe in our Homes and in the World" (we skip the messages). Wednesday night was "Prosperity with a Purpose: Keeping America Prosperous and Protecting Retirement Security," and finally Thursday night was "President with a Purpose: A Strong Leader Who Can Unite Our Country and Get Things Done."

The convention authors deserve credit for their sense of pacing. After the first night, when, for all intents and purposes, only children, minorities, and women were permitted on the podium and when the only subjects that could be broached were diversity and compassion, some participants and viewers found the event soporific. After the second night, liberals were in full gear mocking the convention's "inclusion illusions," while more than a few conservatives had their heads out the window, *Network* style, shouting, "I can't take it anymore." This phase of the Republican Convention must be understood in the light of the propaganda wars of the previous few years. The object of Democratic symbolic labeling during the Clinton years, masterminded by the president himself, was to paint the Republicans as mean-spirited, narrowly partisan, and hostile and insensitive to minorities. The Republican Convention aimed to "de-Gingrichize" the Republican image. This effort was comparable to the one Democrats undertook at their 1984 and 1988 conventions, when they waived flags ad nauseam to counter Republicans' symbolic propaganda casting doubts on their patriotism.

But just as the convention was about to lose its audience, its tone changed. On night three, Dick Cheney's speech offered a dose of much needed partisanship and tossed out at least a small portion of what the television anchors were unanimously labeling "red meat," in contrast to the "vegetarian" diet that had been served up on the first two nights. In addition to taking a shot or two at Clinton and Gore, Cheney made a case for change based on the issues, signaling that the Bush campaign would not walk away from trying to convince the country that, even in good times, it was time for a fresh start. On the final evening, George Bush gave a speech that convinced his followers and many others that he had the "right stuff" to be president. Commentator David Gergen said that Bush had "fired up his party, set forward an agenda for change, and shown he can lead. Unless Gore provides a better answer next week, we have just witnessed the making of our next president."[12] Hardly a Republican walked away from Bush's speech disappointed, an important fact in the close 2000 campaign. Republicans in 1992 and 1996 were widely dissatisfied with their candidates, and Clinton's ability to attract Republican voters in those elections no doubt had as much to do with this dissatisfaction as with Clinton's positive appeal. Gore faced a much harder task attracting Republicans in 2000.

Phase Two: Al Gore Storms Back

If the general election campaign began with Bush's selection of Cheney, Al Gore's comeback began with his vice presidential pick. The subsequent Democratic Convention, held in Los Angeles two weeks after the Republican Convention, was a less perfectly scripted and slightly more haphazard affair. Some speakers went past their appointed times, and thematic programming was not as tight. Initial reactions, while the convention was meeting, were that things were perhaps not going so well. Viewers had to wonder: was the convention about Bill Clinton, or Al Gore? Was it about New Democrats or Old? Was it about "the people," or the Hollywood glitterati peering down from their expensive skyboxes? Yet by its end, and certainly by a few days after the convention, it was clear that something had "happened" in Los Angeles. Al Gore, counted out by many, had managed not only to revive his campaign, but also to seize the initiative and pull out in front of Bush for the first time since polling matchups between these men had begun almost two years before.

How can one reconcile the ordinary character of the Democratic Convention, especially in contrast to the Republican Convention, with the positive effects that it generated? Part of the answer is that the Democrats had far more to gain from having any kind of convention at all, or at least one that was not a disaster. Democrats were far behind in the polls, so they had nowhere to go but up. If conventions are known above all for their ability to rally the troops, and if many Democrats going into the convention were AWOL, then the Los Angeles meeting was bound to help mightily. And it did.

But more was involved. Al Gore succeeded in doing something important to restart his campaign: he emerged as his own man and built a new image as a populist, Old Democrat. His instruments for accomplishing these two goals, apart from the selection of Joe Lieberman as his running mate, were the kiss and the speech. The kiss of Tipper, clocked at seven seconds, called attention to the fact that Al Gore was not Bill Clinton and that the Gores' marriage had none of the singularity of the Clintons' arrangement, which was no doubt a relief to many Americans. Here was a successful man, with a supportive and intelligent wife, and four very attractive children. The family had experienced some hardships—what family has not?—but stood intact as an admirable model of wholesome values. Then came the speech, which was delivered with a willful focus that refused the normal pauses for applause. Its very intensity called attention to Gore's seriousness and commitment to his cause. Without turning his back on anything in the Clinton administration, Gore sought to show in deed, by what he stood for, that he was willing to strike out on his own as one who would "fight for" the people against the powerful.

Gore's surge in the polls following the convention was initially met with surprise by political commentators, as it came after months during which Gore consistently trailed George W. Bush. Once Gore's lead persisted, however, most analysts quickly grew convinced that this new relation between the candidates would hold up through the election. The race, they began to say, was now at last where it "should" be, in line with the "fundamentals" that dictated that good conditions always favor the incumbent party. Gore's rise paralleled the rise of George Bush the elder in 1988, and there was no reason to think that things would be any different this time. The emergence of Gore as the front-runner also vindicated the experts who relied on models to analyze elections, as the models clearly seemed to capture a reality that had been missed by many of those who had dwelt only on this campaign.

In our analysis, we have relied on the models on this point and argued that the fundamentals in the race probably did favor Gore. This assumption helps account for Gore's extraordinary surge at this time, which otherwise seems difficult to explain. It was a surge, we surmise, that could have held up through election day. But the models, we have argued, should be used as an aid to contemporary qualitative analysis, not as a mechanical substitute for it. No historical event with the complexity of a political campaign can be entirely subsumed under a general pattern, as each particular campaign has its own character. Indeed, it is now clear that even at the moment of Gore's surge, there were difficulties with the pure argument deriving from the models. Part of what Gore was doing to pull ahead—at least part of what he was doing at the time that he pulled ahead—violated the model's implicit "rule" (introduced afterwards) to "make the good record of the Clinton administration the centerpiece of the campaign."[13] Gore's populist strategy moved away from this approach.

Where, then, does this leave the analysis? It is of course possible to argue that Gore's success at this stage came in spite of his populist strategy, or that it was a strategy bound to fail. Our view, which is free of the need to force empirical facts to conform to any model, is that Gore's populist strategy was in all likelihood an integral part of his surge. But it is also true that this strategy was precarious, in the sense that it contained built-in difficulties and contradictions that imposed a ceiling on his potential support low enough that it left him little margin for error. With any kind of lapse in the campaign, these contradictions could begin to be effectively exploited. This, we believe, is what happened. No one, of course, will ever be able to prove the case one way or another. Gore's detractors in the Democratic Party (along with many defenders of mathematical models in the academic world) have argued that he followed the wrong course. They insist that Gore could have won easily without this populist phase and, indeed, that he lost because he used it. Another view we find just as compelling, however, is that despite the difficulties of this strategy, Gore needed his populism to have a chance to win. If this is true, then Gore's loss was not due to the defects of this plan, but to his failure to execute it flawlessly.

Gore's recovery caught the Bush organization off guard. While expecting Gore's bounce to make the race close, the Bush team never planned to be trailing by a significant margin. Yet here they were in September, behind by some 5 points, flailing away at Bill Clinton's "shadow" when that shadow had all but disappeared from the race. Bush's loss of initiative was accompanied by some serious bloopers. He sought to impose a schedule for the presidential debates as if he were negotiating from a position of strength to which Al Gore had to accede. In fact, quite the opposite was the case, and, poor debater or not, it was George W. Bush who needed the debates, not Al Gore. Bush was forced to stand down. Bush was also caught in a few of his signature mispronunciations of big words, most notably his disavowal of any "subliminable" intent in a Republican campaign ad that reportedly sought to deliver the subliminal message that Democrats were "rats." He was also hurt in a "major league" way by at least one perfect pronunciation, when he verbally assailed *New York Times* correspondent Adam Clymer in front of an open mike.

Accompanying the reversal of positions between the candidates was a major change in the tone of the press coverage, which up until this period had been less than favorable to Al Gore. A reporting of objective events was no doubt part of the cause, but facts are always structured by one of the four "loves" that influence media interpretation: love of a story, love of a winner, love of an ideology, and love of a candidate. There clearly was a story here—finally. After months of the same script, the whole event now was different, and the press naturally was drawn to the drama. There was the emerging sense too that this was the last turn of fortune in the campaign, and that Al Gore was going to win. Members of the press, like everyone else, admire and respect a winner and have their own professional reasons for staying on good terms with the victor and members of his team. As for ideology, far more of the working press are liberal than conservative, and this preference no doubt plays some role at the margins. Finally, there are the journalists' personal feelings about the candidates. It is true the press never much warmed to Al Gore and in fact possibly even preferred George Bush (although John McCain was the only one reporters truly liked). What all this meant was three out of four of the background influences on press thinking were operating in favor of Al Gore during this period, and three out of four ain't bad.[14]

For the first time, Bush was subjected to a low rumble of grousing by Republican insiders who feared his Texas team was letting the election slip away, and he came under considerable pressure to change his staff and his strategy. The reactions of some conservative intellectuals during this period also reflected a deep pessimism about the future electoral prospects of the conservative movement and the Republican Party. Yes, conservative commentators made perfunctory criticisms of the campaign and raised some of the obvious points about the deficiencies of the candidate. But on balance they were prepared to acknowledge that the candidate was respectable and the campaign was fairly well conceived. The problem, then, had to be the conservative message, or what the American people thought of the conservative message. Conservatism, many concluded, was losing, while liberalism—an older-style, Big Government liberalism at that—was winning. Conservative intellectuals looked to be preparing for a long period in the wilderness, where they might console themselves with the thought that, at least in their hearts, they knew they were right.

Phase Three: Bush Overtakes Gore

Everything turned around for George Bush during the period of the debates. Granted, in the weeks before October 3, Bush's campaign had begun to straighten out its problems and sharpen its message, and with Bush's smooch of Oprah on national TV, he let it be known that he would not concede the strategic kissing war. But the real change came during the debates. Starting with the first debate, a series of little fibs and exaggerations by Gore gave Bush the opening he needed to get a second look by the press and the public. Bush seized the opportunity to exploit not just the troubling aspects of Gore's persona (connecting him once again to Clinton), but also the downside of the Gore "Old Democratic" or populist strategy. Within a couple of weeks, Bush had tied all of these together under the general theme of "trust." The line was that one could not trust Al Gore personally, one could not trust how Clinton-Gore had used the presidency, and finally that Gore, by his Big Government programs and tax plan, showed that he did not trust the American people. Bush was trying this theme before the debate, arguing that he trusted the people, while Gore did not: "The vice president says he wants to help the people. If only he would trust them."[15]

Helping Bush's line of argument, questions of Gore's credibility surfaced in the days before the debate. White House memos became public indicating that in 1995 Gore had solicited large contributions from wealthy trial lawyers by promising to deliver Clinton's veto of a pending tort reform bill. Gore attacked Hollywood one day, then picked up big donations from Hollywood moguls the next. And when Clinton ordered the release of a portion of the nation's strategic oil reserve as a proposed remedy for skyrocketing heating oil costs only a couple of days after Gore had called for such a move on the campaign trail, suspicions were aroused that the president and vice president were playing politics with a national security issue. But most importantly, Gore was caught in three fibs in one week: a story that his mother's arthritis medicine cost more than the same medicine for his dog (he had actually taken an example from a House Democratic policy study); a claim that he had participated in discussions on the oil reserve since its inception (it was begun before he entered Congress); and a reminiscence that a famous union song had served as his lullaby as a baby (he was 27 years old when it was written). Afterwards, Gore's team defended the basic point of the prescription drug illustration, making light of Gore's fabricated personal embellishments. Normally exaggerations of this kind would have been of little consequence. After all, Ronald Reagan, the Great Embellisher, had told a few stories of his own. But things now were different. Given his own "no controlling legal authority" statement and Clinton's testimony about what the meaning of the word "is" is, many Americans were sensitive to the implications of little stretches of truth. Gore was already known to be predisposed to telling such stories, and he had been put on notice, by his own advisers, that he should not do so again. The connection of Gore to Clinton's problems may not have been fair, but was inevitable. According to Charles Cook: "As a friend of mine put it, Bill Clinton lies about big things and does it very well; Al Gore lies about little things and does it very badly. None of his fibs really amount to much, but they remind voters of what they don't like about Clinton."[16] Even more, they reminded voters of the central flaw charged against Gore, that he would say or do anything to get elected.

If Gore's missteps and Bush's new theme laid the groundwork for Bush's surge, bringing him even with Gore by October 3, it was the cumulative effect of the three debates themselves that carried him past the vice president and into a modest lead that lasted until the final weekend. By general consensus Al Gore was supposed to win the debates, and on the initial reaction of those who watched the first one, he probably did win, even though both men looked like they had accomplished what they set out to achieve. As George Will commented afterwards, George Bush "demonstrated that the governor of the second-most populous state can competently address basic questions," thereby putting some fears to rest. But to many, Bush seemed a little unsteady, especially on foreign policy matters, while Gore seemed fully in command, though a little overbearing. ABC News analyst (and former Clinton staffer) George Stephanopoulos declared immediately that Gore had "dominated," and even the conservative *National Review* opined that Gore "won the debate . . . the silver lining for Republicans is that the debate probably won't matter much."[17]

Subsequent analysis changed the initial impression in a dramatic way, making this debate probably the most decisive for any presidential candidate since presidential debating began in 1960. Gore had violated his probation, twice telling stories that were exaggerated or false—one of a trip he took to Texas with the head of FEMA to inspect the fires in that state and another of a young schoolgirl in Sarasota, Florida, forced to stand because of a crowded classroom.[18] Once these problems were revealed, Gore's arrogant behavior—his sighs and eye-rolling—also came to be seen in a different and harsher light. Within a couple of days, with these missteps repeated unmercifully and mocked on the comedy shows, Gore's performance came increasingly to be seen as a disaster. The Gore team went into full damage-control mode, and Gore himself took the extraordinary, and no doubt personally agonizing, step of apologizing for both his misstatements and his behavior. Questions about Gore's character and temperament, often translated by the media as personality and likability, returned to the forefront.

When the transcript of the first debate is studied, it is notable also for casting in high relief an important and fundamental difference between the two men's ideological position on a variety of issues, including taxes, Social Security, energy development, prescription drugs, and campaign finance. Bush continued attacking Gore for heavy-handed new federal programs, while Gore accused Bush of looking out only for the wealthy. It is true that in one sense the two candidates held positions that by historical standards were close to each other. But it is also clear that they began their thinking about politics from quite different theoretical principles. The "classic" split between right and left was never better illustrated than in the two candidates' respective views of who in principle owns the wealth of society.

For Bush the wealth is clearly morally owned by individuals, from which government then takes what is needed. For Gore the wealth is owned collectively and divided according to an egalitarian standard of justice. The following exchange over who owns the national surplus said it all:

> Bush: "My opponent thinks the government—the surplus is the government's money. That's not what I think. I think it's the hard-working people in America's money and I want to share some of that money with you."

> Gore: "I agree that the surplus is the American people's money. It's your money. That's why I don't think we should give nearly half of it to the wealthiest 1 percent, because the other 99 percent have had an awful lot to do with building this surplus and our prosperity."

The second presidential debate, following Richard Cheney's strong performance in the vice presidential debate, was clearly George Bush's best showing—and Gore's weakest. It was Bush's preferred format, with the two men sitting down at a table, which invited a more conversational style. The body language of the candidates was notable here. Bush seemed at ease, more confident and less tentative than in any of his previous outings. It was Gore's demeanor, however, that was most striking. For one thing, as so many remarked, he actually *looked* different, as his makeup artists tried to give him a less plastic and formal appearance than just a week before. And he acted differently. Gore was subdued and a bit hesitant, indeed at moments almost meek. At almost every turn, he was "agreeing" with "Governor Bush." In trying to curb their candidate's aggressiveness, Gore's advisers had seemed to remove his alpha male gene. The lion had become a lamb. After the debate was over, commentators again posed the damaging question about who was the "real" Al Gore. In the first two debates the American people had seen two almost completely different versions.

In the third debate, down two-to-nothing against an opponent considered to be a weak debater, Gore came up with his best performance. Viewers could have no doubts that Gore answered the questions well and was in command of the issues. Supporters were reassured to see the old and more aggressive Al Gore back in action, and his performance certainly stabilized matters. In his own words, he was like Goldilocks (what he meant, of course, was that he was like the bears' porridge that Goldilocks appropriated): too hot the first time, too cold the second time, and just right on the third try. Even then, however, he failed to score a clear win. Like a champion boxer "pumped" for the event, Gore seemed determined to intimidate his opponent, provoking accusations of bad manners when he at one point charged across the stage and planted himself in Governor Bush's face. And Gore's own "Goldilocks" description—an extraordinary admission that three debates had produced three distinct Al Gores—did nothing to allay concerns that he did not quite know who he was.

A major consequence of the debates was to solidify Bush's offensive on the general ideological theme of Big Government. Here we return to the great puzzle or difficulty in assessing Gore's strategy. Gore's campaign was based on trying to have it both ways—on promising a great deal and heating up the rhetoric, yet claiming at the same time that he represented the safer choice and had no intention of overspending or returning to the foibles of Big Government. While Bush had tried to expose this difficulty earlier, without the general opening Gore gave Bush during the debates Gore might well have been able to pull off both sides of this appeal. As the arguments unfolded, however, Gore was exposed for being ideologically farther to the left than he wanted to appear. While Gore continued to score on specific issues, he was often backpedaling on the overall theme of Big Government, which led in the end to criticisms of his strategy from some of the more moderate Democrats. It was more than a little ironic that Bush, who sought throughout his campaign to project a softer, nonideological image, survived his two greatest threats—McCain's victory in New Hampshire and Gore's postconvention surge—only by regrouping on the terrain of limited government ideology.

Phase Four: Gore Closes to a Photo Finish

Al Gore closed the election in the last week, both in the polls and certainly in the election itself, where he finished slightly ahead of Bush. It may be asked whether there was a "real" phase four, in the sense of an actual change, or whether this movement would most likely have occurred whenever the election was held. In favor of the last view is the sudden drop in Nader's support, which followed the usual voter logic of not wasting a vote for a third party in a close race. The strength of this logic was made clear by the fact that as Nader gained in prominence near the end of the campaign, he also lost support. Also arguing in favor of this view is that Gore had the larger reservoir from which to draw among the swayable voters, which by the end had more weak Democrats than weak Republicans. Finally, given the doubts among undecideds about both candidates, there was probably a case of buyer's regret that would come into play: whichever candidate was perceived to be ahead at the end (this was probably Bush) was likely to suffer defections from those having second thoughts.

None of these arguments are inconsistent with the possibility that Bush was harmed by the last-minute "surprise" revelation of an unrevealed DUI arrest 24 years earlier. Bush clearly made a mistake in leaving this piece of his record hanging in the hope that it would remain unexposed. He created an unnecessary vulnerability for himself that allowed a negative story to dominate two or three days of the news during the final week of the campaign.[19] A Gallup poll released November 5 indicated that 10 percent of independent voters declared themselves "less likely" to vote for Bush because of the incident—both a small number and an enormous one, given the closeness of the race.[20]

A few other factors that were far from inevitable probably contributed to Gore's last-minute surge. The weekend before election day, Bush strategist Karl Rove predicted a popular vote victory in the 6–7 percent range and about 320 electoral votes for Bush. Taking the approach of "looking like a winner," Bush seemed to play defense for the last week of the campaign and appeared less aggressive than Gore, who ran a frenetic campaign, turning up the rhetoric to a new level of intensity. Amid the post–November 7 partisan wrangling, more than a few Republican voices could be heard quietly wondering whether Bush had brought the close finish on himself by sitting on his lead.[21] And not all of the return of the Nader voters to Gore was foreordained. Gore made a deliberate appeal to bring them back, to which Republicans may have unwisely contributed by running ads in the Pacific Northwest supporting Nader, a decision that undoubtedly helped remind many straying Democratic voters who it was who had the most to gain if they voted Green.

Gore's advisers pointed out that other vice presidents—Nixon in 1960 and Humphrey in 1968—had surged in the final days as voters focused on the candidates' experience. The discouraging half of the story, from Gore's perspective, was that they had not quite closed enough. In fact, if Gore had going for him the models of political scientists based on economic conditions, he had working against him another sort of historical pattern, just as rooted in a deeper political logic: Since 1916, no incumbent president or vice president had won a close race.[22]

As neither candidate was able to score a real breakthrough in the popular or the electoral vote in 2000, it cannot be said that either camp's strategy was very successful. Or, to be more precise, each candidate achieved what he wanted on certain dimensions, but his gains were canceled by the success of his opponent on other dimensions. Al Gore clearly succeeded in being considered more knowledgeable and more experienced than Bush. He also held the advantage, at the end of the campaign no less than at the beginning, on a series of specific issues. But

Bush was able to negate part of Gore's benefits by linking Gore's character and temperament flaws with the ideological dimension through the medium of "trust" that he enunciated in the debates. Both candidates' strategic successes were, in one sense, equally important since they essentially balanced each other out. Taken in context, though, it is hard to escape the conclusion that Bush's achievement was more noteworthy. His strategy required piecing together all of Gore's weaknesses in one argument. It was just enough to squeak through.

Election Quality and Third Parties

Turnout in 2000 was estimated at 51.2 percent of the voting-age population, up 2.2 percent from the 1996 election, which had been the lowest in modern years. A good part of the increase from 1996 came in the hotly contested battleground states, in which both sides spent large sums of money to get out the vote. As usual, however, the states with the absolute highest participation rates were all located on the northern tier: Minnesota (69%), Maine (67%), Alaska (66%), Wisconsin (67%), Vermont (64%), New Hampshire (62%), and Montana (62%). How legislation that would reduce overall spending might influence turnout remains a troubling issue inside the debate over reform.

Along with this modest increase in voter turnout, those who study campaign quality had other reasons to celebrate the effects of the 2000 campaign, at least if one stops the clock on election day. The Pew Foundation, which has been interested in the question of campaign quality, surveyed Americans on what they thought of the campaign and came up with some surprisingly positive answers. Voters thought there was more discussion of the issues in 2000 than in 1996, and less negative campaigning than in either 1996 or 1992. Overall, Americans were more satisfied with the candidates and the substance of their choice than in any of the elections since 1988.[23] To be sure, the campaign had its few nasty moments, especially at the end, but the conduct overall was tame and civil in comparison to many earlier campaigns. Part of the reason for restraint, of course, was a calculation of electoral advantage. Negative campaigning was "out" by the time the fall campaign began. Al Gore, having run a pretty rough campaign to dispatch Bill Bradley in the primaries, was being watched for nastiness, while the Republicans, who made such a point of calling attention to Gore's tactics, were limited by their own rhetoric. The theme of running a clean campaign became so pronounced that one of the worst charges one campaign could hurl at the other was to accuse it of dirty campaigning—not exactly the stuff of rough politics.

The campaign accordingly ended with the best chance since 1984 for the victor to profit from a general sentiment of goodwill, or at any rate a relative absence of bad will. This opportunity was lost, of course, in the acrimony of the postelection phase. The campaign turned far more partisan after election day than before, and events conspired to leave many with the opinion that the Republicans had stolen the election (and many others with the idea that the Democrats had tried to steal it but failed). Suspicion of the Republicans was particularly strongly felt in the African American community, where charges of "disenfranchisement" became a major theme of the postelection campaign.

When historians look back over the elections of the past decade, one trend on which they will surely remark is the rise and then collapse of the third-party vote. The period of the 1990s stands as one of the high watermarks in American history for third-party activity in presidential elections, due mostly to the performance of Ross Perot and what later became the Reform Party, winning 19 percent of the vote in 1992 and 8 percent in 1996. By contrast, the total third-party vote dropped to some 4 percent in 2000, and the character of third parties seemed unrelated to that of the previous two elections. Most importantly, the major third party in 2000 was not Reform, but the Green Party under Ralph Nader, which polled slightly under 3 percent and which for a good part of the fall campaign was polling in the 5–7 percent range.

The Reform Party failed to make the critical step in 2000 of institutionalizing itself, in the sense of being able to continue as a credible party beyond the candidacy of its founding figure, Ross Perot. With a ticket headed by former Republican Pat Buchanan, the Reform Party netted only 0.43 percent of the national vote, and in no state received more than 3 percent. This collapse was notable because one of the main arguments for the Reform Party in the past—besides anything specific about what the party wanted to do—was simply that the American public wanted a third major option in presidential contests. What remains a matter for speculation after 2000 is whether the Reform Party failed to exploit this niche by its own incompetence and its selection of Pat Buchanan, or whether there was still a niche for the Reform Party at all.

Third parties, as the students who study them know, come in different sizes and shapes. They are the product of one or more of the following: a mood, a personality, a set of particular issues, and a general ideology. Thus the Reform movement of 1992 was a combination of a mood (outsiderism), a strong dose of fascination for the person of Ross Perot, and a concern for the issues of democratic reform of some kind (such as term limits and the deficit). Based on these criteria, some of the conditions that once favored the Reform Party had clearly altered. There was little discontent in 2000 and room for only a mild kind of outsiderism. As for the issues, the budget problem and the deficits had vanished. Insofar as these matters were important for the success of the Reform Party, it might be said that it had suffered the same noble fate of other third parties in American history. If elections are revolutions without bullets, then minor parties play the role of the Marines—the brave few who launch the first assault on an issue but are then wiped out in the process. Still, there was the "new" issue of campaign finance, actually introduced by Perot in 1992 and (especially) 1996 but rising to the forefront in 2000, and it is not inconceivable that a genuine Reform or Independent Party, headed by the dream team of McCain and Ventura, might have made at least a minor stir.

Yet if there was a possible niche open for a reform appeal in 2000, the Reform Party as actually constituted was not the one to fill it. One can point first to the pitiful, but perhaps revealing, spectacle of a party supposedly devoted to reform imploding in the worst kind of personal factionalism and procedural irregularity. After one part of the party took over the machinery under Jesse Ventura, the other parts (including the Perot faction) battled back and relied on an alliance with Pat Buchanan to regain control. Then the Perot people turned on the Buchanan forces and the party split in two, creating the bizarre scenarios of nineteenth-century political fissures in which two rival conventions of the same party are held right down the street from one another. Apart from this organizational fiasco, there was the small problem of the standard-bearer, Pat Buchanan, who was not the best fit with the Reform idea. True enough, Buchanan shared with Perot his opposition to NAFTA and certain themes of economic nationalism, a point on which they had largely converged by 1996. And there was also a remarkable similarity in the profile of the Buchanan and Perot voters in 1996: young, white, male, high school educated independents with below-median income.[24] But for Buchanan to successfully merge with the prior Reform forces, or even with the Perot faction, he would have had to submerge his strong social conservatism—the point on which he and Perot most clearly diverged. Initially, on leaving the GOP and entering the Reform Party thicket, Buchanan had deemphasized these themes in favor of an increasingly heated anticorporate rhetoric. But as time went on, it gradually became clear that his objective was to make the party into a right-wing ideological party, with strong appeals to the anti-abortion cause and opposition to immigration.

As for Pat Buchanan himself, although he was a figure who was well known and who was counted on by some to bring a huge personal following, he could no longer lay claim to being in any sense an outsider. An iron rule of American politics is that you can appeal once as an outsider, a second time as someone on the periphery, but by the third time you are just an ordinary politician. On other aspects of reform issues, Buchanan proudly claimed to be the first "major" party to have a black woman as his vice presidential candidate. That she had once been a member of the John Birch Society in no way changed things, but few of those who were concerned with these sorts of "firsts" were inclined to vote for Pat Buchanan anyhow.

Coming into the 2000 race, the Reform Party offered any potential candidate for the presidency three major assets: a recognized national label name with some legitimacy, a line on many state ballots, and a pot of cash from the Federal Election Commission. These were attractions that led more than a few national politicians to think about vying for the nomination, including not only Jesse Ventura but also the financier and playboy Donald Trump. The attraction of controlling the $12.6 million in federal money due the party in 2000 was one factor keeping the party alive, even as many political factors pleaded for its death. It has been said that the campaign finance law, in respect to third parties, does not give them the money when they need it, but then assures them of money when they do not. For the public funds given, Buchanan received 442,368 votes, averaging about $29 of taxpayer money for each vote. At that rate, federal funding for the major parties would be in the billions.

No one needs to be told that Pat Buchanan is finished in American politics. But what about the Reform Party? Of its three assets—brand name, line on state ballots, and public funds—it has indisputably lost the last two. As for the value of the name, it too now seems to be worth little. In the words of the former party chair and organizer of the Reform Party, Russell Verney, "If the brand name gets tarnished, you may have to step away from it."[25] This statement calls to mind the fate of the Ford Pinto, which of course brings us to Ralph Nader and the Green Party.

The new lead third party was the Green Party, which quadrupled its performance from the 0.7 percent of 1996, when Ralph Nader also ran but did not campaign. Nader, of course, is a minor celebrity in his own right from his days of fighting the Ford Pinto in the 1960s, and he brought a bit of a personal appeal to the party with his small but devoted following of college students and aging hippies. The Greens obviously wanted his name recognition, as Nader himself is not pure Green. In fact, he is not a member of the Green Party and maintains a certain distance from the party's culture, which he has been trying to expand and change. It might

even be said that the two sides reached an old-fashioned political arrangement—or, to alter the metaphor, that each agreed to feed off the other,
symbiotically, as in a finely balanced ecosystem. Nader used the Green
Party organization to secure a place on state ballots and to organize a campaign against corporate power, while the Green Party used his celebrity
and professional, respectable image to draw attention and win positive
media coverage for the party.

Nader's closest competition for the nomination was perhaps Jello Bi-
afra, a former band member with "The Dead Kennedys," who proposed
for a Green administration Madonna as secretary of education and Mar-
ilyn Manson as director of the National Endowment for the Arts.[26] At
the Green Party Convention, Nader endorsed the main planks of the
Green Party platform, which includes saving rain forests, curbing pollution, drastically reducing military spending, and strengthening labor.
But in campaign appearances, he did not dwell nearly as much on environmental issues as on a more general anticorporatist program. As
Nader said on *Larry King Live* (yes, even environmentalists must pay
court to King Larry):

> I think we moved the agenda to focus on something other than harmony ideology,
> to focus on the excessive power of corporations over our country, keeping our
> country down, blocking universal health care, taxpayer money going into good
> things for neighborhoods and communities instead of corporate welfare and sub-
> sidies, like the New York Stock Exchange just getting another billion dollars.[27]

The Green Party, in its present form with its alliance with Nader, is an
ideological type of third party that speaks to many of the concerns of those
on the left. Environmentalism is its friendliest symbol, although only one
of its priorities, and it is combined in the Green Party platform with a program that calls for increased power for citizen groups and strong restraints
on corporations. Environmentalism has been a strong force in America for
quite some time, stronger in many respects than it has been in Europe. But
as a distinct electoral influence the Green movement is light-years ahead
in Europe, where Green parties have emerged in many countries as a major political element on the left. Their progress abroad might suggest a
growing place for them here. Or does it raise again the possibility of American exceptionalism? As it was asked famously early in the twentieth century, in light of the paltry performance of the Socialist Party here, "Why is
there no socialism in America?" Will the question of the early twenty-first
century be, "Why is there no Green Party in America?"[28]

Ralph Nader's role in relation to Al Gore has primarily been discussed
in terms of the "spoiler" question—whether Nader cost Al Gore the elec-

tion because of the way the votes were cast on November 7. But probably the more important story was the influence that the Nader campaign exerted all along on Gore's strategy, as Gore sought to limit defections and to keep potential Nader voters in the fold. Nader's appeal figured importantly in Gore's thinking as early as July, and it had something to do with his adopting a populist stance. Going into the final month of the campaign, pressure from the Nader faction still shaped the content of Gore's campaign, although by the end the strongest counterappeal was based on the practical plea that a vote for Nader was a vote for Bush. [29] What drove Nader's vote down was the closeness of the race, which added reality to the Gore campaign's message.

As for the question of who played the spoiler, it is surprising how hard one must work to put Ralph Nader in that role. True, Nader did cut into Gore's popular vote total. Many Nader voters might have been Gore voters if Nader had not been in the race, although by the time the party bottomed at 2.7 percent, a large part of his vote was Green to the core. Nader ran best among young voters, where he won 5 percent of the vote of the under-30 crowd, and he evidently did well in a few of the liberal latte towns among intellectuals and the wealthy, anticorporate constituency. But there are only two states that Bush won where the sum of the Gore and the Nader vote was greater than Bush's total: New Hampshire and Florida, totaling 29 electoral votes. If, following some of the speculative models, one assumes that only about half of the Nader voters were transferable to Gore, then Nader was a spoiler only in Florida, where everyone and everything else could also be counted a spoiler.[30] If the spoiler argument is to be followed to the bitter end, it should probably be observed that Pat Buchanan might be said to have been a spoiler for George W. Bush. There were four states Gore won, totaling 30 electoral votes, where the Buchanan plus Bush votes were greater than Gore's.

The 2000 Vote: Vote Distribution

Electoral analysis often begins by considering the major changes in the composition of support for the parties from the previous presidential election. If one is searching for trends, such comparisons should be treated with a great deal of caution. Each election year, after all, has its specific candidates and its own set of issues, and it may be these factors that account for the vastly different results between the two elections. Robert Dole, for example, won 41 percent in 1996, in comparison to George W. Bush's 48 percent in 2000, and it is safe to say that part of this difference was the simple result of Bush being a more effective candidate. Still, comparisons between elections are sometimes suggestive of general shifts in party composition. For the 2000 election the task of analysis is made much easier and perhaps more rewarding by the fact that Al Gore received the same percentage of the vote that Bill Clinton did in 1996.

The portrait of the Clinton and Gore vote has many similarities. They fared exactly the same, for example, with women voters, with unmarried voters, with suburban voters, and with a number of other groups as well. Of greater interest, of course, are areas of difference where there is a significant gap between the Clinton-Gore vote for a given category of voters.[31] Table 5.2 provides a list of some of the more notable differences. A few points deserve comment.

First, Gore lost ground in comparison to Clinton in the South, especially among white voters. This change probably reflects in part a long-term trend of change to the Republicans in that region, although it may also have had something to do with a particular southern appeal that Bill Clinton had, but that Al Gore did not. In the end, Gore could not even win Tennessee, his own home state, or Arkansas, Clinton's home state.

Second, in considering their support in ideological terms, Clinton clearly had more cross-party and cross-ideology appeal than Gore, whereas Gore did

Table 5.2.   Some Notable Differences between Clinton 1996 and Gore 2000 Voters

Category	% Voting for Clinton 1n 1996	% Voting for Gore in 2000	Difference
Blacks	84	90	Gore +6
Hispanics	72	65	Clinton +7
18- to 29-Year-Olds	53	48	Clinton +5
60-Year-Olds and Older	48	51	Gore +3
Catholics	53	49	Clinton +4
Republicans	13	8	Clinton +5
Moderates	57	52	Clinton +5
Income >$100,000	38	43	Gore +5
Southerners	46	43	Clinton +3
White Southerners	36	31	Clinton +5
Pop. over 500,000	64	71	Gore +7
Pop. between 50,000 and 500,000	50	57	Gore +7
Suburbs	47	47	Same
Pop. between 10,000 and 50,000	48	38	Clinton +10
Rural Areas	44	37	Clinton +7

Source: 2000 Exit Polls.

a better job at mining his Democratic and liberal base. Gore was a somewhat more polarizing Democrat than Clinton, a fact from which he both profited and lost. On the question of partisan appeal, however, it would almost certainly be a mistake to ascribe too much of this change to the differences between the two Democratic candidates. The more important factor was a change in the attitude of Republicans, who in 2000 were far more enthusiastic about their candidate (and thus less likely to defect) than in 1996 or 1992. Only 39 percent of Republicans expressed satisfaction with the candidates (mostly, of course, their party's candidate) in 1996 compared to 81 percent in 2000.[32] The one "contradictory" trend in this last picture was Gore's performance with wealthy voters, where, despite fears that his populist appeal might alienate them, Gore gained ground against Clinton. This change probably had much to do with the fact that the rich, especially the new rich, had gained their fortunes under the Democrats and were convinced that the nation was on the right track. A growing percentage within the category of the wealthy were also women, who have been more inclined to vote Democratic. This trend had first appeared in 1998, indicating that perhaps some of it may have been due to an upper-class reaction against impeachment and social conservatism.

Finally, the most remarkable shift occurred in the kind of category in which one would not have expected any large change: the place of residence. Gore's vote was far more urban than Clinton's and thus necessarily far less small-town and rural. The suburban vote remained the same. Already in 1996 the Democrats were by far the more urban party, the Republicans the more small-town and rural party. But this gap grew considerably in just four years. What explains this change? Is it mostly candidate-related, or does it indicate a reshuffling of deeper partisan attachments? This development will be important to watch.

The more rewarding form of electoral analysis focuses on the differences in the support for the two major-party candidates in this race, paying particular attention to the lines of division between supporters of the two candidates. Everyone in American politics starts with geography, and rightly so, as the electoral votes are counted by states. The regional patterns of the 1990s remain, with the Democrats being the party now of the East and the West Coast, while the Republicans have become the party of the South and Mountain West. In the South, Bush won all 11 states of the old Confederacy, the first time for Republicans since 1988. While Florida was close, elsewhere this was not the case. Bush won fairly easily in most states and outpolled Gore by more than 3.1 million votes across the region. He also won two states sometimes considered southern, Oklahoma and Kentucky.

The mirror image of the shift of the South toward the Republicans has been the movement of the East into the Democratic Party. Bush managed to win one state, New Hampshire, but otherwise the region went strongly Democratic. The vote in the East was farther from the national average than that of any other region. For years analysts, many from the East, used to speak of the Solid South. Southern analysts may soon start to refer to the Solid East. Additionally, most of the Pacific Coast has become solidly Democratic, with only Oregon's contest in doubt. If Bush outdid his two Republican predecessors, he was far from reconstructing the coalition of the Republican glory years. To some extent, the difference between Bush's coalition and Reagan's was Clinton, a figure who reduced the vulnerability of Democrats on a range of issues. The difference can also be explained almost as well by the ending of the Cold War. The military personnel and defense workers who made Washington and California competitive for Republicans are no longer there, and the issue of patriotism and anticommunism that gave Reagan entrée into the ethnic working class of the East and upper Midwest has subsided.

The second geographical pattern, already referred to, is perhaps even more important. It is the huge difference in voting patterns between small-town and rural America (Bush territory) and urban America (Gore land), with the suburbs evenly split. This tendency appeared across the nation and was only mildly modified by the partisan character of the region. There were, of course, a few exceptions such as some of the Black Belt rural areas in the South and some Hispanic and American Indian counties in the West and a few larger cities that went Republican—Cincinnati, Ohio (Hamilton County) Lexington, Kentucky (Fayette County), and Jacksonville, Florida (Duval County).

This pattern yielded an extraordinary result. Bush carried 2,476 counties against 676 for Gore, who won the popular vote by over a half a million votes. Indeed, it was this extreme geographical concentration of Gore supporters that allowed Bush to win the Electoral College while trailing in the overall popular vote. If stones and trees could vote, George W. Bush would have been chosen president in a landslide. George W. Bush never said what William Jennings Bryan did in his Cross of Gold Speech ("the great cities rest upon our broad and fertile prairies . . . burn down your cities and leave our farms"), but it seemed that the thought might have been in the minds of some who voted for him. This cleavage correlates with and can be explained in part by cultural factors, but the geographic element has an independent effect of its own and will certainly have important consequences. For example, however ingeniously legislators may be in drawing up legislative districts, they all begin from a geographical base and can go only so far in distorting it. The current distribution of support as indicated by the presidential vote points to an enormous number of safe legislative seats in America, even without concerted efforts to make them so.

Turning now to the major lines of cleavage, some of the larger ones—differences between the levels of support for the candidates within a given category of voters of more than 10 percent—are presented below in table 5.3.

It has been observed that, with the exception of the poorest segment of voters, who are strongly Democratic, it is not economic class that influences the vote so much as cultural factors. Some, using a very broad brush, have drawn a picture of a huge cultural divide between voters of a traditionalist disposition and of an experimentalist disposition. As David Frum put it, "the Republicans are the party of those who reject the cultural innovations of the 1970s; the Democrats, of those who accept them." This cultural divide appeared on a number of different elements. One of the most striking divisions was between the unmarried and the married, especially those married with children. Call it family values.

Table 5.3. Noticeable or Important Differences between Bush and Gore in 2000

Category	Bush %	Gore %	Difference
Blacks	8	90	Gore +82
Hispanics	31	67	Gore +36
All Men	53	42	Bush +11
Married Men	54	38	Bush +16
Unmarried Men	46	48	Gore +2
All Women	43	54	Gore +11
Married Women	49	48	Bush +1
Unmarried Women	32	63	Gore +31
All Married People	53	44	Bush +9
All Unmarried People	38	57	Gore +19
Jews	19	79	Gore +60
White Protestants	63	34	Bush +29
No Religion	30	61	Gore +31
Income under $15,000	37	57	Gore +20
Pop. over 500,000	26	71	Gore +45
Pop. between 50,000 and 500,000	40	57	Gore +17
Suburbs	49	47	Bush +2
Population between 10,000 and 50,000	59	38	Bush +21
Rural Areas	59	37	Bush +22
Southerners	55	43	Bush +12
Easterners	39	56	Gore +17

Source: 2000 Exit Polls.

Another cultural influence was religion. Bush won big among white evangelical Protestants, and by somewhat smaller margins among all white Protestants. He lost big among Jewish voters and the wholly secular. He also narrowly won the crucial battleground group of white Catholics. A slightly larger margin there, and he would have won Michigan, Pennsylvania, and Wisconsin, making Florida's agony a footnote. While attention to these traditional groups is warranted, it serves to obscure perhaps a more fundamental cleavage on religious lines: the division between serious believers and nominal believers, as measured (imperfectly) by frequency of church attendance. In this respect, the cultural division between the serious believers and the secularized was a better predictor of the vote than mere membership in religious groups, with Bush winning overwhelmingly among those who attend church at least once a week and Gore winning big among those attending once a month or less. Among Catholics, for example, 57 percent of those who attend weekly mass voted for Bush, while 59 percent of those who do not voted for Gore.[33] Finally, it was a notable development that Muslim Americans were noticed as an important voting bloc, especially in states like New York and Michigan.

Some of the deepest cleavages, however, were demographic rather than cultural or economic class–based. Once, one could practically count the vote by focusing on differential voting patterns among the Irish, Italians, Germans, and Anglos. Today ethnic voting among these white groups is not nearly as marked as it was in the past. But racial voting patterns still differ starkly. While most other categories of national origin–based voting have subsided, racial voting differences have only increased. Not only was Gore's victory among blacks enormous, it was greater than usual. Bush won only 8 percent of the African American vote, the lowest received by any Republican candidate except Barry Goldwater (who had voted against the Civil Rights Act) in 1964, who received 4 percent. In addition, while the nationwide percentage of black voters in 2000 remained the same as in 1996 (10 percent), it jumped in a few key states, most notably Florida. African American voters were 10 percent of the Florida electorate in 1996, but 15 percent in 2000.[34] The rallying of African Americans to Gore is not so easy to understand. Although Gore received a higher percentage of the black vote than Clinton, it is highly unlikely that this comes from a greater affinity for Gore than Clinton. Bill Clinton, whom Toni Morrison called America's "first black president," was enormously popular with black voters. Gore, one can say, was the beneficiary of that popularity, as well as of the goodwill generated from the great gains African Americans made in terms of economics in the second term of the Clinton administration.[35]

The more perplexing point is why George W. Bush did so poorly with African American voters, when he made a greater effort than other Republicans to win African American votes. Indeed, numerous surveys showed widespread black agreement with Bush's positions on Social Security and education, where more blacks than whites support vouchers. Just because the vote for Bush was lower than for previous Republicans, of course, does not necessarily mean that the intensity of opposition to him was great. (A vote, after all, is a binary choice, and it does not measure a degree of intensity.) Yet there was information supplied by some surveys that African Americans came to hold highly unfavorable opinions of Bush.[36] Some speculated that members of the black leadership, threatened by the potential appeal of Bush to their followers, sought to do all that they could to defeat him. There is no question that some of the ads taken out against Bush by black groups were extremely hard-hitting, and these groups were also enormously successful in some areas, as in 1998, in getting out the African American vote.[37] It would be difficult to say now who is in a worse situation on this issue, Republicans or African Americans. The investment of black leaders in the Democratic Party is enormous, and it grew even greater during the postelection campaign when African Americans became the most visible supporters of Gore and the most hostile to George W. Bush. Aside from the obvious dangers in cutting off access to the party that has won the presidency six of the last nine elections, black leaders run the risk of convincing Republicans that they have nothing to lose in appealing to whites much more directly on the basis of racially tinged issues like opposition to affirmative action. If Republicans can gain no more than 10 percent of the black vote no matter what they do, and invariably become targets of race-baiting demagoguery to boost black turnout in every election, they may conclude that they have no choice but to compensate by expanding their white vote.

Gore did much better among Hispanics than Bush, although Bush improved greatly from Dole's score in 1996. Republicans have obviously targeted Latino voters, and George Bush had great success with Hispanics in his races in Texas. Not to be ignored is the fact that, owing perhaps to the Elian Gonzalez affair, George Bush significantly boosted his vote among Cuban Americans in comparison to Dole's support in 1996. Here was another explanation of what delivered Florida to Bush.

Once again in 2000 there was the much-remarked-upon "gender gap," with women favoring Democrats at much higher rates than men. Women in general were, however, much more closely divided than in 1996. Unmarried women, who were much more likely to rely on government services, still backed the Democrats consistently. But Bush was able to partially overcome the gender gap that destroyed Bob Dole by holding down his overall losses among women by winning a tiny margin among married women. Bush also created a "mirror image" gender gap for the first time in presidential elections, winning among men by as large a margin as he lost among women. It was, after all, not only Dole's inability to win women's votes that cost him dearly in 1996, but his inability to open up a corresponding advantage among men.

Finally, the election of 2000 proved to be an election of bases. It had the highest percentage of declared partisans' voting with their candidate: 91 percent of the Republicans voted for Bush and 86 percent of the Democrats voted for Gore. Each candidate held his base to a remarkable degree, more overall than in any election since modern polling has been measuring the electorate. This fact can be overinterpreted. Neither candidate, by historical standards, was especially "far" to one side or the other of the political spectrum. Bush ran well to the middle for a Republican and Gore, while moving to the left, continued to have many centrist appeals. So this was not a case where the candidates were adopting positions that were an especially clear anathema to partisans from the other party. Neither candidate, however, could make a breakthrough with voters from the other party. This result is due on the one hand to the discussed lack of "personal" appeal of either candidate, and on the other to the fact that, compared to the past, more partisans in the electorate are where they "should" be. There are fewer conservative Democrats left in the South, and fewer liberal Republicans left in the North.) Another way of putting this is that the sorting out phase of the longer-term trends of the last era is now reaching its limits. Conservatives nationwide now call themselves Republicans, while liberals nationwide identify with the Democrats. Without inconsistencies between ideological voting and party identification, partisan voting appears to have grown. Party labels have changed—not ideological loyalties.

The electorate today, as we have argued, is almost perfectly balanced in its support for the two parties, with a large swing or floating vote moving between them. Of equal importance, there are almost no leftover forces from the past generating major electoral shifts between the parties. Any increase by one party or another will have to be earned in the future. The condition of a tie today calls to mind the character of politics of the Gilded Age, when the two parties were also closely balanced and locked in tight combat. The three national elections of the 1880s were among the closest in American history. There is, however, this important difference. Today, because of the large floating vote segment in the electorate, the results of any one election provide less indication or predictive value for the results of the next one. But the political conditions between the two eras seem to have an important point in common: only a major change, either of politics or conditions, will be able to give one party or the other a decisive and long-term advantage.

In the end, both parties had some reason for satisfaction in 2000, at least to the extent that it is possible to take satisfaction in a result short of victory. Democrats have established themselves as competitive at the presidential level in a way they were not in the 1980s, even in the absence of Bill Clinton on the ticket. Their hold on urban America is strengthened, their base among blacks and organized labor is mobilized, and they have formed a bicoastal coalition that remains formidable. Republicans have much to celebrate, as well. Bush halted and reversed the Republican presidential free-fall, demonstrating that the cross-country coalition that elected Clinton could be attacked and partially dismantled, at least in the middle of the country. A long-term "New Democratic" majority proved to be a chimera. While conservative proposals for substantial tax cuts and Social Security reform did not receive a "clear mandate"—it is indeed rare that any policy proposals can truthfully be said to have received a mandate in a presidential election—Bush seemed to have made much headway in his arguments for his positions. He touched the "electric third rail" of American politics, Social Security, and lived to tell about it.

Notes

1. Of course, if pressed, proponents of this position would concede that campaigns could matter—if, for example, one candidate ran a truly dreadful race. What these scholars are actually saying, then, is that when both candidates are competent and their mistakes tend to cancel each other out, the net effect of the campaigns is small. Some like to say that these are the *only* elections in which the campaign really matters. But this position seems to us to understate the importance of campaigns, for the simple reason that there are a number of races that fail to become close, not because of the situation but because of the campaigns.

2. There are also very few panel studies of voters that would allow analysts to observe the reactions of the same voters. This method is necessary for an in-depth study of the swayable vote.

3. Measuring this segment precisely is very difficult, as mentioned before, because some voters do not consider themselves swayable until they sway. Postelection surveys here are probably of only limited reliability. It is very interesting to note that voters in 2000 report making up their mind about when to vote at *exactly* the same time as voters in 1996: 11 percent in the last three days, 6 percent in the last week, 13 percent in the last month, and 69 percent before that. The year 2000 therefore may not have had more swayable voters than usual, but had swayable voters who made more of a difference (VNS surveys).

4. Charles Cook, "Buyer's Remorse, Fate, and Close Calls," *National Journal*, October 28, 2000.

5. Barry Goldwater, whose father was Jewish, was raised as a Christian.

6. For example, Thomas Eagleton (1972), Geraldine Ferraro (1984), and Dan Quayle (1988 and 1992) each seemed to hurt their presidential running mates. It is harder to find examples of vice presidential nominees who dramatically helped the ticket, though George H. W. Bush (1980) and Al Gore (1992) were widely acknowledged to be strong choices.

7. Charlie Cook, "Ignore All the Chatter about the No. 2 Spot," *National Journal*, July 1, 2000, 2182; Thomas M. DeFrank, "On Picking No. 2: Don't Make Waves," *Daily News*, July 16, 2000, 24; R. W. Apple Jr., "Decisions on Running Mates Rarely Prove Decisive," *New York Times*, August 9, 2000, A17. Geographical balancing in particular has been discredited as an effective strategy. See Robert L. Dudley and Ronald B. Rapoport, "Vice-Presidential Candidates and the Home State Advantage: Playing Second Banana at Home and on the Road," *American Journal of Political Science* 33 (1989): 537–40. They report that vice presidential candidates bring only about a 0.3 percent advantage in their home state.

8. Frank Bruni with Eric Schmitt, "Looking for Just the Right Fit, Bush Finds It in Dad's Cabinet," *New York Times*, July 25, 2000, A1; Richard L. Berke, "A Bold Move to Set Image: Vice President's Pick Has Air of Integrity," *New York Times*, August 8, 2000, A1; Laurence McQuillan, "Gore Turns to Lieberman," *USA Today*, July 8, 2000, A1; Edwin Chen and Mark Z. Barabak, "Gore Chooses Sen. Lieberman as Running Mate," *Los Angeles Times*, August 8, 2000, A1; David Barstow with Katharine Q. Steelye, "In Selecting a No. 2, No Detail Too Small," *New York Times*, August 9, 2000, A1.

9. William Schneider, "Cheney, Lieberman Have Specific Goals for Debate," October 5, 2000. All Politics Website.

10. Hawthorne wrote a biography for Franklin Pierce; Bancroft wrote one for Martin Van Buren for an intended race after Van Buren had served a term as president.

11. Secondary coverage in the press and television news, as well as face-to-face encounters between people who watched the convention and those who have not, probably serve to transmit the message.

12. David Gergen, "The Making of a President," *U.S. News & World Report*, August 14, 2000, 60.

13. D. W. Miller, "Election Results Leave Political Scientists Defensive over Forecasts," *Chronicle of Higher Education*, November 17, 2000, A24. The quotation is from Professor Helmut Norpoth at Stony Brook University. There is another important point. For those who have actually studied the 1988 campaign, it is not so clear how much the "advice" of the models actually accounts for that result either. It is arguable that George Bush in that campaign made the liberalism of Michael Dukakis as much centerpiece as the record of the Reagan administration.

14. For an account of the working press in the 2000 campaign, see Dana Milbank, *Smashmouth: Two Years in the Gutter with Al Gore and George W. Bush* (New York: Basic Books, 2001).

15. Frank Bruni, "Giving Praise to Clinton, Bush says Gore is Flawed," *New York Times*, September 29, 2000, A20. "This Week," *National Review*, October 9, 2000, p. 8.

16. Charles Cook. "Buyer's Remorse."

17. "This Week," *National Review*, October 23, 2000, p. 10.

18. According to Gore, "I accompanied James Lee Witt down to Texas when those fires broke out." As it turned out, Witt made two inspection trips, but Gore did not accompany him either time. Similarly, Gore cited a girl who "has to stand during class" when science is taught at her amazingly overcrowded school in Sarasota, Florida. But this was not quite right, either. The girl had to stand for one day, as new science equipment was being unloaded.

19. Of course, many harbored strong suspicions that the timing of Bush's setback was not a matter of chance and that Gore's campaign made some of its own good luck here. Journalist Robert Novak reported in a postelection column that the politically connected Democratic judge in Maine who furnished the arrest record to the media through intermediary Tom Connolly had acquired possession of it at least four months before election day. Robert Novak, "How to Work a November Surprise," *Washington Times National Weekly Edition*, November 13–19, 2000, 34.

20. See http://www.gallup.com/poll/releases/pr001105/asp.

21. Richard L. Berke, "G.O.P. Questioning Bush's Campaign," *New York Times*, November 13, 2000, A1.

22. Since Woodrow Wilson's tight reelection victory in 1916, incumbents had either won big, lost big, or lost small (as in 1960, 1968, and 1976). None had won a close race. The underlying logic is that if voters have not embraced the incumbent by late in the campaign, they are looking for an alternative.

23. These statements draw from a poll taken by the Pew Foundation taken from November 10–12. The results are reported and discusses at http://www.peoplepress.org/post00rpt.htm.

24. A county-by-county review of a sample of seven states indicated that there was an overlap ranging from 53 percent to 89 percent in their top half counties. Combining all seven states, they shared two of three top half counties. See Andrew E. Busch, "Outsiderism: Pat Buchanan and Ross Perot in 1992 and 1996," paper presented at the annual meeting of the Midwest Political Science Association, Chicago, Illinois, April 15–17, 1999.

25. Jonathan Salant, "Reform Party Loses Matching Funds," *Associated Press*, November 8, 2000.

26. "Tremble, Langley, Tremble," *The Economist*, July 1, 2000.

27. Ralph Nader on *Larry King Live*, CNN, December 14, 2000.

28. Seymour Martin Lipset, "Still the Exceptional Nation?" *Wilson Quarterly*, Winter 2000.

29. Mike Allen, "Down the Stretch, Gore Gets Specific," *Washington Post*, October 23, 2000.

30. Of the hard core, it has been suggested that about half would have gone to Gore, another 30 percent would not have voted at all, and perhaps some 20 percent would have voted for George Bush.

31. This was a difference of 3 percent or more in a category of some size. Not all categories are listed.

32. The Pew Foundation Postelection Poll. http://www.peoplepress.org/post00rpt.htm.

33. Richard N. Ostling, "American voters polarized by religion, poll indicates," *Denver Rocky Mountain News*, January 26, 2001, 42A. Overall, Bush won 63–36 among those who attend church more than weekly and 57–40 among those who attend

weekly; Gore won by 54–42 among those who attend "seldom" and by 61–32 among those who "never" attend (VNS exit poll).

34. Black turnout in Florida set records—893,000 African Americans cast ballots on November 7, a 65 percent jump over 1996, and, according to exit polls, Gore won an unprecedented 94 percent of the black vote in that state.

35. There is a clear limit to this analysis though, as the black economic condition improved significantly in the second Reagan administration without any similar benefits accruing to the president or his party.

36. A survey by political scientist Michael Dawson of the University of Chicago had 25 percent of African Americans with an unfavorable rating, 42 percent with a highly unfavorable opinion of Bush. *Cleveland Plain Dealer*, November 30, 2000.

37. The NAACP became more active, politically, Then there were the tough ads, relating to the dragging death of James Byrd in Texas, in which Byrd's daughter intoned that "When George W. Bush refused to support hate-crime legislation, it was like my father was killed all over again." The ferocity of this campaign, not easily explained any other way (Bush, after all, supported the death penalty for the perpetrators of the crime), might have been payback for the 1988 campaign of Bush's father when many blacks complained that Bush *père* used the race card by focusing on Willie Horton's furlough.

Chapter Six

The Postelection Campaign:
Bush v. Gore

Americans awoke on November 8 to discover that a new campaign was just getting under way, one that would last five weeks and have as many ups and downs as the original campaign itself. There were two major questions at that moment that no one could answer: who would win, and who would decide who would win. We now know the answer to the first question, but answering the second is not so easy. A longer version, detailing all of the actors and influences along the way, will no doubt be a subject of inquiry for years to come. The short version, thankfully, is much clearer. The last major act in the chain of events that brought George Bush to the presidency was a decision by the United States Supreme Court, fatefully titled *Bush v. Gore*.

The 2000 election is not the only election in American history to have entered a disputed phase after the normal moment of decision. At least three others qualify in this respect: 1800, 1824, and 1876. All were close in the electoral vote, although 1800 is a special case. It was only because of a quirk of the then existing electoral system, in which each elector had two votes for the presidency, that the intended presidential candidate (Thomas Jefferson) tied the intended vice presidential candidate (Aaron Burr). The elections of 1824 and 1876 are more pertinent to the election of 2000. The victorious candidate in all three instances was the one who finished second in the popular vote—John Quincy Adams to Andrew Jackson, Rutherford B. Hayes to Samuel Tilden, and George W. Bush to Al Gore. And in each case, an effort was made by certain supporters of the defeated candidate to cast doubt on the legitimacy of the elected president, either as a prelude to running the next campaign or to undermine the president's grip on the office. There was, however, one important difference among these elections. In 1824 and 1876, the final decisions were reached through a political process: in 1824 by a vote by the House of Representatives acting under the provisions of the runoff system in the Constitution (the Twelfth Amendment), and in 1876 by a determination by Congress (House and Senate) acting under its constitutional authority to count the electoral votes (Article 2). In 2000, the final decisions were made in fact, if not name, by courts of law.

Postelection campaigns must be looked at from two different perspectives. One treats them in the usual tactical-political way as the continuation of a campaign by other means—part public relations, part legal, and part psychological. The analysis focuses on the strategies pursued by the candidates to achieve their objectives, the chief (but not the only) one of which is to win the presidency. The other perspective looks at the event from a "constitutional" viewpoint and considers the systemic issue of resolving the problem of presidential selection. No one needs to be told that the selection of a chief executive is a most delicate matter that, if not handled correctly, can precipitate a crisis that threatens the entire political system. "The system of election applied to the head of the executive power of a great people," Tocqueville wrote, "presents dangers which experience and historians have sufficiently indicated."[1] From the time of the Founding, legislators have sought to put in place an institutional arrangement that would guarantee that a decision about who is elected president is actually made (a matter that we now realize is not as easy as it seems) and ensure, so far as possible, that the decision will be considered as legitimate. This constitutional perspective is higher in rank than the tactical or partisan one, as it concerns a fundamental matter of the public good. Something of the spirit of this ranking was expressed by Senator Robert Torricelli, a Democrat from New Jersey: "I want Al Gore to win the election, but more than that, I want somebody to win this election."[2]

For each of these two perspectives, there is a different standard for judging the actors and participants. In the first case it is, with a nod to Chris Matthews, the "hardball" criterion of how well the candidates and their staffs have advanced their political objective. Did the Gore (or the Bush) organization take the right steps and make the best decisions to bring victory? In the second case, the standard is a more complex measure of virtue and statesmanship—of whether actors tried to serve the larger interests of the nation and whether they actually exercised good judgment or prudence in doing so. Some might take issue with applying this standard to courts by claiming that the highest obligation of a court is to apply the specific parts of the law as it is written or understood. Perhaps. But when courts enter into a constitutional arena as a major actor, we would contend that whatever their own understanding of their function may be, they are still properly judged by this constitutional standard of statesmanship. It would be no real praise of a court to say that it vindicated a secondary principle of law if in doing so it jeopardized the well-being of the nation.

Candidate Strategies and Alternate Centers of Decision-Making Power

The study of the 2000 postelection campaign presents enormous difficulties. While recounting the sequence of events of this period is important, it can have the inadvertent effect of concealing as much as it reveals by focusing attention on what actually happened rather than on what could have happened. But to properly understand this period, it must be seen in light of the situation as it was faced by the actors, who could have no certain idea of what path the process would take. The best way to handle this difficulty is by a circuitous plan of first briefly describing the elements of the strategic situation, then proceeding to recap the events, and finally returning, with the events of what happened in mind, to a closer study of some of the strategic elements.

The strategic situation is best seen in terms of the candidates pursuing their objectives in an environment that consists of a certain set of power centers that might be able to affect the outcome. A word needs to be said about the objectives. The primary objective of both candidates was to win the presidency. But this objective might have been constrained by other considerations. One was a future political career. How much were these candidates willing to risk this time—how far were they willing to push things on their own behalf—if it might adversely affect a subsequent chance to become president? There is reason to think that the calculations of the two men were different. Certainly their situations were. George Bush was governor of Texas, and if he had decided at some point in this contest to limit his combat he would have remained in that position. Even with a loss, a strong case could have been made that Bush had run a good campaign under difficult circumstances. In short, 2000 was far from being his last hurrah. By contrast Al Gore had no official political position if he lost this race. It was clear, too, that many in his party expected him to win and would hold him accountable for "blowing" the election. Finally, in what is damaging to any political career in America, Gore had suffered the embarrassment of losing his own home state and congressional district. Though many Democrats at the time publicly proclaimed Gore the presumptive front-runner in 2004, in fact his future status in politics as a presidential candidate was very much up in the air. And on a psychological level, Gore was a person who seemed to need the presidency to complete himself personally more than did George Bush. In a moment of candor, Gore himself acknowledged this difference: "I'm not like George Bush. If he wins or loses, life goes on. I'll do anything to win."[3]

There were two other constraining objectives. Most immediately, both men wished not only to win the presidency but to be the president, having a sufficient reservoir of support and legitimacy to have a chance to succeed. A delicate problem in this whole process was that the pursuit of the office in certain ways at this period could undermine any prospect of being ultimately accepted by partisans of the other side. As the candidate trying to catch up and change the results, Gore had to take more risks in this regard, and he did. Gore "burned fuel" during the postelection campaign and became less generally acceptable, while George Bush, at least by comparison, was more acceptable. At the same time, Bush perhaps was obliged to pursue a less aggressive strategy because a good part of his appeal for becoming president had been based on his claim that he was a uniter, not a divider, and one who could work with Democrats. Furthermore, though a more distant prospect, both candidates had to be cognizant of the ultimate judgment of history. If they were not, many of their copartisans were. For these reasons, the candidates' objectives cannot literally be described as "to win at almost any cost," although circumstances and temperament might have made this description closer to the truth in Gore's case than in Bush's.

As the candidates surveyed the political environment, they saw eight major power centers that might act to determine the outcome of the campaign.[4] These were:

1. The national political climate (public opinion and the opinion and views of important elites, such as senators and major newspaper editors)
2. Administrative officials in the executive branch of the state government of Florida (the secretary of state, the state election commission, and the attorney general)
3. The county election commissions and commissioners of the different counties of Florida
4. The Florida judicial system (all levels, but culminating in the Florida Supreme Court)
5. The federal judiciary (all levels, but culminating in the U.S. Supreme Court)
6. The Florida legislature (able under the Constitution and federal statute to select a slate of electors)

7. The electors (acting independently and voting differently than they were bound)
8. The U.S. Congress (charged with the counting of the electoral votes and having discretion, as defined by federal law, regarding how and what to count)

Both campaigns clearly understood that they would be competing to control the national political climate (#1). Beyond that, the strategies the candidates devised were based on trying to determine the "venue" in which the decision would be made and in developing tactics to defend in whichever venue one was forced to compete. For example, the Gore campaign was relentless in attempting to have the election played out in the Florida judiciary, especially in the Florida Supreme Court (#4), where it thought it had both a good case and a good chance of receiving a favorable ruling. The Gore campaign was mindful as well of the county election commissions where it thought it might have a clear advantage (#3). There was an intense effort to avoid, by legal tactics and by efforts at delegitimization, a decision process that would be made by state officials (#2) and by the Florida legislature (#6). The Gore team also pursued for a time a plan to coax electors to change their votes (#7), which Gore ultimately repudiated in public even as some Democratic operatives continued to search for potential Republican defectors.

As for the Bush campaign, it would have preferred, of course, to have had no recourse to the courts at all, and to have matters resolved by the executive branch in Florida or, as a last resort, by the Florida legislature. Keeping the courts out quickly proved impossible, however, so the Bush team sought, as part of a defensive strategy, to involve the federal judiciary (#5) as a possible check to the Florida judiciary. Gore's campaign never wanted to enter the arena of the federal courts, but having adopted a strategy that relied so heavily on using state courts, it could not question the legitimacy of that venue.

In most instances the two campaigns had an idea, often a quite clear one, of which power center would favor which candidate. But these estimations did not always turn out as expected. Above all, Gore's team was disappointed by the foot-dragging and lack of zeal of two of the county commissions (Miami-Dade and Palm Beach), which did not act with all the partisan enthusiasm that was hoped for. An arena where a clear estimation was most difficult was the federal judiciary. At the outset, not only was involvement by the federal courts thought to be a long shot, but its proclivities were hard to figure. Bush's team might have some hopes for the U.S. Supreme Court, if anything ever got there, but the disposition of the other courts was much less certain. At a minimum, however, the federal courts might be more favorably inclined than anything likely to come from Florida's highest court.

We contemplated for a time constructing a mathematical model for post-election campaigns that political scientists might consult in the future for predicting the outcome of such events. The equation generated would have been based on a calculation for each of these eight centers of power that would estimate (a) the likelihood that it would come into play, (b) its degree of relative influence, and (c) its likely disposition Ultimately, however, we abandoned this effort, not from any lack of mathematical acumen, but on the grounds that a similar event would be unlikely to occur anytime within the next millennium, if ever again. Instead of a formal model, we substituted a more empirical approach. Graduate students at the University of Virginia, expert in the field of American politics, were asked to use this analysis to calculate the probability of a Gore or a Bush victory. The estimate was to be expressed using a 100-point scale, with 50 being the tipping point between the candidates, so as to simulate voter polls. A reading was taken daily, beginning the day after the election, and, in the current fashion, turned into a tracking poll using a three-day rolling average. Consulted with great interest by leading members of the University of Virginia Government Department, it showed an oscillating pattern reminiscent of some of the polls taken during the final election campaign. Despite trailing in the actual vote in Florida, Gore was judged to be in the lead much of the time (see figure 6.1). The main factor that led students to this determination was their estimate relating to the Florida judiciary. They thought from early on that it was highly likely that the Florida judiciary would come into play, that it would be highly influential in what it could do, and that it was very likely to decide in a way that would help Al Gore. Al Gore thought so, too.

The Events

The Gore campaign showed remarkable speed in putting together a post-election strategy. Indeed, before the long election night had concluded, Gore campaign manager Bill Daley declared, "The campaign continues." Within a day, an initial plan was devised and a legal team was deployed, as waves of Democratic lawyers began an assault on every beach in Florida.

It was astonishing, but not really surprising, to witness how quickly the hare-and-tortoise styles of the two campaigns reasserted themselves in the postelection period. Gore's organization was first out of the blocks and, notwithstanding Warren Christopher as the nominal head of the legal team, flashier and more aggressive. The legal contingent would keep adding talent, so that a week later it was routinely being called the Dream Team, taking over that appellation from the stunning array of legal talent that had assisted in the defense of O. J. Simpson. It would be headed by Superlawyer David Boies (who increasingly took on the duties of spokesman) and included as its constitutional expert Professor Lawrence Tribe of Harvard University Law School. Backing up the Dream Team was a corps of freelance Democratic lawyers, among them the ubiquitous Alan Dershowitz, who were prepared to assist citizens acting in parallel but in a private capacity. The Republican team, headed by former Secretary of State James Baker, was slower in forming, and was routinely said in the press to lack the same punch as the Democrats. Yet by the end, when the last brief had been filed and the last argument made, it was by no means clear that the Democrats owned the advantage.[5] Once again the tortoise had caught up to the hare.

The first element in the Gore strategy was to press the point that Al Gore had won the popular vote. Gore mentioned this point in all of his initial comments, as did President Clinton. The argument was not (at least explicitly) that Gore's majority gave him a claim to the presidency as over and against the result of the electoral vote. Rather, the popular vote majority was used to provide a kind of political and moral high ground that would entitle Gore to pursue with vigor other elements of a legal strategy. Others jumped in to give additional weight to his approach. An ad taken out in the *New York Times*, organized by Professor Sean Wilentz of Princeton and signed by some of the leading constitutional scholars in the nation, featured the following statement: "There is good reason to believe that Vice-President Gore has been elected President by a clear constitutional majority of the popular vote and the Electoral College."[6] This argument never packed quite the positive punch that many in Gore's camp hoped it would, as Americans seemed to accept with remarkable equanimity the prospect of a "minority" president. (Additionally, a number of Democrats had recently been defending the legitimacy of just such a result, expecting that Gore might win the electoral vote while losing the popular vote.) Still, the importance of Gore's popular vote victory should not be underestimated, at least in a negative sense. If Bush had won the national vote, one can be certain that this fact would have been cited in an effort to force Gore to concede, quite possibly with a powerful effect.

The next element in the strategy was to question whether Bush had "really" won Florida as a prelude to some kind of legal challenge in the courts to the final vote count. This strategy initially centered on certain

Figure 6.1. Virginia Graduate Students' Postelection Victory Estimate November 2000–January 2001

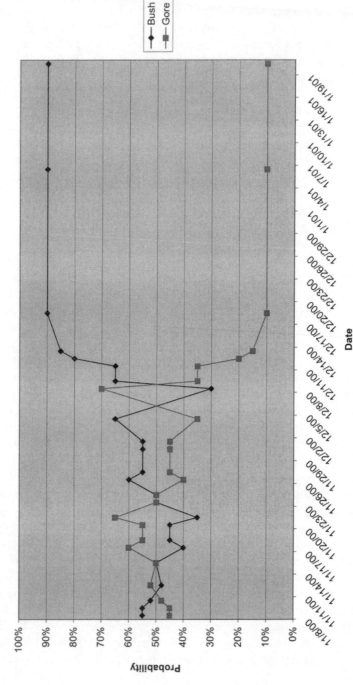

*Note: Bush's probability of victory is never at 100 percent due to one student's refusal to accept the reality of his win.

Figure 6.1. Key Events on the Graph

- Nov. 8th: The morning after: Bush leads by 926 votes; automatic machine recount begins.
- Nov. 9th: Gore requests hand counts in Broward, Miami-Dade, Palm Beach, and Volusia counties.
- Nov. 10th: The machine recount is completed: Bush's lead slips to 327 votes.
- Nov. 12th: Palm Beach and Volusia counties begin their hand recount.
- Nov. 15th: Katherine Harris collects the final votes from all Florida counties.
- Nov. 17th: The Florida Supreme Court issues an injunction, blocking certification of a final vote tally.
- Nov. 18th: Overseas absentee ballots are counted; Bush's lead is back up to 930 votes.
- Nov. 20th: The Florida Supreme Court holds its hearing on Gore's motion to include late hand-recount totals in the official vote certification.
- Nov. 21st: The Florida Supreme Court hands down ruling, extending the certification deadline five days.
- Nov. 24th: The U.S. Supreme Court announces it will hear Bush's appeal of the Florida Supreme Court decision.
- Nov. 25th: The "Brooks Brothers Revolution" erupts, and Miami-Dade County stops its hand recount.
- Nov. 26th: Katherine Harris certifies the vote, giving Bush a 537-vote victory.
- Nov. 27th: Gore contests the certification.
- Nov. 30th: The Florida legislature announces a special session to debate naming Florida's electors themselves.
- Dec. 1st: The U.S. Supreme Court hears oral arguments on the Florida Supreme Court recount deadline extension decision.
- Dec. 4th: Judge N. Sanders Sauls rejects Gore's contestation of the certified results, and the U.S. Supreme Court vacates and remands the Florida Supreme Court's certification deadline extension decision.
- Dec. 8th: The Florida Supreme Court orders manual recounts of all counties with significant numbers of undervotes.
- Dec. 9th: The U.S. Supreme Court halts the manual recounts and schedules oral arguments on Bush's appeal of the Florida Supreme Court order.
- Dec. 11th: The U.S. Supreme Court holds oral arguments in *Bush v. Gore*.
- Dec. 12th: The U.S. Supreme Court rules for Bush, effectively ending the hand recounts.
- Dec. 13th: Gore concedes defeat, and Bush accepts victory.
- Dec. 18th: Individual state electors make official Bush's 271-to-266-vote victory in the Electoral College.
- Jan. 6th: A joint session of Congress opens and agrees to the electoral votes submitted by the states.
- Jan. 20th: Bush is sworn in as the president of the United States.

irregularities on a ballot used in Palm Beach County, which was laid out as a "butterfly" with the names of the candidates listed in two columns with the punch holes in the center. The ballot allegedly created confusion, leading some voters to punch Patrick Buchanan rather than Al Gore or, in their anxiety not to make a mistake, to double punch. Not only was it said that the ballot was confusing, but it was claimed that it was illegal under Florida state law, which required columns.[7] A campaign was launched to build a popular cause with a compelling emotional component. Congressman Robert Wexler, a leading spokesman for the Democrats on this issue, described the Palm Beach situation as follows: "I saw the people who came out of the polling places. They were crying. They were in tears. In hysterics."[8] Gore campaign chairman Bill Daley claimed that Florida courts may find "an injustice unparalleled in our history."[9]

At this point Gore was 1,784 votes behind in the ballot count from election eve, and it was widely known that a recount of the ballots will only very rarely change such a result. The plan at this point was to suggest that something was wrong with the election itself and that the official ballots thwarted the will of the people. Without quite asserting a deliberate fraud, the argument was that a fraud had been perpetrated on the people of Florida and the people of the United States. The premise was that while the formal or official total of the vote may have been (narrowly) in George Bush's favor, there were obstacles that prevented the formal count from expressing the real intentions of those who voted. The core of the message was: In your heart you know he's won. Whether this campaign to soften public opinion was part of an actual legal strategy had not been decided at this point. Some remedy, it was suggested, would have to be found to right this wrong, and Gore supporters floated the possibility of a revote in Palm Beach County or a reassigning of the votes by the courts on the basis of some statistical standard.

The butterfly ballot strategy quickly ran into difficulty, though, when it was reported in short order that the ballot design had been approved by a Democratic election supervisor and that a similar ballot design had been used for many years in Bill Daley's native Chicago. But the biggest problem with this strategy was its appeal beyond the actual vote to the intent of the voter. Although raising this issue served temporarily to mobilize Democrats nationally and to keep the campaign going, many Democratic elites felt uncomfortable with this kind of argument, and Gore soon found himself under some pressure to make the formal recount the test, without going beyond it. The plan of pursuing the butterfly ballot issue as the heart of the Gore legal strategy was slowly being abandoned, and Gore later magnanimously offered in a speech to take this issue off the table (when in fact it had already vanished). Brought by private parties, this suit was ultimately dismissed in Florida's courts. [10]

From butterflies to hand counts (November 9)

A far more promising strategy was then pursued of using the existing law in Florida that allowed for a request for a hand count of votes within the first 72 hours after the election. The Gore team initiated such a request in four selected counties that had voted highly Democratic and that were controlled by Democratic election commissions (Volusia, Broward, Miami-Dade, and Palm Beach). The hand-count strategy proved to be a decisive step and became the centerpiece of the Gore political and legal strategy. It was seen by almost all Democrats and most Americans as being entirely "within" the normal recount process. (Many other states had provisions for hand counts, including Texas, in a law that had been signed by Governor Bush in 1998.) In addition, the argument had the advantages of being simple, democratic, and human. It proposed to count more ballots rather than less, and to rely on human beings rather than machines to make the ultimate decisions. The strategy was therefore sustainable and ensured that the national political climate would not force Gore to concede. Erosion of his political support now stopped.

Above all, of course, the hand-count strategy was attractive to Gore's side because it looked like it could do the job—that is, harvest the votes needed to win. And, after the statewide machine automatic vote recount of November 10, the votes needed to win had shrunk dramatically. Bush's lead fell to just 327 votes.[11] The incredible narrowness of this margin and the fact that totals could shift after a recount were psychological shocks that made Bush's claim to victory look more tenuous. Of course, on Bush's side, it was said that once again Bush had won a real count of the votes in Florida and that this fact was the only material one to be considered. The Bush argument, chanted from Austin to Tallahassee, was: We've counted and recounted the votes, and George Bush has come out ahead. Every election has a winner and a loser, and—no matter how narrow the margin—the winner was George Bush (subject only to the addition of the count of the overseas ballots 10 days hence). Supporters of Al Gore chose to read the 327-vote margin in a different light. If a lead at this level was little more than an arbitrary fiction—and common sense suggests that it was—then why not write the story to make Al Gore the winner, especially when he had the support of more of the people who showed up on election day in Florida? In this way of thinking, it might be defensible to coax the ballots to reveal what was known to be the "real" result.

The shrinking of Bush's total in the statewide recount represents one of many episodes that have yet to be fully explored. Part of the change was accounted for by specific recognition of human error, such as ballots not counted in the first round. But the part of the change that was attributed to the sheer mechanical recount—running the ballots through the counting machines—was still large and defied the normal error margin of mechanical recounts. As with everything else in this phase, supporters of the two candidates drew different conclusions. For Gore adherents this experience proved that a key argument of the Bush side—that one can rely on machines—was false. If the machine vote could change by that much—for example by 682 votes in Palm Beach County—then it surely followed that one should proceed to count the ballots by hand to make sure of the results. For Bush supporters, there was another conclusion: that the machine count of Palm Beach was not the work of machines alone.[12]

Faced with the prospect of a hand count of the ballots in these four counties, the Bush team had now to decide on its own strategy. Some Republicans urged that Bush should respond in kind, requesting recounts in counties where Bush had received large majorities. But such a strategy would have effectively conceded that the two counts of the ballots that had taken place (and which Bush had won) were now no longer the real counts. It would have thrown away the one certain advantage Bush had, which is that he had won, and opened matters to an uncertain outcome. In addition, more of the undercounted ballots in the state were found in Democratic counties being counted by majority Democratic canvassing boards. The Bush team accordingly decided to hunker down and defend by all means possible the vote as it had been counted. It was to be a purely defensive strategy, fighting off attacks from any and all sides. In the realm of public relations, it meant a defense of machine counting over what Secretary Baker referred to delicately as the potential "mischief" involved in human vote counting, especially where there were no set standards of what was to be counted. (One of the incidental benefits of the postelection campaign was the resuscitation of this quaint word in its older sense, which had fallen into disuse.) Admitting its reluctance at involving the courts in this process, the Bush campaign nevertheless took the matter into the federal courts, asking for an injunction to stop the hand counts on equal protection grounds that there were no standards for conducting recounts and that it constituted an unlawful depreciation of the votes in some counties if only votes in selected counties were counted.

Gore's decision to call for hand recounts brought the nation over a threshold, although without really ever having appeared to do so. This was at once the beauty and the danger of this move. Up to this point, with the use of a machine recount and a subsequent counting of the absentee bal-lots, the victor could be known objectively to both sides. While consoling themselves with the thought that Al Gore was the real winner, Democrats could have recognized that going beyond objective standards was impos-sible and that substance (Gore's "real" victory) must occasionally have to bow to form (what the ballots said). The hand recount meant that substance and form would now forever be confused. The recount was within the boundaries of form (it was in the law), but from this point on, neither side could now accept the legitimacy of the count. If Al Gore became president, Republicans would say that the election was stolen, as the determination of ballots by hand—by Democratic hands at that—would mean that the election was fraudulent. If George Bush were to become president, Dem-ocrats would say that it was against not only the real will of the voters (their original position), but also against the form of the law, which, if all ballots were counted, would show more votes for Al Gore.

After the request for the hand recounts was made, the hard questions of detail and implementation remained to be resolved. Would the counties in fact agree to recount the ballots by hand, what standard would they use to count the ballots, and what deadline would apply for turning in a revised count? On the first question, two of the counties temporarily declined, but then finally agreed—no doubt after having been pressed very hard by the Gore team—to undertake the process. On the question of what standard would be used, Florida state law, unlike the law of some other states, had no statutory provisions. Apart from going through the ballots that the ma-chines had counted, there was the question of the ballots that the machine had not counted. Some of these had more than one punch (an overvote), while others did not register a vote for the presidency (an undervote). While many initially believed such details to be of little importance—the thinking being that under any hand count Gore would easily win—it turned out that matters were not that simple. Under a stricter standard, counting ballots only where the chad was hanging out, it was questionable whether Gore would pick up enough of the votes; under a looser standard, counting ballots without the chad fully punched out (so-called "dimpled" or "pregnant" chads), it was far more likely that Gore might prevail. The counties on their own discretion could decide the standards, which they might change.[13]

Keep those deadlines (November 15)

The question of the deadline for turning in the ballots was more crucial still. The secretary of state, Katherine Harris, made it known that the figures were to be submitted by 5 P.M., November 14, as called for by Florida statute. She also said that she had no intention of accepting hand recount totals, as in her opinion these should only have been undertaken in the event of evidence of a showing of a failure in the performance of the machines in the machine recount. The more important point, however, was the deadline itself.

Harris's signal that she was going to insist on the deadline brought a ferocious attack from the Gore campaign. Of the four counties involved, only one, Volusia, had been able to complete its recount by the deadline. Miami-Dade had not even begun, while Palm Beach and Broward were somewhere in midstream. The Gore team immediately challenged Harris's decision, arguing both in court and in public that the decision was arbitrary. In public the Gore attack machine savaged Harris as a party hack who wore too much makeup. Before a Florida circuit court, it was argued that there was an obvious conflict between two parts of the law, one which set the deadline and the other which allowed for a hand recount. As the latter could not possibly be completed in larger counties within the period allowed by the statute, the secretary was obliged to use her discretion to extend the deadline. The circuit court issued a Delphic decision requiring that the secretary exercise her discretion nonarbitrarily, but leaving the judgment about the deadline in her hands. Harris essentially held to the deadline and let it be known that with those figures, plus the additional votes from the overseas ballots to be counted on November 18, she was prepared to certify a final vote for the state on Saturday.

It is impossible to say how much a formal certification at this point would have meant. As there was a growing desire in the country to have the election resolved, it might have offered a clean cutoff point to achieve finality. Certainly the Bush people had attached great importance to the event. They planned a statement by the governor in Austin and a celebration. An open display of victory, they imagined, would bring finality. There were reports, perhaps fictitious, that some in the Democratic Party were also looking for a way to pull the plug on Al Gore, and certification would be the occasion.

Thou shalt not certify (November 17)

On Friday, less than a day before final certification was to take place, the Supreme Court of Florida, acting on its own initiative, took an extraordinary step. It issued an injunction ordering the secretary of state not to proceed with certification on Saturday, and it specifically allowed the hand counting of ballots in Palm Beach and Broward to continue. The court ordered a hearing of the full case for Monday. Florida's Supreme Court had thus stepped in and, temporarily at least, preempted the activity of Florida's executive branch. That a court could feel confident enough to take such a step, knowing that its orders would be followed, speaks volumes about the power of courts in America today. There was a time, only very recently, when such action by a state court would have been highly unlikely. Up to this point, the courts had been involved in the process, but only at the periphery in a careful and modest role of policing parts of the political process. With the Florida Supreme Court's injunction, the judiciary now forced itself front and center into the election. The court's involvement did not mean that other political bodies could not act, but it was clear from now on that courts were in one way or another going to be key decision makers in this election.

Counting the overseas ballots (November 18)

The counting of the overseas ballots, which occurred on November 18, was under law the last event before final certification. The balloting went nearly two to one for George Bush (1,380 to 750), although the number of ballots was not as large as many expected. But their significance—or so the Bush people had hoped—might count in the court of public opinion as much as their numbers. Following the initial shock of realizing that the differences in this election were in tens and hundreds, rather than thousands, everyone now began to get used to thinking in these smaller units. A pickup of over 600 votes almost tripled Bush's lead, now said to be 930, which in this context was huge. Furthermore, as many of these ballots came from military personnel overseas, their "moral" weight might be thought to count more than their numbers. If one were looking for something to serve as an authoritative tiebreaker in a close election, it would be these ballots.

It will not be a surprise to learn that yet another controversy, tinged with passion and bitterness, now erupted over the overseas ballot. In the counting of these ballots, some 1,420 (or more than 40 percent) had been thrown out, many of them coming from people in the military. These disqualifications came with the "help" of lawyers from the Democratic Party—supposedly not directly connected to the Gore campaign—who had been instructed to insist on the strictest of standards and to ensure that all requirements were met. The exclusion of so many military ballots, some allegedly on the smallest of technicalities, created a huge furor, fueled by the Republicans. Speaking for the Bush campaign, Governor Marc Racicot turned up the heat: "The vice president's lawyers have gone to war, in my judgment, against the men and women who serve in our armed forces. The man who would be their commander in chief is fighting to take away the votes from the people he would command."[14] Both sides could find a bit of a contradiction in the views of the others. Republicans, who had been arguing strict legal procedures, now referred to intent. Democrats, who had been arguing intent, now were arguing strict legalism.

This controversy worked in the realm of public opinion to Gore's disadvantage, and several Democrats insisted that every effort should be made to count these ballots. Joe Lieberman was called in to try to soften the effect. But it was no longer clear how much the public relations battle counted in deciding the election. It might now actually be the votes, each and every vote, that mattered. Gore's team surely had succeeded in excluding a certain number of Bush votes. The controversy had another effect; it hardened feelings against Bush among some of the Democratic elite, who winced at old Republican accusations of Democrats' lack of support for the military. Finally, there was a certain racial and ethnic undertone to this controversy as well, an undertone that was being kept just under control all throughout the state of Florida. Why, some asked, was the vote of a soldier worth more than that of an inner-city voter? Why so much concern in one case and not the other? Each side could ask the same questions of the other.

The Florida Supreme Court's first decision: A judicial coup? (November 21)

On Monday, November 20, the full case was argued before the seven-member Florida Supreme Court, which allows for televised hearings. The impressive setting of the court's chambers, together with the fact that the judges posed solid and probing question to lawyers on both teams, left a highly favorable initial impression about the court with both commentators and the American public. In a process that was now looking ever more chaotic and out of control, even more dangerous, many seemed anxious to have somebody step in, with the aura of an impartial umpire, and impose some kind of order, providing a roadmap to a final resolution. The court, which had denied that finality by its injunction on Friday, was now being asked to provide it itself.

Gore's lawyers argued that the court should allow the hand count to continue, a process they said might take another week or so. The court could in effect assume control over the whole election process and, according to David Boies, use its "broad equitable power" to handle the situation and "reconcile the entire statutory scheme." It could set up a new schedule and direct how matters should proceed, creating new deadlines and setting new standards. The Bush team insisted that such a takeover would replace the executive branch with the judicial branch and, in Barry Richard's words, "would have to disregard the most fundamental principles of separation of powers and step into the shoes of both the legislative and executive branches to rewrite these statutes." Richard argued that a ruling in favor of Gore's position would mean that it would "read a statute that says that returns *must* be filed by a date and time certain as though it said *may* be filed, to read a statute that says the secretary of state *may* accept later filed returns as though it says *must* accept late filed returns."[15]

Acting with unusual speed, the Florida Supreme Court issued its ruling the next day, Tuesday, November 21. The decision, made by a unanimous court, was a complete victory for Gore's side. The court set a new deadline for certification of the election on Sunday, November 26, at 5 P.M. (or Monday morning if the secretary of state's office was not open on Sunday). It directed that the hand counts would continue and be included in the final totals. The core of the decision and of the court's animating impulse was summed up as follows: "Twenty-five years ago, this court commented that the will of the people, not a hypertechnical reliance upon statutory provisions, should be our guiding principle in election cases. . . . Our goal today remains the same as it was a quarter of century ago, i.e., to reach a result that reflects the will of the voters, whatever that might be."

Two other notable points stand out about the decision. One was the severe language it directed at the secretary of state, which seemed to go out of its way to criticize her handling of the matter: "To allow the secretary to summarily disenfranchise innocent electors in an effort to punish dilatory board members, as she proposes, misses the constitutional mark. . . . The Constitution eschews punishment by proxy." The other was the clear effort to set up a process that would achieve finality. Courts do not directly administer, but this decision was written so as to make everything work in a certain way that was virtually self-executing.[16] Having spanked Harris, the court was not about to give her the discretion to throw a tantrum.

This decision turned the tide and opened a direct route to a Gore victory. It was the first real moment since the networks had called Florida for Gore early on election eve that Gore and his supporters saw him as the near-certain president-elect. The vice president himself spoke shortly after the decision, in a tone that indicated he was preparing his own claim to the presidency. "I don't know whether Governor Bush or I will prevail, but we do know that our democracy is the winner tonight." Now that things were looking his way, he tried to suggest an end to contestation outside of the Florida court's decision. And he also allowed that it was permissible to begin planning a transition—he would do so—and he invited Governor Bush to join him in a meeting. Shortly after Gore's speech David Boies, now being openly lionized by television commentators as the greatest legal mind of the century (they probably meant the twentieth century), appeared at a press conference. It was the closest thing to a victory dance one could imagine. When asked about the political meaning of the decision, he at first abjured, saying that he was not concerned about the politics of this matter, but the law. But then even this great lawyer betrayed satisfaction, if not triumphalism, when he later let slip, "We have the votes."

Bush's side made no effort to sugarcoat and pretend that the decision said something it never said. The decision from their point of view was beyond spin. It had to be directly attacked. Secretary Baker did not use the words "judicial coup," but the implication was clear nonetheless. The Florida Supreme Court had "pretty well rewritten the Florida electoral code" and "invented a new system for counting the election results." The decision was "unfair and unacceptable." Baker indirectly invited the Florida legislature to enter the picture: "One should not now be surprised if the Florida legislature seeks to affirm the original rules." And the next day Bush's lawyers announced their intention to appeal the decision to the U.S. Supreme Court.

The Florida Supreme Court decision had the effect of launching a fundamental debate on one of the central questions of American politics: is the final word in our political system to be spoken by the judicial or the political branches? To listen to this debate was to have opened a textbook on American government and read excerpts from the classic statements of the role and power of the courts versus the political branches. These arguments were conducted in this instance in the context of state rather than national politics, but the principle was the same. Columnists on one side attacked the notion of judicial finality, especially by a court known to be so activist. As George Will wrote, "By legislating—by airily rewriting Florida's election law and applying it retroactively to this election—the court has thrown down a gauntlet to the state's legislature. . . . It says it acted out of respect for 'the will of the people.' But not the people's will as expressed by the people's elected representatives in the legislature that wrote the election laws. And not the people's will as expressed in the election of the secretary of state to enforce the laws."[17]

Those on the other side spoke in solemn terms of upholding the rule of law (as determined finally by courts) and depicted political action beyond the courts (to the legislature) as a challenge to our very constitutional fabric. The high priest of the Democratic position on this issue was, as ever, the *New York Times* editorial page. By "hinting that the Florida legislature should somehow neutralize the [Florida] Supreme Court's decisions, the Bush campaign risks undermining the rule of law and the office he hopes to occupy."[18] Professor Pamela Karlan of Stanford Law School went further. "To say 'let's go to the Legislature now' is changing the rules a lot more than anything the Florida Supreme Court did," said Karlan. "To cast aspersions on the court reminds me of the 'massive resistance' Southerners engaged in during the 1950s and 1960s in response to civil rights decisions." She added, "We have heard this before, and it wasn't pretty the last time."[19] Karlan's reference to the civil rights struggle was more apt than it seemed, for there is no question that the moral authority that courts in general enjoy in modern America, especially for the left, derives from the role played by federal courts in that period. It was then that the notion of courts as the ultimate arbiter (or "trumper," as they say at the Harvard Law School) began. The Florida Supreme Court, counted now as one of the progressive state courts, was being cast in the sacred model of the Warren Court at the time of the decision of *Brown v. Board of Education*.

The tide turns: "The Brooks Brothers Revolution" (November 25)

Just when it seemed that all was headed in the direction of a Gore victory, everything suddenly turned. Perhaps it was just the sheer role of contingency in human affairs. Or perhaps it was the revenge of administration, of the world of the mundane or routine, against high principle. But however one wishes to explain it, the Florida Supreme Court's electoral process did not bring the finality it promised. Instead it imploded, coming under challenge in the end even from Al Gore's side. The first problem arose from what we suppose should be called a hypertechnicality: the new deadline. The court's due date came too soon for two of the counties to complete their count. Miami-Dade began counting all the ballots, got through about one-fifth of all the precincts by Saturday morning, and then concluded that it could not possibly complete the job by the Sunday evening deadline.[20] Realizing this, the canvassing board made a quick decision to abandon a total recount and remove the 10,750 undervotes from the stack and examine only these ballots. The whole operation would be moved to a more private conference room upstairs.

On hearing about this decision, a large number of Republican operatives who had been shipped into Miami to serve as observers of the recount process kicked up a storm, demonstrating inside the county office building. A couple of hours later, the canvassing board met again and decided 3–0 to discontinue the recount. There was not enough time, they concluded, to do justice to counting all of the undervotes, not to mention the rest of the ballots. On this decision, many believe, may have hinged the outcome of the 2000 election. Without new votes from Miami-Dade, Gore could not win. With them—or so many then believed—he would have won. The canvassing board's decision remains one of the most disappointing for the Democrats, as the board was usually described in the media as being disposed to the Democrats. What precipitated it? Was it the demonstration of a bunch of predominately white males in jacket and ties—what Paul Gigot, in the most memorable phrase of the period, called "the Brooks Brothers Revolution"? Certainly, the demonstration had gotten everyone's attention—that is what a demonstration is supposed to do. But the Democrats chose to see something more sinister. Gore called it "intimidation," while Joe Lieberman argued, "This is a time to honor the rule of law, not surrender to the rule of the mob." [21] The only problem was that those said to be intimidated must have been suffering from a Miami variant of the Stockholm Syndrome, as they themselves never felt they were acting under duress. Canvassing Board Supervisor David Leahy characterized the protest as "noisy and peaceful. . . . I was not intimidated by it. I saw it for what it was." The other members of the board, two judges (Myriam Lehr and Lawrence King) also denied being pressured in their decision.[22]

The second issue was the now old question of the standard that was to be used in counting the ballots, which the Florida Supreme Court had left to the counties to decide. In Broward, which welcomed dimpled and pregnant chads, Gore gained some 567 votes in a process that Republicans claimed bitterly to be completely fraudulent. In Palm Beach County, a stricter standard was used, and Gore made much less progress. The combination of these two events—the refusal of Miami-Dade to recount the votes and the adoption of a stricter standard in Palm Beach—undid Gore's hopes for victory at this stage. Instead of defending the vaunted new electoral process of the Florida Supreme Court, Gore's side went back to court to attack it as unfair.

Certification: Katherine's sweet revenge (November 26)

At last, on Sunday evening November 26, came the long-awaited moment of final certification. Again, even this event, supposedly governed by the ironclad rules of the Florida Supreme Court decision, became a matter of contention. The Supreme Court had specified 5 P.M. as the deadline. But as the day proceeded, it became clear that Palm Beach County, which had been counting for days (but which had taken Thanksgiving day off), would not make the deadline. The county asked for a delay, and others insisted that Harris should exercise her discretion and wait until the next morning.

She refused. Taking Palm Beach figures from the earlier machine recount, the new totals were refigured, and George Bush was given a victory with a margin of 537 votes.

The certification process proceeded with enormous fanfare, in a ceremony replete with seals and flags of the state of Florida, speeches from commissioners, a liberal use of *dulys* and *whereases,* and a public signing of scores of official documents. There could be no doubt of the symbolic warfare going on, and the only question was whether it was a response to or a parody of the Florida Supreme Court hearing earlier in the week. Here sat Katherine Harris behind a huge wooden panel, roughly in the same position as the Florida Supreme Court's chief justice, flanked on each side by other members of the commission. Yes, the executive branch had its dignity too.[23]

Let the contest begin (November 27)

Certification was supposed to be the final moment in the Florida election. Bush tried to treat it as such—sort of—taking to the airwaves to deliver what can only be called a half-victory speech, and not all that impressive of one at that. Gore's strategy was to regard certification as just another little event along the way in what was now regularly being referred to as "the process." Indeed, the whole matter had gone on for so long that no moment could any longer achieve the status of being definitive. There was only "the process," which marched inexorably at its own pace. This numbing effect clearly worked in Gore's favor, and the Gore lawyers announced that they would be moving to the next stage: to contest the election. Again there was the plea for patience, with Gore mentioning in one interview that the matter would be resolved by "mid-December," in another by December 18. The whole matter was brought back to the Florida courts, where a full trial would now be needed before a lower circuit court. The Gore team asked, among things, for a full counting of the undervotes in Miami-Dade County and the inclusion in Gore's totals of the additional votes that had been found in the never-completed recounts in Palm Beach and Miami-Dade.

The Gore team now shifted its public relations strategy. Al Gore himself became much more active, emerging from his reserved statesman's role to fill the airwaves with speeches and interviews, hopping from one morning talk show to the next. Bush, seeing danger, pulled his head back into his shell while Gore's side ratcheted up the rhetoric. Jesse Jackson again spoke of disenfranchisement and called for a Justice Department investigation of the Florida election: "What you will see is a pattern of targeted racial profiling. In a democracy, you can afford to lose an election, but you cannot afford to lose your franchise."[24] Gore endorsed the point: "These cheap and unreliable machines are much more likely to be found in areas of low-income people and minorities and seniors."[25]

The U.S. Supreme Court's first decision (December 4)

For those who love subtlety, nuance, and signals—qualities not generally esteemed in our time—the U.S. Supreme Court's first decision (*Bush v. Palm Beach County Canvassing Board*) is destined to become a classic. One can easily imagine groups of law students twenty years hence sitting in seminars, marveling at how the High Court crafted a decision to send a political-legal (as distinct from a purely legal) message to a lower court, in this case the Florida Supreme Court. The only thing that will mar this adulation is that the Florida Supreme Court, whether from tone deafness or obstinacy, never heard the message. But of that more in a moment.

On November 24, the U.S. Supreme Court agreed to hear the case on the constitutionality of the Florida Supreme Court's decision, before the final certification of votes. By the time the U.S. Supreme Court case was to be heard on December 1, the political situation had changed dramatically and Bush had been certified the winner in Florida. There were many legal analysts who recommended that Bush should now drop the case, as it only served to help extend "the process" and could have little practical benefit to confer. Indeed, with Bush now in the lead in Florida, the whole decision had lost much of its allure. Still, a Supreme Court case is a Supreme Court case, and just as hundreds in the early nineteenth century would wait in line to listen to Daniel Webster deliver his spellbinding arguments before the Marshall Court, so they lined up to watch Laurence Tribe and Theodore Olson be quizzed by our modern justices. So extraordinary was the public interest in this case that the Court for the first time permitted audiotapes to be made of the hearings, which were played on the cable networks afterwards against the backdrop of court-artist renderings of Olson and Tribe and all of the justices. For the first time too, most Americans had a chance to hear the grillings that lawyers receive when standing before the bar of the Supreme Court, which is almost sufficient to make many think that these lawyers earn their fees.

The arguments in the case were legal and technical, actually quite dull, and they seemed light-years removed from the rough and tumble of the political situation. If the whole spectacle were not so fascinating, it would have been easy to pause and ask why anyone was *there*, in a courtroom, and what did any of these arguments have to do with the choice of the next president? Perhaps the only answer was that the Florida Supreme Court had started the whole process of legalization in the first place. The U.S. Supreme Court was thus put in a delicate situation. It was not anxious to overrule a state Supreme Court and its own membership appeared to be deeply divided. Nor did the U.S. Supreme Court want to spend capital or prestige where it was not necessary, and the truth was that for the moment, with Bush having been certified and with the whole matter of the contest under review in Florida's lower courts, the Court had no practical issue to decide at this time. For all its glamor, this decision was a sideshow, far less important than what was going on in the contest trial in Florida.

The Court pronounced a per curiam decision, which meant that it was unanimous. But if it was unanimous, it was not definitive. The Court asked the Supreme Court of Florida to clarify the basis of its decision. "After reviewing the opinion of the Florida Supreme Court, we find that there is considerable uncertainty as to the precise grounds for the decision," the Court wrote. What this meant for the moment was that the existing decision was not operative or real law (though of course many actions had already and were already being taken pursuant to it). It would have to be redone or clarified. In explaining why it asked for this clarification, the Supreme Court also set some guidelines or limits on what the Florida court could or could not take into account in making a decision. It pointed out to the Florida Supreme Court that the proper hierarchy of law in this instance was not the usual one in Florida voting cases, which normally run first from the Florida constitution down to the statute. This hierarchy did not apply because in the selection of electors, the matter is governed by the U.S. Constitution (Article 2, Section 1) and by federal law passed pursuant to it. The U.S. Constitution vests the power to act in this instance not with the state in general, but specifically with the *legislature* of each state, making the statute passed by the Florida legislature the highest authority in the state. That law cannot be interpreted in light of what is found in the Florida constitution, which is what the Florida Supreme Court had seemed to do. (Of course the U.S. Supreme Court never really accused the Florida justices directly of making such an error, but said only that their decision "may be read to indicate" that this is what they had done.) The Supreme Court then "vacated" the decision, and returned it to the Florida court for "further proceeding not inconsistent with this opinion."

What had been decided here? Gore himself chose the now standard tactic of reading into it what he wished: "I think the U.S. Supreme Court ruling was neutral. It may have even been slightly favorable to us."[26] Fortunately, the nation has CNN's legal analysts Roger Cossack and Greta Van

Susteren to set everyone straight on such matters. What had really happened was that the U.S. Supreme Court had strongly suggested that the
Florida Supreme Court had probably rendered an unconstitutional decision. More importantly, the U.S. Supreme Court was putting the Florida
Supreme Court on notice that, within the legal hierarchy of courts, it (the
Florida Supreme Court) was not acting with a free hand, as the court of final resort with no check. The buck did not stop in Tallahassee, but in Washington. The U.S. Supreme Court was watching and, in some sense, super-
vising. In any subsequent decision (on the contest), if the Florida Supreme
Court continued down the same legal path it followed on its November 21
decision, the U.S. Supreme Court might well be willing to hear another appeal from George Bush.

Was this a message that the Florida Supreme Court would receive?
From one perspective, one might have answered in the affirmative. The
Florida court's hand had been weakened. In one week, its vaunted image
had collapsed. Far from being an "august" body, unassailable by any mortal, it looked like a bunch of incompetent, local bumblers, all the more pa-
thetic for their original pretentiousness. The Gore team still wanted to portray it as the court of last resort, but few others saw the court in that way.
On the other hand, there was the possibility that, wounded and filled with
resentment, Florida Supreme Court judges might try to vindicate themselves and call the U.S. Supreme Court's bluff. After all, Florida Supreme
Court judges wear robes, too. With many of them just having had their
terms renewed, what was to stop them from acting as they wanted?

The Florida legislature ready for the rescue (December 8)

While this legal process was unfolding, the Florida legislature, with
large Republican majorities in both houses, agreed to convene on December 8 in a special session. The purpose was to consider the naming of
Florida's slate of electors. The legislature acted under its proclaimed constitutional authority to determine how to select electors, fortified by federal law passed in the wake of the Hayes-Tilden dispute specifying that the
legislature had the right to appoint electors if the state had failed to do so
by other means. Republicans presented this action as a defensive measure,
first as a way of checking the activism of the state high court and second
as an "insurance policy" to guarantee that Florida would actually have
electors in case the dispute was not resolved by December 12 or December 18. As Senate president John McKay said, the goal of the special session was to "ensure that Florida's voters are not disenfranchised from the
2000 presidential election." If the Florida courts somehow named Gore's

electors and the legislature named Bush's, the dispute would have to be settled by Congress. If the two houses of Congress could not agree between the two slates, federal law stipulated that the slate certified by the state's executive branch, which would be the slate chosen by the legislature, was the automatic default pick. It would be almost checkmate for George Bush.

Understanding the danger to Gore's position, Democrats sought to head off the legislature's action with demonstrations and outraged commentary.[27] Failing that, they hoped to delegitimize it. The only way out of the checkmate would be to mobilize public opinion so that Congress would side with the court's slate of electors or so that Bush himself would have to renounce a victory won in that way. The idea was to present a legislative choice of electors as an act beyond the pale, completely partisan, and a part of a fraternal conspiracy between Jeb and George. (Jeb was involved in approving the plan of legislative action and would also certify that slate.) Joe Lieberman touched on all these themes when he said that for the Republican majority in the Florida legislature, now unfortunately encouraged by Governor Jeb Bush, to say they are prepared to put their judgment in place of the judgment of the 6 million voters of Florida is just wrong and sets a terrible precedent. Echoed Gore on CNN: "I can't believe that the people of Florida want to see the expression of their will taken away by politicians. I think you'd see quite a negative response to it."[28] Democrats were inflamed, but Republicans looked prepared to proceed. As Republican state Senator Burt Saunders replied, "This is nuclear war."[29] Like the first Florida Supreme Court decision, this element of the picture provoked a heated theoretical discussion about the relative merits of courts and the elected branches: those who had attacked the court praised the assertiveness of the legislature, while those who lauded the court for its boldness attacked the legislature.

Judge Sauls's ruling and some Saulicisms (December 4)

Though many Americans found the U.S. Supreme Court case and the growing prospect of legislative intervention riveting, the real center of action was in the Florida trial over the contest of the Florida certification of the vote. This trial was in the hands of a Florida circuit court, with N. Sanders Sauls, the presiding judge, a registered Democrat who had been appointed to the bench in 1989 by a Republican, Governor Bob Martinez. Sauls was picked randomly by a computer to preside at the trial. He was a local, born and educated in Florida. His ruling would be crucial, subject only to appeal to the Florida Supreme Court, with which he had clashed in the past.

There was something different about this case. It was in a courtroom that lacked any of the trappings of glory of the U.S. or Florida Supreme Court chambers. It looked a bit like a crowded dentist's waiting room. Then there was the judge. He was folksy, a kind of "real" person in a sea of higher-status sharks. The question many asked was whether Sauls was somehow out of his depth or else a veritable country Solomon. The media took a liking to him as an original, reporting on his hunting habits and his frequent Saulicisms, including: "Let's see now: more lawyers than spectators" and "You lawyers must feel nibbled to death by a duck." When pressed by Gore's over-latted lawyers to pick up the schedule, he told them that "circuit court judges in Florida don't go 24-hours-a-day."

Something else was different, too. There were witnesses in this trial with cross-examination, giving the proceeding a Perry Mason quality. Among those who made their way to the witness stand were two statisticians, an expert on rubber, and, of all things, "a political scientist." As this trial proceeded, it became evident that the legal talent between the two sides was evenly shared. On one side was David Boies. Yet the Bush team had strong lawyers as well, including Barry Richard and the brilliant cross-examiner Phil Beck.

On the afternoon of December 4, only hours after the U.S. Supreme Court had vacated the earlier judgment of the Florida high court, Sauls rejected the Gore contest challenge across-the-board, writing that Gore had presented "no credible statistical evidence and no other competent substantial evidence" that met the legal standard of a reasonable probability that the election result would change if his recount requests were granted.[30] For the Bush legal team, it was total victory. Gore and Lieberman were reeling. They appealed Sauls's decision to the Florida Supreme Court, which they saw as their last and best hope. As Lieberman put it, "This is the court that we took our substantive argument to; they responded favorably. Their judgment has been frustrated by the actions of various parties along the way."[31] The end appeared to be in sight, and Democratic elites edged closer to accepting a Gore defeat.

The Lewis and Clark expedition (December 8)

At the same time, Gore subtly made common cause with two other lawsuits brought from Seminole and Martin Counties that questioned the validity of the absentee ballots. These suits involved charges of illegal conduct by election officials who allowed Republican volunteers to fill in missing voter identification numbers in absentee ballot applications; they asked as relief that all of the absentee ballots be thrown out. Such a remedy would have subtracted more than enough votes from Bush to give the election to Gore. (Democrats sought to invalidate 15,000 absentee votes in Seminole County and 10,000 more in Martin County. Bush won the absentee balloting by 4,797 votes in Seminole and 2,815 votes in Martin.) The plaintiffs were Democrats in these counties, whose legal actions were never officially embraced or backed by the Gore campaign. The suits presented a certain "rhetorical problem" for Gore, as his claim all along had been to count all the votes, not exclude them. (It was the same "conflict" that had appeared in the counting of military ballots.) Nonetheless, in the end the vice president made clear enough that he was interested in these cases and was prepared to win by them, claiming that "more than enough votes were potentially taken away from Democrats because they were not given the same access that Republicans were" to change the outcome of the election.

Called "sleeper cases" by many, these suits came in under the radar and were not heard until near the very end. There was much interest in particular in the Seminole County case, which was heard by a black female judge who had been passed over for promotion by Jeb Bush. The Republicans had even asked for a new judge, fearing bias. Ultimately, though, the two judges—one named Lewis and the other named Clark (Terry Lewis and Nikki Clark)—determined on December 8 that "despite irregularities in the requests for absentee ballots, neither the sanctity of the ballots nor the integrity of the elections has been compromised." The elections "reflect a full and fair expression of the will of the voters."

The Florida Supreme Court's second decision: The revenge of the activists (December 8)

Events of December 8, 2000, seemed to be moving toward a near certain conclusion. Public opinion in the nation had been moving in Bush's direction; all of the important legal decisions of the week had been in Bush's favor; Democrats were now more or less resigned to a Bush presidency; and Gore's own followers were sending up smoke signals. It was Friday afternoon. Only the last piece needed to be put in place for the puzzle finally to be completed. Then came the bombshell.

The Florida Supreme Court reversed Sauls's contest decision by a vote of four to three, with the chief justice writing one of the dissents. The court opinion was so audacious that neither side had any real inkling of what it would be. But while audacious, it had a simple and clear political appeal. The decision simply said, count every undervote in Florida and do it right now. (It also awarded to Gore all of the additional votes he claimed from the partial recounts.)

On the legal side, the Florida majority argued at length that their decision was based completely on an interpretation of Florida statutory law, not the Florida constitution. In so doing they were "answering" the U.S. Supreme Court by saying that they were working well within their jurisdiction. If the Supreme Court had thought it could get its way by sending subtle signals without its majority spending its political capital, the Florida Four had answered: No way. They were throwing the ball back to the U.S. Supreme Court (presumably to the Washington Five). As for the practical problems of actually carrying out this new process, the court responded in one frequently cited footnote: "While we agree that practical difficulties may well end up controlling the outcome of the election, we vigorously disagree that we should abandon our responsibility to resolve this election dispute under the rule of law. We can only do the best we can to carry out our sworn responsibilities to the justice system and its role in this process."[32] No hypertechnicalities were going to stand in the way.

That evening the matter was turned back to the circuit court, and within hours Terry Lewis (Sauls had recused himself) put together a system for recounting the votes that would begin the next morning and be completed by Sunday night. Some votes were to be counted in Tallahassee, others in their respective counties under standards devised within those counties. The turn of events that evening was stunning, comparable to the networks declaring, then undeclaring the race for Bush on election night. Gore, all but out of the running, was revived, and not only revived, but thought likely to win the election.

The U.S. Supreme Court's second decision: The buck stops here (December 12)

By mid-afternoon on Saturday, less than a day after the Florida Supreme Court made its stunning decision, the U.S. Supreme Court issued an order (a stay) to stop the counting, and agreed to hear the case on Monday, December 11. Two points stood out immediately. First, in order to issue the stay and hear the case, five justices—a majority of the Court—had to agree that there was a substantial probability that the plaintiff (Bush) would win his case. Second, by issuing the stay and stopping the count, the U.S. Supreme Court avoided being presented with a fait accompli. Gore's hope (and perhaps the hope of the majority on the Florida Supreme Court, as well) had to have been that it would be nearly impossible to reverse the Florida decision if the recount was complete and it showed Gore the winner.

At about 10 P.M. EST, on Tuesday, December 12—two hours before the "safe-harbor" deadline for certifying electors—the U.S. Supreme Court announced its ruling. By a 7–2 division, the Court concluded that "there are constitutional problems with the recount ordered by the Florida Supreme Court that demand a remedy." The recount scheme established by the December 8 Florida Supreme Court decision was unconstitutional due to equal protection concerns engendered by the lack of statewide recount standards. Of the seven, three also argued that the Florida Supreme Court had violated the Article 2 requirement that legislatures choose the manner for selecting electors: "To attach definitive weight to the pronouncement of a state court, when the very question at issue is whether the court has actually departed from the statutory meaning, would be to abdicate our responsibility to enforce the explicit requirements of Article II." Most decisively, five justices—Rehnquist, Scalia, Thomas, O'Connor, and Kennedy—saw no way to produce a timely remedy. In the end, therefore, the final door on Gore's campaign was shut by five judges.

Dissenting were Justices Stevens, Souter, Ginsburg, and Breyer. In a forceful dissent, Stevens accused the majority of acting "unwisely." He added, ''Preventing the recount from being completed will inevitably cast a cloud on the legitimacy of the election." Stevens went on to say that the Court departed from "rules of judicial restraint that have guided the Court throughout its history. . . . Although we may never know with complete certainty the identity of the winner of this year's presidential election, the identity of the loser is perfectly clear. It is the nation's confidence in the judge as an impartial guardian of the law."

What was perfectly clear was that no one, majority or minority, had wanted to be confronted with this situation. Undoubtedly ruing the refusal of the Florida court to take their earlier hint, the justices said it "sometimes becomes our unsought responsibility to resolve the federal and constitutional issues the judicial system has been forced to confront."

Liberals accused the conservative Court majority of inconsistency, seeing in *Bush v. Gore* a case of judicial activism rather than judicial restraint; a case of ignoring rather than deferring to the power of the states (which of course would mean here the power of the state court); and a hypocritical reliance on a Fourteenth Amendment equal protection argument. It was also argued that the Court had tarnished itself. Conservatives responded that it is not activism to curb activism, and that the real issue was not states' rights but judicial imperialism versus the authority of the elected branches. To decide on behalf of Florida's court, after all, would have been to decide *against* its legislature and executive. In any event, in the eyes of many conservatives, the Court had already tarnished itself with amazing regularity over the previous 40 years, and it was a salutary development if liberals finally noticed that justices are mortal.

Whatever the fine points of legal and constitutional theory, one fact crystalized (that is, after about an hour of fevered instant media analysis grappling with the meaning of the split decision). Altogether, the Supreme Court reaffirmed its importance—no small irony, given the role played in Al Gore's campaign rhetoric by the issue of Supreme Court appointments. Gore had, for all practical purposes, reached the end of the line. A few options might have remained, but none that had a significant likelihood of success or that would have left him in possession of a workable presidency had they succeeded. An overwhelming proportion of Americans indicated they accepted the result and that they would see Bush as the legitimate president. Above the wailing and gnashing of teeth of some Gore partisans could be heard a general sigh of relief by the public at large. Indeed, curiously, the people seemed to want the contest decided by courts rather than by the elected branches at either the state or federal level. The vice president "should act now and concede," said Ed Rendell, general chairman of the Democratic National Committee. "Clearly the race for the presidency has come to an end. George Bush is going to be the next president of the United States," added Senator Bob Torricelli (D-N.J).

The National Political Climate

Let us return now to consider one of the central elements of power in the strategic situation that the candidates faced: the national political climate. The national political climate is a combination of two interacting parts: public opinion and elite opinion. Public opinion at any point might have been subject to a move from elite opinion—say, if two or three Democratic senators had publicly announced that it was time for Gore to concede. But elite opinion was also subject to pressure from public opinion, as Democratic leaders were far less likely to make such a request as long as Gore's support among voters at large, and especially among core Democratic partisans, remained strong.

Both organizations knew from the beginning of the postelection period that the campaign would involve both a legal aspect and a political aspect. Probably the predominant view was that it would be the national political climate that would somehow resolve the election, forcing one of the candidates to leave the race. The national political climate never played this role—not, we would suggest, because it lacked the power, but because it could never be decisively mobilized one way or the other. The political climate reached, if not a pure stalemate, then something short of what was required to force a resolution. Once this occurred, the legal elements came more and more into play, and events in the legal process—who won what case, what lawyer made what argument—began to shape the national political climate. But like a sleeping giant, the national political climate was always lying dormant in the background, capable of being roused from its slumber. Each side would from time to time seek to awaken it, while the other would sing its patented lullabies.

Both campaigns had a maximalist objective and a minimalist objective for the national political climate. Bush's maximal strategy was to generate enough pressure from elites and from public opinion to force Gore into a concession. In doing so, the Bush campaign stressed the need for finality and stability, hinting vaguely at the danger of a looming crisis if the election were not soon resolved. Gore's maximal strategy was to create a powerful national sentiment that he was the real winner of the election and was being denied the presidency by fraud or legal technicalities. With a clear sentiment of this kind operating, somehow or other Gore could be assured that the legal matters would be resolved in his favor and that Bush would be driven from the race. Turning to the minimal objectives, Bush's aim was to keep public opinion favorable toward him as the more legitimate one to be president, allowing him if chosen to assume the office on a stronger ground. Gore's minimal strategy was to secure sufficient support from elites and public opinion to give him the leeway to pursue all legal options open to him—or, to put it negatively, to avoid having these options short-circuited or foreclosed. Stressing patience and fairness, he would stretch the election out until a possible break in his favor.

How well did either candidate meet his objectives? If we look first at Bush's side, he needed elite opinion (particularly from Democrats) to, as it were, pressure or force Gore to concede, and he needed support from the public to pressure the elites. It was a difficult gambit, as it involved forging public opinion into an active force to compel action. It was made more complicated by the fact that Bush's appeals to the general good were seen also as serving his own interest in becoming president. This does not mean that the arguments were specious, but it does mean that they were more difficult to accept. Indeed, to push too hard with this kind of argument could backfire, and Bush slowly came to the realization that it was better to tread lightly. Indeed, he came to see early on that signs of his behaving too presidential were perceived to be presumptuous. By the end of November, the Bush team had come to the calculation that "if Republicans are not clamoring for Gore to quit, Democrats will be more likely to ask him to give up the fight."[33]

Yet if Bush never succeeded in his maximal objective of forcing Gore out, he did hold his ground in public opinion. Part of this achievement was due to finding the correct tone, and that tone was to lie low. Bush spent a lot of time at his ranch dressed in his cowboy hat and cowboy boots, holding various high-level meetings in what he would not quite call a transition. After certification, Bush began to rise in the polls, as did—especially—Dick Cheney. (Cheney's rise was not affected by the mild heart attack he suffered on November 22.) As of December 2, 56 percent had a favorable view of Bush as against 40 percent unfavorable, whereas Gore had fallen to more unfavorable (52 percent) than favorable (46 percent). Cheney was at 58 percent favorable as compared with just 40 percent for Joe Lieberman.[34] By this time, the Bush campaign saw public opinion in a different way. Its approval was important for after the election, to supply a foundation for Bush's presidency, should he be elected.

Let us now turn to Gore's side. On the maximal strategy, Gore initially tried, but never even came close, to generating a huge and general groundswell in his favor for becoming president. Many reasons could be offered, besides the obvious one that turning public opinion into an instrument of pressure is a difficult proposition under any circumstances. It is fair to say as well that there was never an enormous positive enthusiasm for Al Gore, however much many admired and respected him. But the truth is that Gore's staff never thought they could win over the national political climate by a purely positive campaign anyhow. If public opinion was to be aroused, it would have to be on a campaign of anger at a stolen election, in the spirit of Andrew Jackson in 1824 or some of Samuel Tilden's supporters in 1876. Gore's side was clearly willing to play hardball in this sense—look at the roughing up of Katherine Harris—and they did not falter for lack of will. Our primary explanation for why this negative campaign failed is that it lacked a villain or perpetrator of the crime. If an election is stolen, then someone has to be stealing it. You cannot wage a successful stolen election campaign on the strength of a passive verb. Yet this was just the problem that Gore and the Democrats faced. Every time they looked for a "thief," it turned out to be a Democrat or an impersonal force. Who had disenfranchised the citizens of Palm Beach with the butterfly ballot? Not the Republicans, but a Democratic election official trying to do her best to help those whom she harmed. Who had decided not to count the ballots in some of the counties? Not a plot of Republican officials, but Democrats or neutral civil servants. Who had installed the sub-par voting equipment? Mostly Democrats in Democratic counties. And so it went. Apart from a few efforts to depict Katherine Harris as the Princess of Darkness, or some shouting guys in suits as a dangerous mob, no one in the Gore camp could ever put a "face" on the injustice they had suffered.

Failing in the maximal strategy, Gore fell back on the defensive or minimal strategy. That objective was to achieve enough support from public opinion and from elite opinion (particularly from his own party) to give him the room or leeway to pursue and maintain the legal strategy. As long as he was behind and trying to overcome the existing vote counts, he needed to buy time and avert the development of a sentiment of impatience. He had to convince the elites to stand by him—not to desert and start a stampede—and convince enough of the public that his requests for more time were legitimate. Here he was enormously successful. At the outset, many thought that the country would give him a few days. Gore himself told Americans in mid-November that things would be settled with finality "in days, not weeks."[35] Who would have thought it possible that, at the end of November he would be telling Americans to be patient and that a resolution might not come until December 12 or possibly even December 18? Core Democrats stuck with him, and in some sense moved even closer to him as the process went on. Gore relied heavily on black supporters and on labor unions, and as these constituencies rallied to him few elite Democrats wanted to put themselves at the front of a charge to force Gore out. The political debt Gore would have owed these groups if he had won would have been enormous.

An Appraisal of Constitutional Statesmanship

It is always difficult to step out of the pundits' role of commenting on political strategies and assume the historian's responsibility of judging the virtue and prudence of political actors. It is not just that personal biases can always cloud one's views; it is also that the kinds of judgments that are required are usually difficult to make and subject to uncertainty. Yet in a case like this one, where the nation teetered on the edge of crisis, questions of this kind cannot be avoided. They are every bit as much a part of the election story of 2000 as an analysis of the candidates' fund-raising strategies or their calculations of which states and groups to target in the political campaign.

To introduce a minimum of system into an inquiry that cannot be made systematic, we can at least say where we are looking and what we are looking for. We are looking for some of the points in this process—we call them potential "stopping points"—where an identifiable actor could either have done (or desisted from doing) something that could have had a direct effect on bringing the election to a close and ending it on terms that could widely be regarded as legitimate. We will survey some of the actors—candidates, the elites, the courts—who confronted such stopping points, beginning with the candidates. Of all the actors involved, the candidates should perhaps be treated with the greatest degree of indulgence. They, after all, had the most personally at stake, and—even discounting for the self-serving character to the argument—they had a strong obligation to their supporters to fight hard for the cause. Indeed, any electoral system must assume a driving ambition on the candidates' part, which it is the system's job in large measure to control. Still, an attitude of indulgence is not the same as a willingness to exonerate the candidates from all personal responsibility. These people were vying for the office of president of the United States, where there is still a lingering hope, if no longer a firm expectation, that (in the old-fashioned words of *The Federalist*) the position will be filled "by characters pre-eminent for ability and virtue."[36]

It is not a matter of virtue or anything else to say that George Bush in 2000 falls largely outside the orbit of most of these judgments. It may well be that some of his early attempts to appear too soon like the president-elect grated on some—they didn't work, in any case—but these are not matters that involve action at what we have called a stopping point. By and large Bush was not involved in many stopping points. His major "action" was this: he won the vote in Florida and then he took all reasonable steps to hold on, parrying the stratagems of his opponent while engaging in no major action that anyone can say was objectionable. There are nonetheless points where some might argue that he could have gone out of his way to help bring the election to a conclusion. He could have agreed with Al Gore's proposal at one point for a statewide hand count. This plan would have meant giving up a huge legal advantage, which is perhaps more than anyone has reason to expect. But more importantly, it was never clear that the candidates had the legal right to reach such an agreement on their own. Nor was there any consensus on what the standards for taking such a count would be. Bush was never, really, in a position to bring the election to a full stop.

Al Gore, by the nature of his situation as the one who lost the election on November 7, obviously was confronted with more real stopping points along the way. Indeed, he was continually being pressured by some to be the "statesman," and in the Gore camp the term statesman was seen as a euphemism for surrender. Gore was being "instructed" by many wise elder figures, mostly Republicans, to take the noble course and act like Richard Nixon supposedly did in 1960, putting country over personal ambition. In the end, Gore ignored all these pleadings, seeing them either as mere partisan gambits or as inapplicable to the nature of this specific case, which was different from any of the others. There were at least five stopping points, specific and general, that Gore confronted. He could have (1) declined the automatic recount provided under Florida law, (2) desisted from asking for any hand recounts, (3) desisted from engaging in a public opinion war suggesting a stolen election campaign, (4) desisted from contesting the election once it was certified, and (5) desisted from a concession after *Bush v. Gore*. As it was, Gore did indeed choose to keep going at the first four stopping points, but finally accepted the near-inevitable and made the decision to withdraw at the fifth.

How do we judge these cases? As for the first stopping point, it would have been unjust and unnecessary for Gore to give away freely what he was entitled to and indeed almost required to accept under the law. Americans had no trouble in waiting for the automatic recount and for a counting of the overseas ballots. If it took that long to settle the election, this was not due to an attack on the legitimacy of the process, but was purely a result of how close it was. The second stopping point—the hand recount—presents greater difficulties. A consequence of proceeding here was that the legitimacy of both men's presidencies would now be more difficult to establish. Gore could no longer proceed without in some way harming George Bush, should Bush eventually win. And yet, Gore was seemingly convinced that he really had won this election. To have asked him to sacrifice not just his personal ambitions but what he strongly believed was the justice of the case may have been an easy request for Republicans, but not so easy for the candidate himself. The third stopping point is more general and refers to the public relations campaign Gore waged. It may be argued that the need to keep the campaign going required tactics of this kind. But this argument does not justify the means. The public campaign here had some disturbing implications. When it became clear that there had never been a plot to steal the election from Gore, then an attack on the electoral process would—even without intending to—undermine a Bush presidency. Although this ploy was necessary for Gore, it was destructive of Bush. If there were problems with America's voting system—and there were—George Bush was not responsible for them any more than Al Gore was. (Neither, really, was Jeb Bush, as Florida's system was certainly no worse than that of many other states in the nation.) In pursuing his own goal of becoming president, Gore was ensuring that Bush should be asked to pay the price. Still, Gore's supporters might plausibly argue that this price was not exorbitant and that Gore's rightful claim to the office made such measures defensible.

The fourth stopping point was at certification. Some of the same considerations apply here as at the point of asking for a hand recount, only the arguments for accepting this moment as an appropriate stopping point gain some weight. After all, the first Florida Supreme Court decision had given

Gore the rules he wanted, so at this point Gore had a graceful out, even with his supporters. The more important point now became the stress on the nation. Time was beginning to run out for a reasonable transition, and Gore had to up the rhetorical stakes to stay in. Just to stay alive and keep core Democrats with him, he had to anger more Republicans and independents. Even if his cause were just, at some point the questions had to be asked about how many would accept him as president and how effective a president he could be. And in pursuing that possibility, was he making it more and more likely that many would not now be able to accept Bush, either? In short, was this becoming a version of destroying the presidency in order to save it?

At the fifth stopping point after the U.S. Supreme Court decision in *Bush v. Gore*, Gore did avail himself of the opportunity to withdraw and put an end to the election. But as we have been hesitant to assign blame, so here we should be reluctant to bestow praise. The accounts of the last day suggest that Gore and his advisers considered all options and only concluded that he should not continue with his challenge because there was no chance of succeeding, not because of a larger concern for ending the election crisis. On the other hand, after his defeat, not only did Gore act with great decorum and grace, giving a fine concession speech, but he did not undertake any campaign to undermine the legitimacy of Bush's election. This attitude stood in striking contrast to President Clinton, who with no personal stake and every reason to uphold the dignity of the office, elected gratuitously to turn on his successor and contend that under a full counting of the votes Gore should be president.

There are two caveats on this complicated judgment on Gore that should be mentioned. First, to see Gore's postelection behavior as a mixed bag, not too blameworthy, presupposes that Gore really believed that he was the true winner of Florida under the actual ballots cast and that he expected the hand counts to be fairly and appropriately conducted. It is one thing to count the votes as they are, but something quite different to count them in a way to try to make up for votes that Gore might have believed people *intended* for him. Given the wide latitude enjoyed by county canvassing boards, and control of the most important boards by Democrats, some suggested that Gore actually expected that the Democratic machinery would "manufacture" enough votes to put him over the top, by means fair or foul. If this was what was in mind, then a reasonable appraisal of Gore's statesmanship in this period must, needless to say, undergo a substantial downward revision. Second, a question must be raised about the overall tenor of Gore's approach, independent from analyzing the individual stopping points. The sum might be greater than the parts. While it might be possible to justify each of Gore's decisions, by the end he gave many Americans reason to wonder whether there was any point at which he would stand down for the good of the country. Connected with this impression was the sense that Gore was willing to search, with the aid of courts, for any way to dispense with formalities and controlling legal authority, from laws to deadlines to certifications. Whether this example will prove harmful in the long run cannot yet be known, but it will necessarily affect the way Gore's postelection campaign will be assessed by history.

What of the national elite, the elder statesmen? Perhaps, from the Republican side, there were too many too soon who were trying to push Gore into a concession. In fact the much-cited parallels between the cases of 1960 and 2000, while correctly drawn in certain respects, were incomplete. Nixon required victories in more than one state, and his case rested solely on the allegations of fraud, a difficult case to prove even if it was correct; Gore needed only Florida, and he believed that only a recount of existing ballots was necessary. Once the appeal for Gore to match Nixon's magnanimity fell short, Republican elites had little to say, although they did weigh in against the Florida Supreme Court ruling. The Democratic elite also got caught. Once Gore adopted the strategy of demanding the hand count, a strategy working inside the law, there was no easy way for Democrats to play statesmen. From that point until *Bush v. Gore*, they lacked any clear ground on which to take a stand. They simply turned the issue over to the courts and Al Gore's legal team, and sat on the sidelines. They gave up any chance for striking a political deal, implicit or otherwise (perhaps because they did not really have any political deal in mind). Furthermore, as Gore energized his base, the first Democrat to break ranks would have faced the wrath of key constituencies. No one was willing to take the risk. In any case, for much of the time Gore's chances looked good, so why rock the boat?

Only one subset of the Democratic elite—a very irregular subset, at that—thoroughly distinguished itself by its conduct after the election. Many black leaders—especially Jesse Jackson, who was ubiquitous, and Al Sharpton—actively sought to racialize the contest. Jackson decried the situation as "another Selma, " "disenfranchisement," and "tyranny," accused Bush of trying to "steal" the election, and said after the U.S. Supreme Court hearing on December 11, "We will take to the streets right now, we will delegitimize Bush, discredit him, do whatever it takes, but never accept him."[37] No major Democrat spoke out against Jackson's presence, and it was clear that if Gore himself was not to win, the object was to make Bush a weaker president. This strategy fits with the one some partisans had used in 1824 and 1876.

Let us turn next to the Florida Supreme Court. The two stopping points it faced were the two cases that came before it, and in both cases it elected to throw fuel on a fire that was down to its smoldering embers. Indeed, in both instances what must be called to mind is that the Florida Supreme Court went out of its way to make its decisions, overturning lower court decisions. A court is entitled, perhaps even obliged, to defend the rule of law, but it works within an institutional setting. It cannot be said that the Florida Supreme Court was under an undue legal compulsion to act in either case. Its intention, or the effect of its action, was to "legalize" the decision-making process of the postelection stage and bring it primarily under the purview of courts. In its first decision, it tried to vindicate a principle it held to be almost sacred. It was a far reach, almost as far as one can imagine that a court could go, but it represented the kind of vigorous judicial activism that many have come to admire.

The second decision is another matter altogether. A judgment of prudence requires looking at the specific circumstances at the time of an action and at the alternatives of each possible path of action. Think here of where matters stood in the country on Friday afternoon December 8. Everything finally was set for resolution. The American people were ready; public opinion was resolved that, under the circumstances, Bush should be president. The Democrats by and large were resolved. The other court matters (Lewis and Clark) had been decided against Gore. On top of all of this the Florida Supreme Court had the perfect legal justification for restraint, as a higher court is supposed to respect the decision of a lower court—Judge Sauls's decision—unless the plaintiffs overcome a heavy burden of proof.[38] In addition, the judges had had their chance the last time, and it had not worked—in part because of certain "practical" or real-life constraints of time and detail. What entitled them to a second exercise of will, that by anyone's estimate involved a far more complicated order than the first? Even if a kind of justice had been on their side, the question remained of how justice can be implemented. They themselves had been responsible for the chaos by their first decision. They themselves had proven to the world that the details of implementation (administration) were far more important than they had anticipated, yet here they were at the last moment throwing new orders, with new and untested schemes of implementation, into the air. Like riverboat gamblers, they chose to double the bet, whatever the risks.

On the other side, what good could possibly have followed from this decision? Possibly, just possibly, there could have been a legitimate outcome: a smooth counting of the votes with a clear result. But more probably, more disputes would have erupted over which ballots were to be counted, accompanied most likely by accusations of real fraud. A change to Gore would almost certainly have brought in the Florida legislature and pushed the election to the counting of the ballots in Congress. The new president (still likely to be Bush) would take office with even less legitimacy and without a significant transition period. Another likely consequence of this decision was that it would bring in the U.S. Supreme Court, which in fact occurred. This result must have been known and expected, at least by realistic jurists, as the Supreme Court had more or less issued a warning to go no further. Indeed, Florida Chief Justice Charles T. Wells predicted in his dissenting opinion that the decision would come under renewed constitutional scrutiny—scrutiny that it could not withstand.

If this decision does not show pride, rigidity, pique, obstinacy, it surely displays a simple lack of judgment. The decision never helped Al Gore, but it did hurt George Bush. It did not help the Florida Supreme Court, but it did hurt the U.S. Supreme Court. The most one can say is that these four members of the majority were determined to go down in a noble cause, guns blazing, while destroying everything around them. It is rare in the history of a court that its chief justice would go as far as to accuse his own court of creating a "constitutional crisis" that "will do damage to our country, our state, and to this court as an institution." Above all, the decision suggests that courts may have acquired simply too much power, and have grown accustomed to using it unchecked—and hence carelessly, if not dangerously.

This brings us finally to the U.S. Supreme Court. Its bluff had been called, and now it believed it had to act. It was thrown into a particularly difficult situation, having to stop vote counting in Florida while it was going on. Yet just as the perfect should not be made the enemy of the good, so the worse should not be made the enemy of the bad. No doubt there are a hundred ways in which, on its own terms, one might argue that *Bush v. Gore* was a bad decision. Legal and political scholars will have no difficulty in pointing out that it was badly written and badly argued. Not only this, but it may well produce unwelcome results, especially for the authors. It is likely to be regarded as at least a half-assault on the principle of federalism, and the legal basis of the decision, which is an equal protection claim, strengthens the most activist and nationalizing principle that the federal courts have developed.

But to say all of this is gratuitous and means next to nothing. A prudential decision must be judged by its effects in a specific context. Would the consequences of not acting have on balance been worse? The Court had a stopping point at its disposal, and it finally was the actor that took the opportunity to use it and bring the 2000 election to an end. If that end was not easily regarded as legitimate in an absolute sense, it was likely to be more legitimate than any other end now on the horizon. The Court knew, for better or worse, that it had the reservoir of respect to end the contest without entering a real crisis, and that it was perhaps the only institution at that point in a position to do so. If not the Supreme Court, then who? And if not then, then when?

It is said that the Court's decision may have harmed the principle of federalism. Perhaps, although in this case it is also true that the state action is one that touches directly and fully on a national matter, which is the election of the president. It is said also that the decision was a raw exercise of judicial activism. There is something to this criticism as well. But the argument would have been stronger if the Court were attempting to short-circuit a genuine political process. But this was not the case. The Court stepped in this time, as it had tried to do more gently in its first decision, not to undermine a political process but to curb a judicial process. It was trying to stop activism from the Florida court, and it is fair to ask which course of action—acting or not acting —would have encouraged more judicial activism in this country. If this was activism checking activism, so be it. There is a paradox here, but if pondering this paradox serves to curb activism altogether, more will have been gained from *Bush v. Gore* than anyone thought.

Notes

1. Alexis de Tocqueville, *Democracy in America*, ed. J. P. Mayer (New York: HarperPerennial, 1988), p. 127.

2. David S. Broder and Ceci Connolly, "Democrats Urge Gore Not to Push It Too Far; Line Drawn Between Recounts, Lawsuits," *Washington Post*, November 11, 2000, p. A1.

3. Evan Thomas, with Eleanor Clift, T. Trent Gegax, Adam Rogers, and Peter Goldman, "What a Long, Strange Trip," *Newsweek*, November 20, 2000, p. 30. Bush, these authors concluded, was less driven. "If this doesn't work out," he told one of them "I've got a life."

4. We focus here on Florida and exclude the possibility of Bush taking any legal or political action in some of the other close states. Bush kept this possibility alive for a time, leaving open the option of recounts in Wisconsin, Iowa, and Oregon, but then finally decided to drop it and stick exclusively with Florida.

5. The Republican team included Benjamin Ginsberg, George Terwilliger, Theodore Olson, and Barry Richard—certainly an illustrious group in its own right.

6. The signers included such academic notables as Bruce Ackerman, Cass Sunstein, Ronald Dworkin, and Michael Walzer, although they were apparently unaware of this sentence when they signed the ad. History may track Wilentz down and condemn him for his trickery.

7. According to a *Miami Herald* analysis, Gore outpolled Buchanan 167–1 across Florida. However, in Palm Beach that difference was a less-pronounced 79–1, with some precincts showing margins as low as five-to-one. Most Florida counties where

Buchanan made inroads went solidly to Bush, but the Palm Beach County vote favored Gore. That Buchanan would do so well in Palm Beach, considering its pro-Gore results, is a statistical improbability, the *Herald* analysis concluded; http://www.herald.com/ broward.htm/content/archive/news/elect2000/decision/splash.htm. Whether the statistically unlikely result was the consequence of voter confusion, as Democrats alleged, or of some other factor will be one of those issues for historians to debate.

8. http://www.herald.com/broward.htm/content/archive/news/elect2000/decision/ splash.htm.

9. John Marelius, "Digging in for long fight" *San Diego Union-Tribune*, November 10, 2000, p. A1.

10. The butterfly ballot suit was dismissed by a Florida District Court. The decision was upheld on appeal to the Florida Supreme Court. The Florida Supreme Court said, "We conclude as a matter of law that the Palm Beach County Ballot does not constitute substantial noncompliance with the statutory requirement mandating the voiding of the election." *Supreme Court of Florida Fladell v. Palm Beach County Canvassing Board*, Per Curiam Opinion, December 1, 2000.

11. In the recount there were 3,583 more votes for Gore, 2,250 more for Bush, or 70 percent more for Gore.

12. This charge was offered by the *Weekly Standard*: "In our bones, we're pretty sure what happened here. In the middle of the night of November 8, Democratic ultraloyalists . . . watched a fevered Bill Daley announce that things were still close in Florida . . . and read this hint for what it was." David Tell, "The Gore Coup," *Weekly Standard*, November 27, 2000.

13. The Florida courts were brought into this process as well to determine which standard might be used, and they generally turned the matter back to the canvassing boards.

14. Paul West, "Absentees push Bush lead to 930," *Baltimore Sun*, November 19, 2000.

15. Michael Kranish and Susan Milligan, "Asking the Hard Questions," *Boston Globe*, November 21, 2000, p. A1.

16. The only issue that the Florida Supreme Court did not take up directly was the standard to be used in the counting of the ballots, i.e., the stricter or looser standard, which was to be left to the discretion of the local canvassing boards and to the decisions of lower courts. But even here Democrats tried to claim that the spirit of the decision was in the Democrats' direction. The Court cited a 1990 opinion of the Illinois Supreme Court in which that court said that "to invalidate a ballot which clearly reflects the voter's intent, simply because a machine cannot read it, would subordinate substance to form and promote the means at the expense of the end."

17. George F. Will, "This Willful Court," *Washington Post*, November 23, 2000, p. A43.

18. "Reckless Republican Rhetoric," *New York Times*, November 23, 2000, p. A30.

19. Henry Weinstein and David Savage, "Judicial Legitimacy May Be Next Hue and Cry," *Los Angeles Times*, November 22, 2000, p. A1.

20. Gore had picked up some 157 votes to that point, although the precincts counted were among the most heavily Democratic in the county.

21. "Lieberman's Remarks on Protesters," *New York Times*, November 25, 2000, p. A15.

22. Mike Clary, "America Waits," *Los Angeles Times,* November 26, 2000, p. A 17.

23. Palm Beach finished a couple of hours later and it was announced—though never officially—that the recount had shown Al Gore gaining 215 votes on Governor Bush. Yet this Sunday evening total was informal and did not take place after all the required checking and rechecking of added totals. In fact, two days later—Wednesday—after the controversy died down, Palm Beach County released final results Wednesday from its presidential recount: an extra 188 votes for Al Gore.

24. "Gore Looks Again to Florida's High Court," *St. Louis Post-Dispatch*, November 30, 2000, p. A1.

25. John Mintz; Dan Keating " Ballot Spoilage Likelier For Blacks," *Washington Post*, December 3, 2000, p. A1.

26. "Excerpts from Washington Press Session" *Boston Globe*, December 6, 2000, p. A27.

27. http://www.washingtonpost.com/wp-srv/aponline/20001205/aponline021054_000.htm.

28. Karen Branch-Brioso, "Legislature in Florida will vote on calling special session," *St. Louis Post Dispatch*, November 30, 2000, p. A1.

29. Kenneth T. Walsh, "Confusion Reigns," *U.S. News & World Report*, December 18, 2000, p. 25.

30. Judge Sauls's ruling of December 4, 2000. It can be found at http://www.nytimes.com/2000/12/05/politics/05CTEX.html.

31. http://www.washtimes.com/national/default-2000125163046.htm.

32. *Gore v. Harris.* December 8, 2000. http://www.flcourts.org/pubinfo/election/OP-SC00-2431.pdf.

33. *Washington Post*, December 7, 2000.

34. Gallup Poll of December 2–4, 2000. http://www.gallup.com/poll/releases/pr00 1206.asp.

35. Speech of November 15, 2000, *Washington Post*, November 16, 2000, p. A28.

36. *Federalist* 68.

37. *Denver Post*, December 16, 2000, p. B7.

38. One subsequent nonpartisan ballot count seemed to verify Sauls's conclusion. *A Palm Beach Post* review of undervotes in Miami-Dade County, using a liberal standard of chad counting, showed Bush with a gain of six votes. Of course, the recounting of Florida's votes has only just begun. Clay Lambert, "Paper's Count," *Denver Rocky Mountain News*, January 14, 2001, p. 56A.

Chapter Seven

Congressional and State Elections

In the year of the Perfect Tie at the presidential level, the elections for U.S. Congress and state governments were equally indicative of the divisions in the nation. For the first time since 1881, the U.S. Senate was evenly divided between the two parties. In the U.S. House, the split was 221–212 in favor of the Republicans, giving them the smallest majority in that body since 1953. Even at the state level, partisan control of state legislatures was as closely split as possible. Republicans and Democrats each had full control of 17 state legislatures. The legislatures in the remaining 15 states were divided, with either a Republican House and Democratic Senate, a Democratic House and Republican Senate, or bodies that were literally tied between the two parties. Only among the governorships did either party hold a clear advantage. Here, the Republicans retained a 29–19 edge over the Democrats, with two independents.

In one sense, these results can be seen as a Republican victory: 2000 marked the fourth consecutive election in which the GOP held control of both houses of Congress.[1] Republicans were in a much stronger position at the state level than they were after the last pre-redistricting election in 1990. Furthermore, Republicans attained these results less than two years after many pundits (and more than a few Democrats) had declared them doomed as a result of public backlash against impeachment. At the same time, however, the 2000 election was the third consecutive election in which Democrats gained seats in the U.S. House. The Democrats in 2000 also defeated five incumbent Republican senators, completely eliminating the once strong Republican majority in that body. Another such victory, and the Republicans will be in the minority.

Interestingly, the close congressional division was in certain respects a consequence of, or was at least related to, the close presidential contest.

Coattails did not seem to be a factor except perhaps in a few races, and even then the effects were not unidirectional. Gore might have provided slight coattails for Democrats in some races, mostly in the Senate, while some slight Bush coattails outside of urban areas might have helped hold down net Republican losses in the House. More importantly, unlike in 1996, the very closeness of the presidential race right up to election day made it difficult for voters to swing decisively toward one congressional party or the other as a calculated counterweight to the probable presidential winner.

The Strategic Environment at the Beginning of the Congressional Campaign

A major part of the story of the 2000 congressional and state elections is the recovery of the congressional Republican Party from its public relations debacles of the winter of 1998–99. As the race for 2000 began immediately after the 1998 midterms, at least four interrelated factors favored the Democrats in their pursuit of congressional control. First was the previous unwillingness of the Republicans to drop impeachment charges against the president. Not only did most House Republicans genuinely consider Clinton guilty of acting outside the law, but many also understood the importance that the issue held to their conservative Christian base. But the Democrats counterattacked. Taking advantage of widespread public weariness with the Monica Lewinsky scandal, Democrats sought to portray Republicans as rigid, out of touch, extreme, and mean-spirited. Additionally, for every Democrat and independent voter who was angry at the impeachment spectacle, there was a Republican somewhere who was just as frustrated with the Republicans in the Senate for failing to vigorously press the case against the president. No one was happy. These sentiments combined to produce low public approval ratings for Congress as an institution, which registered at only 41 percent favorable in February 1999. In essence, Republicans gambled that the public would come around to their point of view. Democrats, on the other hand, had reason to hope that the unpleasant aftertaste of impeachment would linger. It was even reported that Bill Clinton, bent on revenge, planned to target the 13 House impeachment managers for political extinction.

Secondly, as the 105th Congress drew to a close, it appeared (and *appeared* is the key word) that Bill Clinton controlled the agenda. Budget negotiations in October 1998 concluded in what was widely interpreted as a Clinton victory, as the president used the implied threat of a government shutdown to gain funds for some of his top priorities, including a down payment on the hiring of 100,000 additional teachers. Conscious of having been labeled too confrontational during the 1995–96 government shutdowns, congressional Republicans may have overcompensated by acquiescing too much. They were so wary of facing another crisis that any threat of an impasse led to instant retreat. If we look at the larger picture, however, it is not clear that Clinton had gained anything other than a small tactical victory. Nevertheless, the budget collapse by the Republicans was viewed by many activists to be part of a demoralizing pattern stretching back at least to 1996. Democrats were given fresh reason to believe that Bill Clinton, despite his troubles, had not lost his golden touch.

These first two factors converged in the third: Republican losses in the midterm elections of November 1998. Throughout 1998, Republicans and many nonpartisan analysts had predicted the GOP might gain 10 to 15 House seats and a handful of Senate seats that year. In early October, shortly after release of the Starr Report, some Republicans, including House Speaker Newt Gingrich, claimed that Republicans might gain as many as 30 to 40 House seats. Real prospects also existed for Republicans to gain 5 seats in the Senate, enough to attain a filibuster-proof majority of 60 seats. But when the votes were actually counted on election day, Republicans had lost 5 House seats and made no gains in the Senate. Not since 1934 had the party controlling the White House actually *gained* seats in the U.S. House in a midterm election. Subsequent analysis showed that Democratic successes were a result of increased turnout by black voters and organized labor, who were mobilized largely in reaction to impeachment. In particular, a last-minute decision by Gingrich to air television ads trying to capitalize on the Clinton scandal almost certainly backfired. On the other hand, turnout of Republicans and conservatives was down, which some attributed to the collapse of the party's position in the budget talks a few weeks earlier.[2]

The 1998 elections appeared to hurt Republicans' hopes for 2000 in a variety of ways. Most obviously, their House majority was narrowed at a time when they should have been able to count on a modest increase, meaning that Democrats needed to gain far fewer seats than expected to take control in 2000. The difference between the 15 seats the Republicans hoped to gain (with good reason, given historical precedent) and the 5 seats they actually lost, meant that the gap between the parties going into 2000 was some 40 votes smaller than many Republicans expected. The Republicans' inability to expand their Senate majority in 1998, while less remarked upon, was no less portentous. With no seat pickups in 1998, there was no buffer against probable Republican losses among the large crop of marginal 1994 Republican senators up for reelection in 2000. In the short term, the unexpected Democratic victories in 1998 gave that party momentum. Democrats were confident and on the offensive. They were well positioned on the ascendant issues, and could use their 1998 successes to raise the necessary sums to compete two years later.

Finally, the combination of the election debacle of 1998 and the ongoing impeachment saga precipitated a leadership upheaval within the Republican conference, the fourth factor pointing to trouble for Republicans in 2000. Within 48 hours of election day, Newt Gingrich resigned as Speaker, leaving the way open for House Appropriations Committee Chairman Robert Livingston of Louisiana to take over control of the House. But before Livingston even had an opportunity to officially become Speaker, he too resigned when an old extramarital affair became public on the eve of the House's impeachment vote. Thus, in a strange way, Clinton's shenanigans brought down not one, but two, Republican House Speakers, while Clinton himself survived.

Altogether, then, by February 1999, the congressional Republicans were in disarray. Their public image was in tatters. Their leadership was in chaos. Their legislative strategy was in question. Their majority was narrowed, and their opponents were on the march.

The Republican Recovery

The recovery of the congressional Republicans from this low point was, in certain respects, not difficult to foresee, though it was rarely predicted. Key long-term factors, such as the underlying distribution of partisan and ideological loyalties within the electorate, and incumbency advantages in congressional contests, had not fundamentally changed after 1998. Most of the Republicans' troubles, in fact, were the consequence of short-term factors, such as flawed leadership and poor tactical decisions, that were within the Republicans' own control. Being the victims of self-inflicted and short-term wounds did not, of course, mean the Republicans would automatically recover in time for the 2000 elections. But it did mean that recovery was possible.

The Republican turnaround began as the public wrath against the Republicans' position on impeachment subsided. The Republicans' gamble in a sense appeared to pay off. A year after the trial, the percentage of Americans who approved of the impeachment vote in the House had grown from a definite minority of 37 percent to a small plurality of 50 percent, although most Americans still said the Senate was right not to remove Clinton.[3] What's more, by late 1999 the passions of those on both sides of the impeachment struggle had cooled, as issues like gun control, tax cuts, and HMO reform returned to center stage. Democrats, who had earlier threatened to mount a full-scale assault on the House impeachment managers, could not even find challengers in some of their districts, and quickly toned down their rhetoric.

Within this framework, Republicans set out to repair the other damage of their own making. One of the most important decisions was the selection of the new House Speaker, seven-term veteran Representative Dennis Hastert of Illinois. While Hastert was unknown outside of Washington, he had the perfect pedigree for uniting the party. He was well liked and respected by moderates and conservatives in the Republican caucus, and he was a protégé of Bob Michel of Illinois, the mild-mannered former Minority Leader, as well as the more confrontational and conservative current Majority Whip, Tom DeLay of Texas. Hastert lacked Newt Gingrich's flamboyance, but the very qualities that made it possible for Gingrich to take power arguably made it impossible for him to exercise it effectively. Hastert's different, less visible and less confrontational, style of leadership was perhaps a better way to lead the House. Though he came under early criticism from some Republicans who feared he was not aggressive enough, Hastert quickly scored high marks for unifying House Republicans and demonstrating tactical acumen. *Congressional Quarterly* reported that the new Speaker's "patient, team-building style inspired remarkable loyalty."[4] This understated style did have a downside; in July 2000, a year and a half after he became Speaker, fully 67 percent of Americans still did not recognize the Speaker's name.[5] But, as Republican Congressman John Linder of Georgia noted, "We don't have any of the real highs and real lows [of the Gingrich era, either]. That's good."[6]

With the Republican leadership situation stabilized, congressional Republicans fought Bill Clinton to a draw in most respects during the remainder of 1999 and in 2000. In 1999, they passed a large across-the-board tax cut that was vetoed but allowed them to go on the offensive for the first time since 1996.[7] In repassing particularly popular portions of that tax cut, including the abolition of the estate tax and the "marriage penalty," the Republicans forced even more difficult vetoes from President Clinton. They also won a round against the president, passing a repeal of the Social Security earnings cap—in essence, cutting taxes for the elderly. This was a position that not even Clinton dared oppose.

Republicans also succeeded in turning President Clinton's tactical brilliance against him in a form of political jujitsu. In 1999, to defuse calls for larger tax cuts, Clinton had declared his intention to effectively lower the size of the available budget surplus by cordoning off the portion of it coming from excess Social Security revenue. During the budget fight of 1999, Republicans accepted this proposal and made it their own. They then promptly pointed out that Clinton's own spending requests encroached on that same limit. In the end, the Republicans used this fact to block some of Clinton's additional proposals and even forced him to accept a small across-the-board cut in discretionary spending.

The improvement in the Republican position can also be seen by comparing public responses to a poll question asked during the annual budget dustup in 1998 and in 1999. In November 1998, a Gallup poll found that, by a slim 43 to 40 percent margin, the public believed the policies of the congressional Republicans represented the right direction for the country. This might be considered a positive result, except for the fact that the public approved of Clinton's policies by a 70 to 22 percent margin. Less than a year later, however, in October 1999, the Republicans dramatically strengthened their position, both absolutely and relative to the president. Evaluations of Clinton's policies fell to 60 percent positive as against 35 percent negative, while the Republicans' image improved to a margin of 54 percent positive to 35 percent negative. In one year, a 27-point gap favoring Clinton's positions on issues was reduced to a 6-point gap, with each side in 1999 having equal numbers of negative responses.[8]

Throughout 2000, Republicans feared that Clinton would engineer another budget crisis, including a government shutdown, as an "October surprise" to help Al Gore and Democratic congressional candidates. In the end, no such thing happened. This dog did not bite for two main reasons. First, the government stayed open partly because congressional Republicans had earlier in the year acceded to many of Clinton's original budget requests. Second, there was no shutdown, despite Clinton's calls for additional spending in the fall, because of the Republicans' strengthened position. Rather than either accept the bait of a confrontation or cave into Clinton, Republicans simply passed a series of continuing resolutions funding the government at current levels until after election day. The headway George W. Bush was making in his campaign against the atmosphere of bitter partisanship of the Clinton years gave Republicans added leverage. A confrontation provoked by the president might have boomeranged, hurting Gore more than the Republicans. The weapon of the budget, used so successfully against the Republicans in 1996, was largely neutralized in late 2000.

Taking a broader view, the congressional Republicans in 1999–2000 were able to dispose of most of Bill Clinton's high-priority agenda without suffering too much criticism for being obstructionist or a "do-nothing"

Congress. *Congressional Quarterly* reported, "None of the major initiatives in [Clinton's] State of the Union address—overhauling Social Security and Medicare, raising the minimum wage, tightening regulation of health maintenance organizations (HMOs), or raising tobacco-related revenue—became law. Few ever came up for a vote."[9] Congress also refused to pass the president's campaign finance proposal or gun control plan (even in the wake of the Columbine High School shooting), rejected the Comprehensive Nuclear Test Ban Treaty, and stopped most of the rest of Clinton's laundry list of new federal programs outlined in his 1999 and 2000 State of the Union addresses. Altogether, Clinton's congressional support score fell to 37.8 percent in 1999, the second lowest percentage in the 47 years *Congressional Quarterly* has been calculating such scores (the lowest was also held by Clinton for 1995, the first year of the Republican Congress).[10]

Sometimes Republicans sought cover for voting against the president by operating behind the curtain of bicameralism. The House, but not the Senate, passed HMO legislation and campaign finance reform, while gun control passed in the Senate, but not in the House. Undesirable but popular proposals were also buried in the obscure graveyard of conference committees. Amendments were offered allowing vulnerable members to obtain political cover without fundamentally changing the outcome. Some Republicans were even able to run reelection campaigns partially on HMO reform and other "Democratic" issues. In other words, Republicans adopted many of the same legislative tactics that Democrats had developed to help maintain their pre-1994 majorities amid the ebb and flow of public opinion.

The Republicans also benefited from the general contentment of the nation. They could plausibly argue that they were due as much credit for the generally good economic times as the Democratic administration. Indeed, some wore the "do-nothing" label as a badge of honor, hearkening back to the old colonial saw that "no man's life, liberty, or property is safe as long as the legislature is in session." Above all, Republicans benefited from, and used to their advantage, the politics of the Perfect Tie: however popular some of Clinton's proposals may have been in the polls, there was no groundswell of opinion demanding them, and Clinton was unable or unwilling to exert himself to try to create such a groundswell. In an environment in which action breeds reaction, and in which competing negative coalitions mobilize in response to any significant threat to the status quo, the congressional Republicans arguably made a virtue out of necessity. In 1999–2000, they concluded that the best offense was a good defense.

At the same time, congressional Democrats calculated, gambled, and ended up losing. Confident of victory in 2000, they seemed to have adopted (though not publicly) a strategy of holding out for everything at the risk of ending up with nothing. As one senior White House official intimated, House Democrats were "not of a mind to get too many accomplishments."[11] Consequently, compromises that might have been possible on issues like gun control, HMOs, or prescription drugs were never consummated. While these issues remained legislatively alive after November 7, there could be little doubt that Democrats were in a weaker position to pursue them than they were at many points during the 106th Congress.

The 2000 Campaign

While the broader context of political conditions gradually moved in the direction of the Republicans, there was a narrower campaign context that largely favored the Democrats. The Democratic advantages were to be found in the situation of retirements in the House, in a form of the "six-year itch" in the Senate, and in the unequal success in fund-raising efforts.

Because of the power of House incumbency, the potential for parties to pick up seats is closely tied to the occurrence of "open seats," or districts in which the incumbent has chosen to retire. In 1994 and 1996, the retirement picture strongly favored Republicans and contributed to their takeover and then maintenance of House control. In 1998, House open seats were evenly divided between Republicans and Democrats. But in 2000, there were many more Republicans retiring (26) than Democrats (only 9), raising the possibility of large Democratic gains in formerly Republican districts.[12]

This disparity was partly the consequence of Democratic efforts, spearheaded by House Minority Leader Richard Gephardt and Democratic Congressional Campaign Committee (DCCC) Chairman Patrick Kennedy, to dissuade numerous Democratic House members from retiring in 2000 with the promise of achieving majority status, and the Chairmanships and perks that senior members receive from it. Indeed, "the minority leader personally pleaded with a collection of senior Democrats to postpone retirement to take one more shot at the GOP."[13] Even Tom Davis, head of the National Republican Congressional Committee, conceded that Democrats did a "good job disciplining their members to stay where they are."[14]

By contrast the number of Republicans who chose to retire or run for other office was the largest since 1958. In some cases, members of the class of 1994, who campaigned on a self-imposed six-year term limit that came due in 2000, made those decisions. In other cases, more senior members faced a Republican conference rule, instituted in 1995, that limited committee chairs to six years, making a continued career in the House less attractive. Many members decided to move on to other pastures, some private and some political, instead of taking a lower-ranked position on another committee. Of the 26 Republicans leaving the House, 6 had been elected in 1994 and another 8 had been committee or subcommittee chairs, including Bill Archer of Texas (Ways and Means), Tom Bliley of Virginia (Commerce), William Goodling of Pennsylvania (Education and the Workforce), and John Kasich of Ohio (Budget), who left to run for president. It is ironic (or perhaps fitting) that the issue of term limits—hot in 1994 but moribund in 2000—threatened to hurt most the Republicans, who had benefited from it six years earlier.

Overall, however, the threat posed to the House GOP by retirements was often overstated. As it turned out, the partisan and demographic makeup of most of the open seat districts made them essentially noncompetitive. NRCC head Tom Davis declared (a bit too optimistically) that Republicans were only concerned about three of the Republican open seats. Nationally, coming into 2000, there were perhaps no more than 30 truly competitive House races.[15] GOP losses in 1996 and 1998 meant that many of the most vulnerable Republican House members elected unexpectedly in 1994 had already been defeated.

In the Senate, most analysts considered the Republican majority secure. In August 1999, Charles Cook, editor of the *Cook Report*, argued that Republicans "couldn't lose their majority in the Senate if they tried."[16] But there were 19 Republican seats up for election in 2000, compared to only 15 Democratic seats. More to the point, the GOP faced the hidden danger of the "six-year itch," in a modified form. The "six-year itch" is the appellation usually given to the tendency of the president's party to lose a large number of Senate seats in his second midterm election (six years after gaining office). In essence, the theory goes, the national momentum reflected in the president's original election coattails produces a bumper crop of Senate victories, many by marginal candidates who could not have won on their own. Six years later, when they have to run without a national tide to support them, many lose.[17]

The itch bothering Republicans in 2000 was a little different. The Republican Senate majority did not owe its victory to presidential coattails, but instead to a swelling antipresidential sentiment in the 1994 midterm elections. The same principle, however, applied. After the tide receded, a number of vulnerable Republicans were in danger of being left high and dry. These included Senators Rick Santorum of Pennsylvania, Spencer Abraham of Michigan, Rod Grams of Minnesota, and John Ashcroft of Missouri. A few senior Republican senators, such as Slade Gorton of

Washington, Conrad Burns of Montana, and William Roth of Delaware, also appeared vulnerable, having won reelection in 1994 due heavily to the anti-Clinton surge.

The Democrats were in a better situation with far fewer weak incumbents to defend. Only Virginia's Democratic Senator Charles Robb seemed vulnerable, and only a couple of the Democratic retirements presented a chance for an open seat pickup. In Nevada, Republicans hoped that former Congressman John Ensign, who lost a 1998 Senate bid by about 400 votes, would succeed the second time around to fill a seat vacated by Democrat Richard Bryan. And in New York, all eyes were fixed on Daniel Patrick Moynihan's retirement, which set up a potentially riveting (although ultimately abortive) race between First Lady Hillary Clinton and New York City Mayor Rudolph Giuliani. As one Republican noted, "We've beat all the easy ones," as all of the Democrats up for reelection in 2000 had already survived their toughest challenge in 1994.[18]

In terms of candidate quality—widely defined as political experience and fund-raising capacity—the Democrats in 2000 seemed to have an advantage in the key Senate races and fielded a fairly strong crop of candidates in the House. In the Senate in particular, the Democrats continued to pursue their previous strategy of putting forward independently wealthy, and therefore self-financing, candidates. In New Jersey, Jon Corzine, former head of the Goldman Sachs investment firm, spent $30 million, most of it his own money, to win his primary against a well-known former governor. He then went on to spend another $30 million to defeat Republican Congressman Bob Franks in the general election. In Minnesota, Mark Dayton, heir of the Dayton-Hudson fortune, spent $10 million of his personal fortune against Republican Rod Grams. Finally, in Washington State, millionaire Internet executive (and former one-term House member) Maria Cantwell took on Republican Slade Gorton, committing more than $5 million of her own funds to that race. In other contests, Democrats relied on big-name political figures who had already won statewide election at least once. Popular Governors Mel Carnahan of Missouri and Thomas Carper of Delaware, former Governor Ben Nelson of Nebraska, and state Insurance Commissioner Bob Nelson of Florida all had statewide name recognition and experienced political organizations backing them.

Aggressive fund-raising by Democratic campaign committees also gave the Democrats an early monetary advantage over the Republicans for the first time since the Democrats lost majority status in 1994. By mid-2000, the DCCC had raised nearly $30 million, compared to the only $16 million raised by their Republican counterpart, the National Republican Congressional Committee (NRCC). By the end of the campaign, the DCCC had raised a record $84 million, much of it from business donors who might have preferred Republicans, but were hedging their bets. In 1997–98, business and corporate associations gave nearly two-thirds of their House election contributions to Republicans. By July 2000, however, their giving was about evenly divided, with the DCCC holding a slight edge,[19] and by September 2000, at least 21 large political action committees that had given at least 75 percent of their House campaign donations to Republicans in the 1997–98 election cycle had fallen below that mark for the 1999–2000 cycle.[20] DCCC Chairman Patrick Kennedy declared, "This is happening because of the very real perception that we're about to take the House back."[21] A big push at the end allowed the NRCC to catch up with and surpass DCCC fund-raising, but for most of 2000, House Democrats were well positioned. At the same time, the Democratic Senatorial Campaign Committee (DSCC) out-raised and out-spent its Republican counterpart.[22] Additionally, major groups favoring Democrats, especially the AFL-CIO, spent tens of millions more than comparable groups favoring the Republicans.

The six-year Senate itch combined with strong Democratic candidate recruitment to put the Democrats in a good position to compete for Senate control, though it took analysts a long time to perceive that it was the Senate rather than the House where GOP control was shakiest. As the campaign for Congress unfolded, most speculation centered on whether the Democrats would make good on their promise to seize control of the House. Only after the July 2000 death of Georgia's Republican Senator Paul Coverdell, and the appointment of popular Democrat Zell Miller to replace him, did talk of eliminating the now 54–46 GOP majority seriously begin. Republicans stabilized their prospects in the House by targeting Democratic open seats and capitalizing on their improved public standing. In October 2000, 49 percent of Americans approved of Congress, compared to 42 percent who disapproved—a complete reversal from February of 1999, when Congress had a paltry 41 percent approval, 53 percent disapproval rating. What's more, after trailing for most of the summer and early fall, House Republicans in mid-October established a modest lead in the Gallup poll's generic House vote question.[23]

Just when the Democratic drive in the House appeared to be stalling, Republican vulnerability in the Senate burst into the open. By early October, Democrats spoke openly about the possibility of Senate control, though it remained a long shot. Democrats had to win almost every close race against a Republican incumbent and not lose any of their own seats, but such an outcome suddenly seemed within reach. Even on election day, no one could predict with certainty who would gain control of either house of Congress.

The lack of any national theme and the apparent disconnection of the congressional races from the presidential election contributed to what analyst Bob Benenson called "the most amorphous—and unpredictable—congressional campaign in recent memory."[24] Since the 1800s, the typical pattern of American politics was for a party's congressional fortunes to wax or wane with the fortunes of its presidential candidate. This once-strong phenomenon of "coattails" meant that presidential and congressional party wings, like magnets properly oriented, pursued a strategy of "attraction," pushing similar themes, running national campaigns, and rising or falling together. As the twentieth century wore on, however, a new kind of model emerged. This model posited a separation between the presidential and congressional campaigns, as if the magnets were simply placed too far apart from each other to exert a significant pull. It often took the form of a strong incumbent president hoping to remain above the lowly fortunes of his copartisans in the congressional minority, or of a congressional majority seeking to avoid the undertow of a sinking presidential nominee. This separation has therefore not usually been a strategy embraced by a whole party. Rather, it is advanced by whichever faction is stronger, hoping to avoid being pulled down by the weaker partner.

In 1996 the parties experimented with a third strategy of "repulsion," as the presidential candidates and their congressional parties appearing like two magnets wrongly oriented and hence actively pushing each other away. One of Bill Clinton's key campaign themes was built around the assumption of continued Republican congressional control, as Clinton called on Americans to reelect him to check Newt Gingrich. Once congressional Republicans were sure that Clinton was going to win, they turned this argument around, using Bob Dole's weakness as a reason for voters to reelect a GOP Congress, saying in effect, "Don't give Bill Clinton a blank check." However well the strategy of "repulsion" might fit with the modern American preference for divided government, it can only be used under certain circumstances. Voters have to know—or at least think that they know—who will control either the presidency or the Congress in order for a party to call for support in one body as a check against a sure win for the other party in the other institution. Alberto Alesina and Howard Rosenthal argue that it is this certainty about control of the presidency that accounts for the tendency of the president's party to lose seats in midterm elections.[25] A looming presidential landslide can have the same effect. A clear presidential winner shows swing voters which congressional party they must vote for in order to maintain partisan balance in government. But in 2000 the conditions necessary for such a voter calculation, let alone for conscious strategies of repulsion by the parties, did not exist. In fact, the 40 percent of voters indicating a preference for divided government in 2000 split their votes evenly between the Republican and Democratic congressional candidates, perhaps due to the inability to judge which candidate or party was actually in the lead for either the presidency or the Congress.[26]

It is clear that the traditional model of attraction cannot be used to describe the 2000 campaign. Neither Al Gore nor George W. Bush made a conscious effort to highlight his congressional party. Gore was never popular in Congress, even among Democrats, and he did not necessarily want to highlight the parade of far-left Democrats in line for House committee chairmanships. For his part, Bush was from the gubernatorial, rather than the congressional, wing of the Republican Party and he did not wish to be too closely associated with either congressional leaders or with Washington in general. Bush was once even reported to have ducked out a side door after a meeting with Republican congressional leaders, rather than risk being photographed with them. Journalists Cokie and Steven V. Roberts remarked as the campaign drew to a close, "There is a reason neither presidential candidate is saying anything about electing a Congress of his party—it would scare the voters."[27]

Consequently, because the attraction model and the repulsion model do not come close to explaining the 2000 campaign, only the model of separation will do. Even then, it was a novel form of separation, practiced equally by both components of both parties—not heavily by one of the two institutions against the other. Indeed, one would be hard-pressed to think of another instance when all actors separated themselves from the fate of their copartisans as uniformly and as completely as in 2000, without actually running away from them. This nonadversarial separation of the presidential and congressional campaigns was helped by the substantially fragmented nature of the national presidential campaigns. Both Bush and Gore crafted individualized messages for local delivery in many of the key swing states, and largely ignored the other states. It is therefore not always clear that there could be a coherent national message to which congressional campaigns could easily attach themselves, even if one was desired. Adding to this separation of campaigns, the congressional parties did not run well-coordinated races with their presidential nominees. Congressional Republicans, who had hoped in 1999 that Bush would have long coattails, concluded by the end of the primary season that he would likely have none. Most Republican congressional candidates shied away from Bush's tax cut and Social Security plans, though many may have supported them privately. Tom Davis, Republican campaign chairman, pointed out that Republican candidates deliberately ran "highly localized campaigns tailored to each district's demographics and political predilections."[28] In the Rhode Island

Senate race, for example, the National Republican Senatorial Committee even bankrolled an advertisement for Lincoln Chafee praising him for "voting against his own party for a patient's bill of rights."[29] Democrats had somewhat greater unity on issues, but hardly on themes: Al Gore's decision to wage a "fight" against everything "big" (except of course Big Government) was echoed in few districts, and his vocal support for gun control and unrestricted abortion was a liability in much of nonurban America. The upshot was separation writ large. Congressional candidates were on their own, and for the most part, that is the way they wanted it.

In the end, the Republicans in 2000 lost only two House seats, retaining a majority of 221–212 with two independents. One of those independents is, however, actually a gain for the Republicans. Former conservative Democrat Virgil Goode of Virginia abandoned his party partway through the 106th Congress. He promptly endorsed Republicans for state and national office, and joined the Republican caucus in the House. Additionally, another Democrat, James Traficant of Ohio, voted for Dennis Hastert as Speaker in January 2001, signaling his deep disaffection with his own party, and prompting his removal from the Democratic caucus. In the end, the Democratic drive to exact vengeance on the House impeachment managers also fell far short. Of the 13 Republican members targeted, only two lost their next election. Jim Rogan of California was defeated in a race that would have been very difficult with or without impeachment, due to the Democratic registration advantage in his district; and Bill McCollum, trying to move up from the House to the Senate, lost his election bid in Florida to a better-known and more popular Democrat (Bill Nelson). The race would also have been difficult for McCollum regardless of his impeachment participation. Altogether, Republicans won 49.2 percent of the national House vote to the Democrats' 47.9 percent, a slight improvement for the GOP over its 1998 performance.[30]

Republicans held on by aggressively attacking Democratic open seats and a few vulnerable incumbents, especially in the East. Republicans captured 6 of 9 Democratic open seats, while holding on to 20 of their own 26. There was little anti-incumbent mood, as only two Democratic and four Republican House incumbents were defeated. This marked the smallest number of Republican incumbents defeated since 1988 (if one excludes the abnormal year of 1994, when none lost). Including the three incumbents who lost primaries earlier in the year (but not including retirements) the House as a whole had a 97.8 percent incumbent retention rate in 2000.[31] The number of incoming House freshmen, 41, equaled the number elected in 1998, but represented a much smaller class than was elected in 1992 (110), 1994 (86), or 1996 (89). Not least, Republicans were helped by several narrow victories, including four of the five races so close that recounts had not determined the winner a week later.[32] As David Plouffe, executive director of the DCCC, explained, "We lost a lot of very close races."[33]

Exit polls showed that House Republicans won among all men (54–44), white men (59–38), those aged 30–44 who came of age in the Reagan years (50–47), married people with children (57–41), independents (49–46), 1996 Perot voters (64–30), gun owners (60–39), Protestants (56–42), white Catholics (52–46), and people across faiths who attend religious services regularly. They also won the votes of the 53 percent of the electorate who said government should do less rather than more by a margin of 69–28. Republicans did best in the South (55–43) and worst in the Northeast (40–56), and were roughly even with Democrats in the Midwest and West. In each of these areas, the Republican House vote was not significantly different in 2000 than it had been in 1996 or 1998, although the GOP gained a net 3 points among white men and a net 4 points among Catholics compared to 1998.[34] While 70 percent said Bill Clinton was not a factor in their votes, the remainder said by nearly a two-to-one margin that they were voting "to oppose Clinton," and 85 percent of these voted for Republican House candidates. Finally, Republicans held solid majorities among the 7 in 9 voters who believed the economy would be the same or worse one year from now. Additionally, in another sign that partisan loyalties remained high in 2000, about 85 percent of Bush and Gore supporters voted for House and presidential candidates of the same party, while only about 12 percent split their tickets.

In the Senate, the Democrats made a net pickup of four seats, bringing them into a 50–50 split. In this case, however, 50–50 was a tie mathematically, but not politically. The Democrats needed 51 members to keep the Republicans from controlling the chamber, because when Bush won, so did Republican vice presidential candidate Dick Cheney. Constitutionally, the vice president is the presiding officer of the Senate and is entitled to cast a vote in the event of a tie. Had Gore won, Senate Democrats would also have been out of luck. In order to assume the vice presidency, Joseph Lieberman would have had to resign from his Connecticut Senate seat. Connecticut's Republican governor would then have appointed Lieberman's replacement, giving the Republicans a 51–49 edge. Indeed, some Democrats privately blasted Lieberman for refusing to give up his Senate seat to run for vice president on the theory that Democrats would have won the seat with another nominee.

Nevertheless, in 2000, the Democrats came closer to holding the majority in the Senate than almost anyone was willing to predict, even a few months before. They defeated five of the six incumbent Republicans they had heavily targeted—Roth of Delaware, Grams of Minnesota, Gorton of

Washington, Abraham of Michigan, and Ashcroft of Missouri, while only Burns of Montana survived. They also took away a Republican open seat in Florida, while giving up only two seats of their own: incumbent Virginia Senator Charles Robb, who lost to popular former Governor George Allen, and the Nevada open seat won by Republican John Ensign.

There was a large number of unusually interesting Senate races in 2000. In New York, Hillary Clinton won by a margin that surprised many observers. She had long trailed Rudolph Giuliani until Giuliani dropped out in May due to a combination of marital woes and prostate cancer. Her new opponent, Long Island Congressman Rick Lazio, held his own for months until slipping behind in mid-October. He then seemed to stage something of a comeback, in no small part connected to Mideast troubles that resurrected the charge that Hillary Clinton was too friendly to the Palestinians. In the end, Clinton's star appeal, campaign strategy, and liberalism in one of America's most liberal states won out, with help from an unexpectedly good showing in traditionally Republican upstate New York.

In Missouri, the death of the Democratic nominee, Governor Mel Carnahan, in an October 16 airplane crash seemed at first to doom Democratic chances in the Senate. However, the new Democratic governor, Roger Wilson, promised to appoint Carnahan's widow Jean to the Senate seat if Carnahan received the most votes on election day. When she accepted that offer on October 30, she became the de facto Democratic nominee despite not appearing on the ballot. In the meantime, Ashcroft suspended his efforts altogether for eight days, and then shifted to a soft, positive campaign. When he lost by a 50–48 margin, he declined to contest the results, despite the legal question of whether a dead man could actually win an election, and despite charges of fraud coupled with a controversial decision by a judge to hold open the polls past the normal closing time in heavily Democratic St. Louis.

All three Democratic multimillionaires won, although two of the races were very close. Dayton in Minnesota, the only easy winner, captured 49 percent of the vote to 44 percent for Grams. Corzine in New Jersey broke the record for Senate campaigns by spending more than $60 million ($50 million of it his own), vastly outstripping Michael Huffington's previous record of $30 million in 1994. Despite outspending his opponent Bob Franks by a ratio of 10 to 1, Corzine only managed to win by 3 percent, 50 to 47. Finally, the Cantwell-Gorton race was the closest in the nation and the last outcome to be determined, as the vote totals shifted back and forth for three weeks between the two candidates. When the final absentee ballot was counted, Cantwell had won by 2,229 votes out of 2.4 million cast. It was Cantwell's seesaw victory that finally established that the Senate would be split 50–50.

Democrats tried mightily to claim a mandate from the results. An aide to Senate Democratic leader Thomas Daschle (S.Dak.) argued, "All these candidates ran and won on our issues. It is also a referendum on the failure [of Congress] to do anything."[35] There was also, as we will see below, some reason to believe that Al Gore helped at least a few of the Democratic upset winners in the Senate. On the other hand, the 50–50 split is hard to describe as a Democratic mandate or a referendum, especially in the context of Republican victories for the House and presidency. Republicans could (and did) make the case that the Senate outcome "reflected the idiosyncrasies of the candidates or their home states" more than they did the overall weakness of Republican issues in the electorate.[36]

Rarely have so many congressional elections depended so heavily on unpredictable factors outside of human control. If Al Gore had reason to curse a variety of flukes that might (or might not) have cost him victory in Florida, Senate Republicans had at least as much reason to rue the vagaries of fate that led to their losses. Had Senator Paul Coverdell not died unexpectedly in office, the net four-seat Democratic gain would have left Republicans in clear, though still tenuous, control. Would a living Mel Carnahan, who won by a narrow margin as a ghost, still have defeated John Ashcroft? Would Rudy Giuliani have beaten Hillary, had he not been struck by prostate cancer in mid-campaign? Would William Roth of Delaware have lost had the 79-year-old senator not fallen twice, once on television, reminding voters of his advanced age? Would Spencer Abraham have lost in Michigan had the United Auto Workers not written into their contract a provision making election day a paid holiday? Would Slade Gorton have gained the sliver of votes he needed in Washington had the networks not all but declared the race for Gore hours before polls on the West Coast had closed? In the end, of course, these questions—though tantalizing—were irrelevant. Unable to demand a hand recount of death certificates, unwilling to pursue a court order to revote in Missouri or Washington, Republicans had to live with their luck. Nor should the flurry of odd circumstances obscure the fact that Republican losses in 2000 were not terribly surprising after the high number of unexpected Republican victories in 1994. In a sense, the Senate merely returned to a type of equilibrium. But rarely has equilibrium meant such exact equality.

The Congressional Results and Presidential Coattails

It might seem absurd to address the question of presidential coattails in the 2000 election. The winning presidential candidate did not lead the national popular vote, shifts in Congress were relatively small, and there was little attempt by either party to fashion a coherent national campaign. Yet beneath the surface, there was some connection—though a confused one—between the presidential results and the congressional results. It is probable that several Democratic Senate candidates were pulled over the finish line as an incidental by-product of "get out the vote" efforts by organized labor and minority groups on behalf of Al Gore. In the eight key Democratic wins—the six pickups plus the open seat victories in New Jersey and New York—Gore ran ahead of his party's Senate candidate in four contests. Moreover, three of these four were among the closest Senate races in 2000: Maria Cantwell's 0.09 percentage point margin of victory in Washington state, Debbie Stabenow's 49–48 percent victory over incumbent Spencer Abraham in Michigan, and Jon Corzine's narrow victory over Republican Bob Franks in New Jersey. In that race, Franks himself attributed his narrow loss to Gore's 16-point blowout of Bush in the Garden State.[37] This claim has some merit, as Gore's last-minute rise in the polls seems to have transferred momentum to Democratic Senate candidates. As late as one week before election day, *Congressional Quarterly* rated only Florida and Minnesota leaning Democratic, while Delaware, Michigan, Missouri, and Washington were rated as having "no clear favorite."[38] The Democrats eventually won all of them.

Gore's surge also appeared to help Democrats in the House, as a 5-point Republican lead in the Gallup poll's generic House ballot evaporated the weekend before election day.[39] In addition, Gore's crushing victory in California probably helped prevent a net loss of Democratic seats in that body. The Democrats picked up 5 House seats in the Golden State, including three of the four Republican incumbents defeated nationwide. Nevertheless, House Democrats widely blamed Gore for their inability to make the overall inroads they expected. Some blamed Al Gore for distancing himself too much from Clinton, while others blamed him for not distancing himself enough. Some relatively conservative Democrats cited Gore's position on gun control for their losses in Kentucky, Florida, and West Virginia. Others pointed out more generally that Gore's intense focus on urban voters left Democratic candidates in rural and suburban areas without the support they needed.[40] While Democrats won the urban House vote 62–36 percent, they lost both the critical suburbs 48–50 percent, and rural areas 37–59 percent.[41]

These two strains of argument—that Gore helped Democrats in the Senate and hurt Democrats in the House—might seem impossibly contradictory, but they are not. Indeed, this outcome bears a resemblance to the structure of the presidential election. In the Electoral College, since popular votes are not transferable across state boundaries, a candidate is better off winning by small margins in many states than by large margins in a small number of states. An imbalanced distribution of votes can give one candidate the lead in the popular vote while he is losing in the Electoral College. Likewise, in congressional elections, Democrats could win a state by padding their urban margins, hence winning the Senate seat, without affecting the outcome in the rest of the state, and hence many of the state's House districts. The urban margins for Democrats created by labor and minorities contributed to statewide totals but could not cross district lines.

In Gore's case, his appeal needed to be broader to boost House Democrats, not just deeper in the already Democratic urban areas. Yet a look at the electoral map shows Gore lost nearly four-fifths of the counties in the United States. By choosing to play to his base, Gore made more difficult the kind of broad-reaching success that could deliver both the House and the Electoral College. As it was, 63 House Democrats compared to only 34 Republicans won with more than 75 percent of the vote in 2000. Conversely, while only 79 Democrats won with less than 65 percent of the vote, 110 Republicans did.[42] Taken together, these differences indicate a broader distribution of Republican House votes compared to Democratic House votes in 2000. If this analysis is correct, it might be possible to speak of slight Bush coattails in the House, manifested not as seats gained, but as a better performance than expected; to blame Gore's weakness outside of urban America is another way of crediting Bush's strength there.

The 2000 election confirmed what many already suspected: that significant presidential coattails are now the exception rather than the rule. Indeed, winning presidential parties have lost seats in the House and/or Senate in the last four presidential elections. Not since 1980, when Ronald Reagan's Republicans gained 33 House seats and 12 Senate seats—enough to win outright control of the Senate and working control of the House— have serious coattails really been evident. This weakening of presidential coattails has coincided with, and is perhaps related to, a long-term weakening of the midterm election pattern. Even excluding 1998, when the president's party actually picked up seats, most recent midterms have shown lower than average shifts against the president's party. The 1994 election, which saw a large swing against Democrats, would have been not at all unusual 50 or 100 years ago, but today it stands as something of an exception.

There are several possible explanations for the fact that the formerly common congressional swings have only taken place once in a presidential year (1980) and once in a midterm year (1994) over the last two decades. One is that the growing power of congressional incumbency has insulated Congress from wild electoral swings most of the time. Only when public frustrations reach a boiling point do large swings break through this institutional defense. It may also be that national conditions have not provided fertile ground for frequent, large changes in Congress. The peace and prosperity enjoyed by America for most of the past 20 years have bred a certain electoral contentment. Another explanation is that the low seat shifts in recent congressional elections have reinforced each other. As presidential coattails declined, fewer marginal in-party congressmen, vulnerable in the next midterm election, were elected. With fewer marginal seats, fewer incumbents are defeated. Finally, the predominance of divided government, occurring 18 out of the past 20 years, may have also contributed to stability in Congress. If there is truth to the argument that a small but decisive bloc of middle-ground voters deliberately choose divided government, there is no reason for them to bolster the presidential winner's party in Congress. Two years later, there is little reason for them to shift massively against the president's party, either, since his opponents already control Congress. (This interpretation helps explain 1994, the one midterm since 1980 in which the president's party did control Congress.) These are only some possible explanations, and needless to say, they are not mutually exclusive.

Congressional Prospects

Given the extremely close division in both houses of Congress, no one can say that the party majorities established on November 7, 2000, will necessarily endure until the 2002 midterm elections, especially in the Senate. A few untimely deaths, a party switch or two, or a handful of presidential appointments of members of Congress to executive positions could tip the balance against the Republicans, or further against the Democrats.

At this point, the outcome of the 2002 midterm elections is as unpredictable as it could be decisive. Favoring the Democrats in the Senate will be the fact that of the 34 seats now scheduled to be up for election, 20 are held by Republicans compared to only 14 by Democrats. In the House, all 435 seats will, as always, be up for election. Republicans are potentially vulnerable here as well, for more House Republicans won narrow victories than did Democrats in 2000. Democrats in both houses will have in their favor the midterm election pattern, where the incumbent party usually loses seats, though it is a more consistent pattern in the House than in the Senate. Democrats can now try to hold Republicans responsible for the operation of the entire government, just as Republicans held Democrats accountable to devastating effect in 1993 and 1994 (though this tack might be mitigated a bit by the power-sharing arrangement in the Senate). Finally, enduring anger among Democratic Party activists and donors over the presidential outcome of 2000 may fill campaign coffers and mobilize the vote. This anger and uncertainty will also make it tempting for congressional Democrats in 2001 and 2002 to delay and obstruct the new president in hopes of creating a disaster for which he will be blamed. Indeed, in the wake of the Democrats' failure to reclaim the House in 2000, some Democrats argued, "We just weren't mean and tough enough in defining what the Republicans were, what they really stood for, and why they can't get much done."[43]

Any bold predictions that fury will sweep Democrats to assured victory in 2002 are eerily similar to the equally bold predictions that anger over impeachment would doom congressional Republicans in 2000. And Republicans will have a few things going for them, as well. For one thing, if the Democrats do become too obstructionist and obsessively spiteful over Gore's loss, they will diminish themselves and make it easier for Bush to split their party and claim the center. Also, congressional Republicans will no longer face a skilled opposition president committed to using his considerable power to undermine their political position. Moreover, having lost House seats in the last three congressional elections, the number of vulnerable Republicans has dwindled. Additionally in the Republicans' favor, the midterm election pattern, as described above, has itself weakened, and by most accounts Republicans stand to make gains in the congressional redistricting process affecting the House in 2002.

It is also unlikely that the number of Republican open seats will outpace the number of Democratic open seats in 2002, owing to the passed deadline for self-imposed term limits of several 1994 freshman, and to the likely retirement of many Democrats who stayed in the House based on unfulfilled promises of majorities in 1996, 1998, and 2000. As *Congressional Quarterly* observed, "Before Election Day, even Democrats acknowledged that failing to retake the House this year could trigger a slew of retirements over the next two years."[44] For example, New York Democrat Charles Rangel, in line to become House Ways and Means Committee chairman, remarked that many of the same Democrats who had put off retirement in 2000 "would likely leave."[45] The most that can be said is that if the first two years of the Bush presidency are as disastrous as the first two years of the Clinton presidency, due either to self-inflicted wounds or external events, Democrats stand to make gains that would propel them into control of the Congress. If not, all bets are off.

State Elections

Even as congressional elections in 2000 tilted slightly toward the Democrats, elections at the state level tilted toward the Republicans. Because public attention was focused primarily on the presidential race and secondarily on Congress, the nationwide competition for governorships and state legislative seats escaped broad public notice almost entirely. This competition—featuring races for 11 governorships and 5,918 legislative seats—did not, however, escape the notice of the parties, which devoted considerable resources to improving their positions in the states.

The importance of these elections was obvious for two reasons. First, over the past 20 years, state governments and the principle of federalism have regained some of the ground lost in the centralizing period from the New Deal through the 1970s. As one analyst remarked, "Every important domestic policy innovation in the decade of the '90s has come from the states, and there is little indication that [it] will change" given the close partisan division of Congress.[46] Second, the state elections of 2000 had the potential to quite directly affect the party division in the U.S. House. Every state is faced with the decennial task of the redistricting of U.S. House seats that will affect the 2002 elections. The 2000 census results mandated that four states will gain two congressional seats (Arizona, Florida, Georgia, and Texas) and another four will gain one (California, Colorado, Nevada, and North Carolina), while two states lose two (New York and Pennsylvania) and eight states lose one each (Connecticut, Illinois, Indiana, Michigan, Mississippi, Ohio, Oklahoma, and Wisconsin). This shift largely reflects a continued movement of population from the Rust Belt to the Sun Belt.[47] Even in the remaining 32 states, where the number of House members will remain the same, new districts will have to be drawn to account for internal population shifts. In 44 states, state legislatures and governors are responsible for redistricting. That means that whichever party made gains at the state level in 2000 could, in theory, translate those gains into more House seats in 2002. In light of this fact, it is not surprising that each of the major parties plowed an estimated $2 million into state legislative races nationally.[48]

The Republicans lost one governorship in 2000, but retained a lead of 29–19 over the Democrats (with two independents). In the state legislatures, the Republicans made a net gain of about 70 seats nationwide, a modest figure given the number of seats at stake. Most of their gains came in the South and Midwest, though the Republicans also picked up 16 seats, enough for a newly minted majority, in the Vermont state House as part of a local backlash against the legislature's court-mandated bill allowing "civil unions" for homosexuals. More importantly to the congressional redistricting process, Republicans improved their relative position in terms of control of legislative bodies. Prior to the election, Democrats controlled 19 legislatures and Republicans 17, with 13 split (Nebraska's unicameral legislature is nonpartisan). After election day, each party controlled 17 legislatures with 15 split. Furthermore, Republicans completely control 13 state governments—including governor, state House, and state Senate—while the Democrats completely control just 9.[49]

Two facts about state elections in 2000 particularly stand out. First, the results show a minimal change in what was already a very close division in state legislatures. The politics of the Perfect Tie were very much in evidence. As scholar Alan Rosenthal argued, "We are in a period of competitive politics. . . . Two-thirds of the 99 legislative chambers are competitive. Either party can win."[50] At the end of the day, Democrats held 51.6 percent in state Senates and 51.9 percent in state Houses.[51] Kevin Mack, executive director of the Democratic Legislative Campaign Committee, said, "We fought this thing hard, and we fought it to a draw," a conclusion generally shared by Tom Hofeller of the Republican National Committee.[52] Or, as an analyst for the National Conference of State Legislatures put it, "The story was how successfully the two parties did in terms of protecting their majority in states they already held."[53]

Second, the other notable feature of the 2000 state elections was that this level of parity between the parties in the legislatures, coupled with the large Republican advantage in governorships, means that Republicans are in a much better position at the state level in 2000 than they were 10 or 20 years before, during the last two congressional redistrictings. Indeed, not since 1952 (the year of Eisenhower's first landslide) have Democrats controlled so few state legislatures.[54] In this process, the big win of 1994 was crucial, giving Republicans a huge boost at the state level that they have struggled, mostly successfully, in maintaining ever since.

The question on the minds of many political analysts then is, what specific effect will these factors have on Congress? The virtually unanimous conclusion is that Republicans will benefit in redistricting for 2002, making a net gain of anywhere from four to ten House seats nationally.[55] A few cautions, however, are in order: courts have increasingly intervened in redistricting battles, the status of the 1982 Voting Rights Act amendments requiring minority–majority districts is uncertain, and demographic and political shifts can quickly undo the best-laid plans of partisan redistricters. A great deal of uncertainty therefore hangs over the final outcome of the process. Nevertheless, most analysts agree that Republican gains give them an advantage.[56] Furthermore, Republican parity in state legislatures bodes well for the party's long-term chances in Congress in another way: state legislatures are the major breeding ground and "farm teams" for competitive congressional candidates, at least for the House. On the other hand, it is not clear how long Republicans will hold their majority in governorships. As in Congress, many governors will face the midterm curse in 2002, when nearly three-fourths of governorships will be up for grabs.

The congressional and state elections of 2000 essentially reinforced the conclusions drawn from the presidential election. For at least a moment on November 7, there was a mathematical parity between the two parties. Americans divided their votes almost evenly, and split control of the institutions with near precision.

Furthermore, this unusual outcome of parity was achieved in Congress and the states in an election that produced very little overall partisan change: a net shift of 4 U.S. Senate seats, 2 U.S. House seats, 1 governorship, and 70 state legislative seats out of nearly 6,000 such seats at stake. As commentator William Schneider said, "A close split has become even closer."[57] Yet the competitiveness of American politics below the presidential level was narrowly confined, with perhaps only 30 U.S. House seats in play and control of redistricting hinging on perhaps 75 key state races.[58]

Given the closeness of the presidential race, the sharply differing geographical coalitions assembled by the two candidates, and the nearly complete localization of other contests, it is of little surprise that coattails were difficult to identify. Democrats gained in the Senate largely on the basis of Gore's strength in urban areas. Yet Republicans held Democrats to a draw in the House and made modest gains in the states. Just as the disparity between the performance of Senate and House Democrats was largely due to the extreme geographical concentration of Gore's vote, one might surmise that Republican state legislative pickups can partly be accounted for by the same factor.

In both Congress and the states, the shadow of 1994 looms large. The outsized Republican gains made in that year have since eroded somewhat, leading to Democratic satisfaction that the Republican momentum stalled short of undisputed majority status. On the other hand, Republicans have protected most of their gains, remaining in control of Congress and in a majority of governorships, while winning an even split of legislatures. Compared with 1994, Republicans have slipped a bit, but compared with ten, twenty, or even forty years ago, they are quite healthy indeed, and they are poised to remain competitive for the foreseeable future.

Notes

1. Even though the Senate is split 50–50, Vice President Dick Cheney will cast tie-breaking votes, giving the Republicans control of the body. While the Republican leader will be the floor leader and Republicans will chair all Senate committees, the party leadership did in early 2001 agree to give Democrats equal representation on all Senate committees.

2. Paul R. Abramson, John H. Aldrich, and David W. Rohde, *Change and Continuity in the 1996 and 1998 Elections* (Washington, D.C.: CQ Press, 1999), pp. 257–60.

3. Keating Holland, "A year after Clinton impeachment, public approval grows of House decision," December 16, 1999. http://www.cnn.com/1999/ALLPOLITICS/stories/12/16/impeach.poll.

4. "Clinton Comes Up Short In a Year of Politics Over Substance," *Congressional Quarterly Almanac*, Vol. 55 1999 (Washington, D.C.: CQ Press, 2000), p. B3.

5. Karen Foerstel, "Hastert and the Limits of Persuasion," *CQ Weekly Report*, September 23, 2000, p. 2254.

6. Foerstel, "Hastert and the Limits of Persuasion," p. 2254.

7. While observers noted correctly that the groundswell of public support Republicans anticipated did not materialize, Gallup polls showed that about two-thirds of Americans approved of the tax cut and said they wanted Clinton to sign it. http://www.gallup.com/poll/releases/pr990812.asp.

8. See www.Gallup.com.

9. "Clinton Comes Up Short," p. B3.

10. "Clinton Comes Up Short," p. B3.

11. "Clinton Comes Up Short," p. B4.

12. Since you cannot beat someone with no one, another small advantage for the Democrats in 2000 was that Democratic candidates ran unopposed by Republicans in 33 seats as compared to 30 Republicans who were unopposed by Democrats. But as most of these cases occurred in districts that were already considered safe, the Democratic advantage here was not very important.

13. Karen Foerstel, "Gephardt's Charge," *CQ Weekly Report*, November 4, 2000, p. 2578.

14. Gregory L. Giroux, "Balance Hangs in a Few Races," *CQ Weekly Report*, January 1, 2000, p. 12.

15. Giroux, "Balance Hangs," p. 12.

16. John Gizzi, "The Congress: Split Decision?" *The World & I*, November 2000, p. 31.

17. An example of this phenomenon could be seen in the 1980s. Reagan coattails brought in a net gain of nine U.S. senators for the Republicans, enough to take control of the Senate, but then lost eight seats and Senate control in the 1986 midterm elections.

18. Andrew Taylor, "Democrats Hope for Majority In Defiance of History," *CQ Weekly Report*, January 1, 2000, p. 16.

19. Karen Foerstel and Derek Willis, "DCCC Rakes in New Money As Business Hedges Its Bets," *CQ Weekly Report*, July 15, 2000, p. 1708.

20. Derek Willis, "The 75 Percent Dissolution," *CQ Weekly Report*, September 23, 2000, pp. 2193–94.

21. Foerstel and Willis, "DCCC Rakes In New Money," p. 1708.

22. Center for Responsive Politics. http://www.opensecrets.org/index.asp.

23. http://www.gallup.com/poll/trends/ptjobapp_cong.asp; http://www.gallup.com/poll/releases/pr001106.asp.

24. Bob Benenson, "Proudly Worn Party Label Missing in Key Contests," *CQ Weekly Report*, September 23, 2000, p. 2183.

25. Alberto Alesina and Howard Rosenthal, *Partisan Politics, Divided Government, and the Economy* (Cambridge: Cambridge University Press, 1995). Alesina and Rosenthal argue specifically that this balancing is done in hopes of forging a moderate macroeconomic policy, but the argument itself can easily be applied to partisan control generally.

26. Voter News Service exit poll. http://www.cnn.com/ELECTION/2000/results/index.epolls.html.

27. Cokie and Steven V. Roberts, "Why candidates ignoring Congress," *Denver Rocky Mountain News*, November 5, 2000, p. B1.

28. See Gregory L. Giroux, "GOP Maintains Thin Edge," *CQ Weekly Report*, November 11, 2000, p. 2652.

29. Benenson, "Proudly Worn Party Label Missing," p. 2182.

30. At the same time, third parties won 5 percent or more of the vote in 73 House districts in 2000, up from 44 districts in 1996.

31. Giroux, "GOP Maintains Thin Edge," p. 2652.

32. Giroux, "GOP Maintains Thin Edge," p. 2652; "Cantwell-Gorton Count Continues; GOP Leads in 4 of 5 Close House Races," *CQ Weekly Report*, November 18, 2000, pp. 2726–27.

33. Giroux, "GOP Maintains Thin Edge," p. 2652.

34. Voter News Service exit poll. http://www.cnn.com/ELECTION/2000/results/index.epolls.html; Will Lester, Exit polls: Democrats improve performance among key voter groups," *Detroit News*, November 7, 1998.

35. Kirk Victor, Margaret Kriz, and Michael Posner, "A Split Senate," *The National Journal*, November 11, 2000, p. 3563.

36. Victor, Kriz, and Posner, "A Split Senate," p. 3563.

37. Ralph Siegel, "Franks Considers Running for Governor; says Bush's Deficit Led to Senate Defeat," *The Record*, November 10, 2000, p. A20.

38. "19 GOP Senate Seats in Play," *CQ Weekly Report*, November 4, 2000, p. 2585.

39. See http://www.gallup.com/poll/releases/pr001106.asp.

40. Ethan Wallison, "After Failing to Take Back House Majority, Dismayed Democrats Point Fingers at Gore," *Roll Call*, December 14, 2000; see also David Hess, "Gephardt's Private Agony," *The National Journal*, November 18, 2000, p. 3674.

41. Voter News Service exit poll. http://www.cnn.com/ELECTION/2000/results/index.epolls.html.

42. "Small Room for Compromise," *CQ Weekly Report*, November 11, 2000, p. 2655.

43. Hess, "Gephardt's Private Agony," p. 3674.

44. Karen Foerstel, "The Limits of Outreach," *CQ Weekly Report*, November 11, 2000, p. 2650.

45. Foestel, "Gephardt's Charge," p. 2578.

46. Karen Hansen, "Election 2000—The States Are Crucial," *State Legislatures*, September 2000, p. 16.

47. The new apportionment will be in effect for the 2002 congressional elections.

48. Hansen, "Election 2000," p. 17.

49. Suzanne Dougherty, "GOP Primed for Redistricting," *CQ Weekly Report*, November 11, 2000, p. 2671; Karen Hansen, "The New American Political Parity," *State Legislatures*, December 2000, p. 12.

50. Hansen, "Election 2000," p. 19.

51. "Partisan Control of State Legislatures," *State Legislatures*, December 2000, p. 14.

52. Hansen, "The New Political Parity," p. 15.

53. Dougherty, "GOP Primed for Redistricting," p. 2671.

54. Hansen, "The New Political Parity," p. 15.

55. See Michael Janofsky, "G.O.P. Gains A Future Edge in Redistricting," *New York Times*, November 10, 2000, p. B10. Dougherty, "GOP Primed for Redistricting;" Hansen, "The New Political Parity," p. 15.

56. Janofsky, "G.O.P. Gains A Future Edge in Redistricting, p. B10."

57. Hansen, "The New Political Parity," p. 12.

58. Giroux, "Balance Hangs on a Few Races," p. 12; Hansen, "The New Political Parity," p. 15.

Chapter Eight

Electoral Reform

In the wake of the controversy surrounding the 2000 national election, the idea of electoral reform is on the lips of every politician in America. As political correspondent John Harwood writes, "There's little doubt that swelling calls for reform will lead officials at every level—federal, state, and local—to re-examine all of the ways American elections are conducted."[1] Emblematic of this eclectic call for reform, the National Association of Secretaries of State established a voting reform task force charged with examining no fewer than seven items—uniform polling hours, voting methods, technology, standardized ballots, poll staffing, voter education, and election-night media coverage—and even that list did not exhaust all of the issues.[2]

All, of course, are in favor of reform—who is ever against it?—but few people have begun to think about what actual reform might really mean. As they do, some of the complexities and problems related to electoral changes will begin to become clear, and many would-be reformers will likely reconsider their initial enthusiasm. Some are even likely to find themselves to be ardent defenders of many aspects of the status quo. For not far beneath the arcana of electoral process lie fundamental and enduring theoretical questions about the importance of federalism, the meaning and proper scope of the franchise, and whether American democracy should be simple and plebiscitary or complex and representative. In any case, the word reform is little more than an empty vessel into which virtually any content can be poured. The important question is, what kind of reform? And at what cost, monetary or political?

Given the incrementalist bias of the American system, major electoral reform is rare in America, requiring the confluence of two factors: an electoral crisis or misfire that casts doubt on the legitimacy of the results,

and great political power and energy held by those who most want to enact electoral change. Arguably, the 2000 election satisfied only the first of
these criteria. Substantial potential for change remains, though it is far
from clear what form these changes will take. Democrats originally
framed the reform issue as a way to correct a defect in the electoral
process that had produced the "wrong"—or illegitimate—winner, successfully drawing attention to problems in Florida and the discrepancy between the Electoral College vote and the national aggregate popular vote.
Consequently, the first items on the Democratic reform agenda were
changes in the Electoral College and the way votes were cast and counted.
But Democrats have not been alone in calling for change; and the reform
movement has become sprawling. Never before in American history have
so many of the institutional mechanisms of election been simultaneously
challenged in the aftermath of a single vote. Only time will tell whether
this brief moment of public attention will be seized by reformers, or
whether, like many storms in American political history, this too will pass
over without leaving any significant institutional traces. We can at least
survey the range of possibilities.

Vote Casting and Counting

In the view of several analysts, the 2000 election exposed the fact that "the
nation's voting system is deeply dysfunctional . . . a jumble of different
technologies and methodologies."[3] In particular, the close race in Florida,
ultimately decisive to the outcome of the presidential election, demonstrated the degree to which the U.S. electoral system is massively decentralized. It is a reminder that presidential elections are not nationally run
contests, but a patchwork of mechanics and methods that vary not only
from state to state, but from county to county. In Florida, some counties
used single-column ballots and others used two-columned butterfly ballots. Some Floridians used punch cards to vote, while others used optical
scanners. When the automatic recount was undertaken, there was no clear
standard to guide it. Some counties rescanned all ballots, while others simply retabulated their mathematical calculations based on the original scanning. When hand recounts were finally undertaken in a few counties, no
standard guided that process either, allowing each three-member canvassing board to select its own criteria for countable votes—criteria that could
and did change even in the midst of the recount. When one multiplies those
variations across 50 states—Florida was the center of attention, after all,
because its vote was close, not because it was uniquely bungled—it is clear

that there is no uniformity of election procedure to speak of. Normally, these disparities are relatively inconsequential. In 2000, they riveted the nation's attention.

Democrats cried foul in Florida for two reasons. First, they alleged ballot and vote counting problems were greatest in some heavily Democratic counties, costing Al Gore precious votes. As evidence, Democrats pointed to the fact that voters using the punch card system were three times as likely to cast an invalid vote, or "undervote," in the presidential race as voters in counties using optical scanners (3.7 percent to 1.2 percent).[4] Second, because those counties also tended to have high concentrations of racial minorities, Democrats and others contended that these disparities amounted to a disenfranchisement of minorities. Democrats pointed not only to the "undervotes" but to the "overvotes," which were disqualified because they contained votes for more than one candidate. In Florida, an unusually large number of overvotes were found in Palm Beach County and heavily black precincts of Duval County, and some Democrats blamed these irregularities on confusion caused by the butterfly ballot or the "lack of sophistication" of the voters. Democrats could not allege intentional disenfranchisement, since the county commissioners and election officials from these areas were almost all Democrats. But it was troubling even to many nonpartisan observers that mechanical error might have cost Gore the presidency by throwing out disproportionate numbers of black votes.

In response, some political figures and analysts have called for greater uniformity of ballots and voting machines, at least for presidential elections. The most modest reform proposal came from Senators Robert Torricelli (D-N.J.) and Mitch McConnell (R-Ky.), who agreed to join forces to push for federal funding to help municipalities modernize their voting systems. Calling the current patchwork "antediluvian," Senator Charles Schumer (N.Y.) also promised to propose legislation requiring the Federal Election Commission to study voting technology, as well as other election issues, and make recommendations to state and local election officials, followed by a matching-grant program to help pay for new equipment. Other lawmakers joined in with a variety of proposals to study election issues, including Representatives Peter DeFazio (D-Oreg.), Jim Leach (R-Iowa), and Representative Jerrold Nadler (D-N.Y.), and Senators Barbara Boxer (D-Calif.), and Arlen Specter (R-Pa.).[5] Some legal analysts even argued that the reasoning of the Supreme Court's *Bush v. Gore* decision, though originally pertaining to the Florida recount, could be used to mandate uniform voting mechanisms on equal protection grounds (though the Court explicitly denied that its decision should be read as setting a broader precedent).

These reforms would not come cheaply. National replacement of the most antiquated technology—lever machines and punch card systems—would carry a $6 billion price tag.[6] More costly still could be the toll of reform on the principle of federalism. Election administration is one of the few realms of local government that has avoided significant intrusion from Washington, and the surrender of that part of federalism is not a step to be taken lightly. Though proponents of federal funding disclaimed any intention of pulling strings from the banks of the Potomac—Schumer, for example, said, "There will be no national mandate"[7]—skeptics argue that control follows money almost as surely as night follows day, and that such control could easily over time be asserted on other election issues, encompassing aspects well beyond the technical issue of voting mechanics. An important question for reformers will be not just how elections should be conducted, but what level of government should be responsible for conducting them.

In any event, it seems likely that pressure will grow on many municipalities, especially those using the now irreparably tainted punch cards and butterfly ballots, to move in a new direction, with or without federal funds. Those preferring state action already have a model in Oklahoma, which mandated a decade ago that all counties use the most up-to-date optical scanning ballots and machines, as well as specifying strict and uniform standards for vote counting.[8] Others propose mandating a common presidential ballot for use across the United States, though such proposals face enormous logistical hurdles. Kathleen M. Sullivan, dean of the Stanford Law School, argues that the Constitution should be amended to allow Congress to set the time, place, and manner of presidential elections, as it already can do respecting congressional elections.[9] Absent such an amendment, however, it is not clear that Congress can do much to standardize election procedures. Furthermore, adoption of such an amendment might violate the principle of separation of powers, since it would give Congress unusual influence over the selection of the president.

Proposals for change have not been limited to the mechanics of the electoral process. Other reformers have sought to eliminate a variety of formal and informal barriers to voting that they believe have disproportionately harmed the poor and racial minorities. Many would-be reformers took up causes that had no direct connection to events in the 2000 election. Among these were the 15-hour voting window used by New York State, same-day voter registration, and weekend elections. House Minority Leader Richard Gephardt even called Tuesday elections "unacceptable."[10] Some especially broad-minded reform advocates took up the unlikely cause of the voting rights of felons. In all but two states, felons are barred from voting while serving their sentences, and in 13 states, felons are not automatically eligible to vote after their sentences expire. This has resulted in the disenfranchisement of one-third of black males in Alabama and Florida, and 13 percent nationwide.[11] Before the 2000 elections in Florida, state election officials undertook a program to purge felons from the registration rolls, a program that came under attack from civil rights groups and even some county officials for being "too aggressive."[12] While some reformers hope to lighten the voting restrictions on felons, most politicians will no doubt proceed very carefully on this issue.

Yet if Democrats felt they had disproportionate reason to object to the disparity of voting systems or other barriers to voting for heavily Democratic constituencies, Republicans could point to Florida and elsewhere for evidence that other types of election reforms were needed. Some Republicans focused primarily on Florida's flawed recount procedures. Republican observers bemoaned the ongoing spectacle in Broward County, where Democratic-dominated vote counters seemed at times willing to use all means short of tarot cards and Ouija boards to "divine" the voters' intent to choose Al Gore for president. Ultimately, seven of nine U.S. Supreme Court justices agreed that Florida's recount procedures were so uneven as to be unconstitutional. In light of the Florida debacle, many state legislatures likely will revisit their procedures regarding recounts, driven by a desire to avoid the chaos and potential for partisan manipulation endemic in Florida and a desire to conform to the Supreme Court's ruling in *Bush v. Gore*, which insisted that the counting of votes be undertaken in a uniform and predictable fashion.

Efforts to bring greater uniformity to voting, however, will necessarily run at cross-purposes with one of the most important trends in election mechanics over the last two decades: the growing tendency of states and municipalities to experiment with voting innovations. Thirty years ago, despite variations of method, almost all Americans voted on the same day, in the secrecy of the ballot booth. Today, millions of Americans vote in states or localities that use *unrestricted absentee voting* (in which one requests an absentee ballot for no specific reason); *walk-in early voting* (in which one can vote days before the statutory election day in an election office or satellite site); and *mail-ballot elections* (in which every eligible voter is automatically mailed a ballot). For the first time, voters in some jurisdictions also experimented with Internet voting: the Arizona Democratic primary was conducted by Internet, and the Pentagon conducted an experiment in Internet voting for servicemen overseas.

Approximately half of the 50 states use one or more of these innovations, and they are generally very popular. In California alone, approximately one-fourth of voters (or about three million people) voted absentee in 2000, while in Washington State, about half did. Oregon in 2000 eliminated the ballot booth altogether and for the first time in a presidential general election used only mail ballots. Texas and many other states offering walk-in early voting consistently report that about one-fourth of voters take advantage of the opportunity. Almost all of the voters who use these innovations cast their ballots days or even weeks before the formal "election day." In the case of unrestricted absentee and mail-ballot elections, there is no guarantee that votes are marked without coercion from parents, spouses, or political activists, nor is there an ironclad guarantee that they are marked by the voter for whom the ballot was intended. Furthermore, ballots designed for home use are not always consistent with ballots used in polling places. For example, advanced electronic or computerized voting machines can be used in polling places, but can hardly be sent to people's homes.[13] Yet, though these innovations have drawbacks, they are likely to remain. Given the popular appeal of voter convenience, it is hard to imagine that the trend toward individualized voting options will be easily reversed.

Voter fraud was another problem that came to the forefront in 2000. Had George W. Bush lost the election by a handful of electoral votes, "fraud" might well have been the watchword, rather than "chads." Considered by many Americans to be a relic dating back to the heyday of the party machine, voter fraud has made something of a comeback in recent years. In Wisconsin, for example, there were voluminous reports that Democratic activists bribed homeless men and that college students at Marquette University voted multiple times, abetted by Wisconsin's same-day voter registration scheme.[14] In Connecticut, a law allowing same-day registration for presidential voters was so poorly enforced that there were calls for state and federal investigations, as election clerks complained that "they had no way to check whether people were voting more than once or in a town where they don't live."[15] Allegations of fraud also abounded in Florida. Despite complaints that Florida's program to purge felons from the registration rolls was too aggressive, there was evidence that several thousand felons might have voted anyway, with three-fourths of them registered Democrats. The *Miami Herald* also reported in late December that it had uncovered firm evidence of 144 ineligible voters being allowed to sign in and vote at polls where they were not registered—including someone posing as a Haitian immigrant who had been dead for over three years.[16] This sample comprised only 138 of Miami-Dade County's 617 precincts. Perhaps more disturbingly, statisticians offered an intriguing argument that the large number of "overvotes" in Palm Beach County (about 19,000) was most likely not the result of confusion, but of organized fraud carried out by election workers who punched the Gore hole in reams of already-voted ballots on their way to be counted. The result: a Gore vote remained a Gore vote, a blank ballot became a Gore vote, and a vote for anyone else became void. One statistical analysis estimated that this sort of fraud may have cost Bush up to 15,000 votes in Palm Beach County.[17] Republicans also had reason to be suspicious that even the initial mechanical recount had been rigged against them in some counties. The probability of Gore correctly gaining a net of over 600 votes in Palm Beach, as he did in the first recount, was estimated to be 149 million to one.[18]

The methods of remote voting described above, like unrestricted absentee voting, mail-ballot elections, and Internet voting, all pose a heightened risk of abuse. In the 2000 election, perhaps the most egregious example came in Oregon, when "unidentified people collected ballots from hundreds of voters on the street in Portland during the election day rush. The mysterious ballot collectors then put their haul in cardboard boxes and disappeared."[19] As the *Wall Street Journal* observed in its December 2000 series on election reform, "the growth of absentee voting has provided new opportunities to cheat. It has also spawned a mini-industry of consultants who get out the absentee vote, sometimes using questionable techniques."[20] Indeed, since 1996, at least two dozen cases of absentee ballot fraud have been exposed in 17 states. In one case, Miami's 1997 mayoral election was overturned when 4,500 fraudulent absentee ballots were thrown out. In another, a Texas woman serving as an absentee vote "broker" for a district attorney candidate in early 2000 collected and sent 240 votes from mostly elderly, often non-English-speaking voters in south Texas.[21] Associated with this problem—though few in either party will say so openly—was the manipulation of immigration for political purposes that took place throughout the 1990s. In 1996 alone, as many as a million immigrants were rushed through the naturalization process at the behest of Vice President Gore so they could vote in November, presumably for Democrats.[22] Additionally, in the fall of 2000, several Internet sites such as voteauction.com, which promised to sell the cumulative votes of groups of voters in key states to the highest bidder, were sued and temporarily shut down by various state courts.[23]

These problems—and the widespread perception of rampant fraud is itself a problem for democratic legitimacy, leaving aside its accuracy—are difficult to combat because of the general loosening of registration requirements. The 1993 National Voter Registration Act prohibited local election officials from purging the registration rolls of nonactive voters more than once every six years. Furthermore, attempts to prevent ineligible people from voting have almost uniformly come under attack by spokespersons for minority groups. In keeping with this pattern, the investigation of the Texas vote broker, a Hispanic, led to charges of "racism" and "intimidation."[24] White liberals have tended to remain silent or join in the recriminations, perhaps seeing the phenomenon as an electoral form of affirmative action that gives minorities extra votes to make up for earlier disenfranchisement. Whatever the explanation, it is clear that reform is not the same thing to everyone, and that not everyone will welcome every conceivable reform with equal enthusiasm. As Cokie and Steven V. Roberts observe, "Democrats want every vote to count; Republicans want every vote to count only once."[25]

There are some relatively uncontroversial remedies for certain aspects of the problem of burgeoning fraud. Some states, for example, have prohibited campaign offices from requesting absentee ballot applications and have hampered vote brokers by delaying the release of absentee ballot lists. Michigan has, for the sum of $8 million, constructed a state voter registration database that can reduce the potential for both fraud and the inadvertent purging of legitimate voters.[26] Simply replacing the punch card system would eliminate the sort of fast, easy double-punching fraud that may have occurred in Palm Beach and elsewhere. But any more stringent measures to prevent either individual or organized vote fraud—such as several proposals at the state and federal levels to tighten registration and voting requirements—will have to swim against the prevailing tide. Americans may have to choose between convenience and a uniform and secure ballot, between an expanded electorate and a legally valid one.[27]

Electoral College Reform

Within days of November 7, a chorus of critics led by Senator-elect Hillary Rodham Clinton suggested that it was time to replace the Electoral College with a national popular vote that would assign victory, simply and straightforwardly, to the candidate who won the most votes nationwide. The popularity of this reform gained strength as Americans realized that 2000 would be only the second clear case in which the popular vote winner lost the election in the Electoral College.[28]

Before examining competing claims, it is important to note that reforming the rules can very easily lead to new and different outcomes. Consequently, it cannot be said with any degree of assurance that Al Gore would have won the presidency if the popular vote had been decisive. This is because both campaigns in 2000 based their plans on the requirements established by the Electoral College, pursuing a state-based electoral vote-maximization strategy rather than a national popular vote-maximization strategy. George Bush did not campaign in Texas, and Al Gore spent no money in New York. Both candidates ignored these "safe" states in favor of closer contests in what became known as the battleground states. Under a vote-maximization strategy, the campaigns would have been conducted in a very different way, which might have altered voter turnout, intrastate voting, and ultimately the national popular vote count.

In any event, the argument for abolition of the Electoral College is unambiguous. The current system makes it possible for a candidate to assume the presidency even though more Americans voted for his opponent, raising fundamental questions about consent of the governed and the democratic legitimacy of the result. Democratic Senator Richard Durbin of Illinois called the Electoral College a "dinosaur," and about three of every five Americans seem to agree.[29] While this argument had noticeably greater resonance in 2000 than the last time such a situation clearly occurred, there are two good reasons to believe that little will come of efforts to replace the Electoral College.

The first reason is theoretical. If the argument against the Electoral College has the advantage of democratic simplicity, the argument for it is no less endowed with a constitutional, republican elegance. The United States of America is a federal republic, or what James Madison termed a "compound republic" falling somewhere between a unitary regime and a confederation of coequal states. This compound republic has numerous institutional manifestations, of which the Electoral College is but one example. Using a formula allocating electors on the basis of congressional representation, the Electoral College recognizes both the population of a state and its autonomous political standing. This compromise gives populous states more electoral votes, but grants smaller states a greater number of electors than is warranted by their populations.[30]

This means that the Electoral College has, on the surface, a disproportionate bias in favor of small states. However, it is not quite as simple as all that. For years, liberals believed that the Electoral College helped them by giving influence to heavily Democratic voting blocs like blacks and Jews who could tip the balance in the big, closely divided industrial battlegrounds; indeed, right up until November 7, analysts had suggested that it was George Bush who might win the popular vote and Al Gore who might win the Electoral College. Perhaps the most fundamental bias of the Electoral College is this: It is not sufficient to win in a few big states by huge margins. Since almost all states give their electoral votes on a winner-take-all basis, the system works in favor of candidates who win in a lot of places, even by modest margins, and against candidates whose support is deep but narrow. For reasons both of federalism and major party moderation, many analysts consider this bias a good thing for American politics.[31]

In the end, however, this bias cost Gore the presidency. Gore trailed in the aggregate popular vote from coast to coast until returns came in from California, where he pulled ahead only because he won that state by a 1.3 million vote margin. Gore lost the rest of America by nearly a million votes, winning only 20 of 50 states and about one-fifth of America's counties, so that one could fly from Washington, D.C., to San Francisco without ever crossing a Gore state before reaching California. Gore's support might have been deep in a few places, but it was much more narrowly concentrated than Bush's. Consequently, it is not obvious that "the will of the people" was thwarted in his defeat, at least if one takes federalism seriously. Furthermore, one might say that in the American system the most fundamental, legitimate, and enduring embodiment of the will of the people is the Constitution itself. If this is true, then the claim that the outcome of a presidential election is "illegitimate," even though it conformed to the process established by the Constitution, must be considered in some sense an anti-constitutional argument.

Whatever the theoretical merits of the argument favoring the Electoral College, the facts of the case in 2000 expose the second, more practical reason that it is unlikely to be replaced with a national popular vote. Such a reform would require a two-thirds majority in each house of Congress and ratification by 38 of 50 state legislatures. Neither scenario is very likely. The Senate is even more heavily weighted toward the small states than the Electoral College itself, and these states would not easily forfeit their influence over the presidential race. And due to the bicameral make-up of the state legislatures, as few as 13 legislative chambers out of 99 could block any constitutional amendment. It is hard to imagine a scenario in which this bare minimum could not be mobilized in defense of an Electoral College system that seemed to operate, even in this highly contentious election, to the benefit of 30 states. The Electoral College has survived approximately 700 proposed amendments over the last two centuries. Even opponents of the Electoral College such as Congressman Jerrold Nadler of New York acknowledge that abolition "won't happen because the small states won't agree to it."[32]

A more realistic possibility would be for a greater number of states to adopt the electoral vote allocation scheme used by Maine and Nebraska, in which it is possible for a state to split its electoral votes between competing candidates. Two votes go to the statewide winner and one to the winner within each congressional district. Supporters hope this scheme would be a little less likely to produce a plurality-loser. But in order to adopt such a plan, states would have to risk surrendering much of their influence over the election process, which is currently guaranteed by the winner-take-all rule. States such as California, Texas, New York, and Florida would be reluctant to embrace this division of their Electoral College power, as would small states. Even if some state lawmakers can support the plan in the abstract, they are not likely to implement it unless many other states are already doing so, producing a classic catch-22. Such a reform would also bring the question of presidential elections into the congressional redistricting process every 10 years; and parties would almost surely begin to consider district lines from the point of view of maximizing electoral votes. That might be good or bad, but it would surely be significant and would drastically change the whole redistricting calculus. Above all, this reform might not even achieve the intended purpose of making presidential elections more reflective of the popular will by reducing the likelihood of a plurality-loser. Depending on how party coalitions are concentrated, it could have the opposite effect. One party could win a state by building up large majorities in a few congressional districts, yet still lose most of the districts (which is exactly how Democrats did better in the Senate than in the House in 2000).

Another plan offered by former Senator Daniel Patrick Moynihan would leave the Electoral College intact, but allot a specified number of "bonus" electoral votes to the winner of the national popular vote. This plan seems like a finely crafted compromise, but its rationale can be readily attacked. If the bonus is not enough to put a plurality-loser over the top—in the 2000 race, Gore would gave needed a 5-point bonus to win the presidency—then it is superfluous. But if the bonus is enough to negate the normal functioning of the Electoral College in close cases, then the Electoral College becomes superfluous.

Finally, opponents of the present system have pointed out that nothing constitutionally prevents electors from voting their own preference, disregarding the popular vote in their state. The "faithless elector" is a rare breed—before 2000, there were only nine in American history, and their votes have never been decisive. Yet, speculation swirled around the possibility that a handful of Bush's electors might defect to Gore, swinging the election to the vice president (Gore only needed three of Bush's 271 electors). Democratic operative Bob Beckel, Walter Mondale's 1984 campaign manager, openly recruited such defectors. Conservative radio personality Rush Limbaugh even reported on his December 8 show that his Democratic sources claimed Beckel had actually succeeded in persuading three Republican electors to jump ship. For a time, then, it appeared possible that 2000 would see both of the nightmares of reformers come true—a plurality-loser, and faithless electors tipping an election—though of course, had it happened, the two phenomena would have canceled each other out. Calls were renewed by some to amend the Constitution, keeping the electoral vote system but eliminating the human electors, or else requiring them to support their state's choice. This proposal seemed unlikely to succeed, given the lack of urgency; and in the end, the only faithless elector was a Gore elector from the District of Columbia who voted a blank ballot to protest the lack of D.C. statehood.

While short-term prospects for Electoral College reform are dim, a crucial question is whether 2000 was an aberration not just historically (as clearly it was) but from this point forward. It is conceivable (though not probable) that population shifts and demographic and geographical voting patterns make the scenario of 2000 one that may be repeated more frequently in the near future. Had the upcoming reapportionment of House seats been in effect in 2000, George Bush would actually have received seven more electoral votes with exactly the same popular-vote division. Should the plurality-loser phenomenon become commonplace, supporters of the Electoral College may find it more difficult to defend the institution. That outcome, however, would depend on a continuation of the extraordinary parity of the two parties.

Reporting of Election Results

As if there were not enough controversies surrounding the 2000 election, the reporting of election results by the major news media also came under assault. Goaded by faulty exit polls and incomplete returns, the television networks made a series of mistakes that diminished their journalistic reputations and may have affected the outcome of the election itself. The networks' early call for Gore in Florida, which was later reversed, and their sluggishness in calling several Bush states in the East might have generated at least three important electoral consequences. First, because the networks called Florida for Gore before the polls had closed in the heavily pro-Bush Florida panhandle, Bush may have been deprived of hundreds or thousands of votes that could have sealed his win in that state and prevented most of the postelection wrangling and bitterness. Second, network calls that made it appear as if Gore had essentially won the election may have depressed Republican turnout in the West, costing Bush wins in New Mexico, Wisconsin, and Iowa, as well as possibly costing Republicans a smattering of House seats in California, and two or three

Senate seats, such as Slade Gorton's seat in Washington. Third, a number of Republicans, including Bush adviser Karl Rove, argued that the early network calls might have been responsible for Gore's exceedingly narrow national popular vote margin, a margin with no electoral meaning but plenty of political significance.

While Republicans seemed to have the most reason to complain, Democrats objected to one premature projection, when the networks finally crowned Bush the winner of the presidency at about 2 A.M. EST. The polls were already closed around the nation when that projection was made, but it helped shape public opinion in the weeks ahead, contributing to the impression that Bush was the presumptive winner and that Gore was the one trying to wrest away the prize by all available means.

Of course, it is impossible to prove any of these effects. The only way to know what would have occurred without premature network projections on election night would be to go back in time, rerun the election without the projections, and see what happens. But this fact did not keep numerous observers from calling for changes in the way election-night projections are made. Congressman Billy Tauzin (R-La.) promised to hold committee hearings in the new Congress on the subject, and threatened to grill network executives about their procedures and possible partisan bias.

A number of solutions are potentially available. Congress could consider passing a law prohibiting election projections until all polls in the continental United States have closed. But such a law would probably violate the First Amendment. Alternatively, Congress could try establishing a nationwide poll closing time or prohibiting state and local election officials from releasing federal election returns until a certain time. Either solution could attain the desired result, but it is not clear that Congress has the constitutional authority to enact them, since Congress has power to regulate only the time, place, and manner of congressional elections, and not presidential elections. A more modest response would be for networks to reach a voluntary agreement to revise their procedures, or for Congress to rely on public pressure to force a network agreement. This approach may be the most promising; within a month of election day, two networks had already dropped out of the Voter News Service exit polling consortium.

Campaign Finance Reform

Candidates spent a record amount of money in the 2000 presidential and congressional elections, with over $900 million expended just by the two parties' national election committees.[33] Supporters of campaign finance reform hoped that these numbers (though smaller than national expenditures for a variety of consumer items like potato chips) would provide ammunition for a renewed assault on the nation's laws regarding the funding of federal campaigns. This effort has been driven by the conviction that there is too much money in politics, and that six- or seven-figure contributions by interested donors can have a corrupting influence on the parties. Consider, for example, the $600,000 contribution to the Democratic National Committee by the head of Loral Corporation during the 1996 election cycle. In short order, a pending export license sought by Loral to provide sensitive satellite technology to China was approved by President Clinton over the objections of both the Departments of State and Defense. When questioned, Clinton would say only that he did not approve Loral's license "solely" because of the contribution.

Reform efforts will doubtlessly focus on the McCain-Feingold Bill. It proposes to ban all soft-money contributions to the parties—that is, money donated for generic "party-building" purposes that falls outside the normal regulations and limits of federal campaign contributions. Many congressional Republicans oppose the bill, believing it would place them at a disadvantage in future elections. But in certain respects prospects for passage of some version of McCain-Feingold seem favorable. John McCain's strong showing in the 2000 Republican primaries strengthened the hand of the reformers, and the congressional balance after November tilted a bit in that direction. Indeed, McCain announced that he would use his prerogatives as a senator to insist on early consideration of the issue in the 107th Congress, promising "blood on the floor of the Senate" if he was thwarted. Furthermore, Republican resistance might weaken (though Democratic enthusiasm might also wane) as it becomes more widely understood that Democrats actually relied on soft money more than Republicans did in 2000. Democrats raised more than half of their money as soft money, while Republicans raised most of their funds as hard money.[34] George W. Bush has expressed a willingness to consider a version of campaign finance reform, including a ban of soft money from corporations and labor unions tied to a "paycheck protection" measure making it harder for organized labor to use union dues for political purposes. But this paycheck protection provision may prove a deal-killer for Democrats.

During the 2000 campaign, Bush also proposed raising the hard-money individual contribution limit, which has remained static at $1,000 since 1974. His proposal took note of a fact about campaign finance that seldom makes its way into a public discussion dominated by the view that there is too much money in politics. One problem of the finance system, arising primarily during the presidential nominating phase, is not too much money but too little. To be more precise, a key reason that so many otherwise viable candidates are unable to compete is that they are forced to raise money in such small increments that there are not enough contributors to go around. Current finance rules would have made it impossible for outsider George McGovern to raise $400,000 from one contributor at a critical point in his 1972 campaign. Likewise, congressional challengers, who typically gain a greater marginal benefit from campaign spending than do incumbents, cannot make a race competitive by tapping a few early, highly committed contributors. Without higher individual limits, candidates are increasingly dependent on assistance from their national parties, much of it funded through soft-money contributions.

These two competing interpretations of campaign finance—that there is too much money in elections, and that there is too little—are difficult to reconcile in any one package, which helps explain the lack of action on the issue. Any campaign finance reform that does not address both sides could easily create more problems than it solves. For instance, restricting soft money without raising the individual contribution limit would make life much harder for congressional challengers. With Congress so closely divided, both parties are positioned to stop any changes they believe would hurt them—yet virtually every imaginable change in campaign finance law is bound to disproportionately benefit, or seem to disproportionately benefit, one of the parties.

Major Party Nominating Reform

Lost in the national angst over the general election was the fact that one of the major parties, the Republicans, came very close to ordering a complete rehaul of their nominating process in 2000. The intended target of the reform was the ubiquity of "front-loading," the process described in chapter 2 in which states compete to schedule their primaries as early as possible. Republican leaders, including National Committee Chairman Jim Nicholson, argued that both candidates and voters are hurt by front-loading. Candidates who cannot raise large sums of money up front cannot compete, while voters are given very little time to assess the candidates or to take account of shifting circumstances. Once a nominee is decided, or a challenger concedes, all subsequent primaries are essentially meaningless. As Professor Robert Loevy has shown, only 10 states were relevant in all of the three most recent nominating campaigns. A full 22 states were irrelevant in all three years, voting after the nomination was already locked up.[35]

To prevent front-loading, reformers must overcome a tremendous collective-action problem. States have little reason to push back the date of their primaries if other states are not doing so, especially if it will diminish their influence over the nomination. The Republican National Convention in 1996 tried to create a new incentive structure by allotting bonus delegates (either 10, 7.5, or 5 percent of a state's delegation) to states that held their primaries later in the primary calendar. But this tiny carrot failed to have any effect. States reasoned that extra delegates served no purpose if primaries were held after the nominee was decided.

In 1998–99, there was also much talk of scheduling large regional primaries. The most notable of these attempts took place in the Rocky Mountain West, where Utah Governor Mike Leavitt led a drive to form a Rocky Mountain primary joining the states of Arizona, Colorado, Idaho, Montana, Nevada, New Mexico, Utah, and Wyoming. But once California announced its intention to move ahead to March 7, Leavitt abandoned any thought of scheduling the primary later in the season. March 10 was set as the date, and in the end he attracted only three of the original eight states. Legislatures in the other five states rejected the move for mostly parochial reasons, including favorite-son considerations, conflicts with national Democratic Party rules, an unwillingness to shift forward primaries for state offices at the same time, and logistical concerns such as cost.[36] The failure of both the RNC bonus delegate plan and the regional primary plan demonstrated the difficulty of modifying the nominating system through a decentralized and voluntary process.

Having tried a carrot and failing, the RNC took the unusual step (for Republicans) of proposing a stick. Following up on the 1996 RNC Task Force on Primaries, RNC Chairman Jim Nicholson in 1999 appointed an advisory commission on the Presidential Nomination Process. Headed by former RNC Chairman and U.S. Senator Bill Brock, the advisory commission held hearings and examined a variety of options for dealing with front-loading. Alternatives that were considered included mandating a single national primary or rotating regional primaries, requiring states to hold their primaries roughly in order of size (called the "small states first" or "Delaware" plan), implementing a system of proportional representation, and holding the national convention before the primaries. In the last proposal, the convention would be an assembly of party activists who would screen candidates, and primaries would select the nominee from among that pool.

After months of deliberation, the RNC advisory commission recommended in May 2000 that the party adopt the "small states first" plan, establishing a window of March through June (soon revised to February through May) and mandating a 45 to 90 percent reduction in delegate allocations for states that did not comply with the new schedule. This proposal represented a drastic change in approach for Republicans, who have traditionally shied away from centrally imposed mandates. In the commission's view, the "small states first" option was most likely to reduce the "entry fee" for candidates and least likely to produce a premature victory by one of the candidates. The advisory commission's report asserted that "the Delaware Plan has potential to soften many of the problems that have come to plague the current nominating process: frontloading, compression, low voter turnout, early media frenzy, excessive 'tarmac and media ad' campaigning, emphasis on early need for large sums of money, and a condensed time window for the actual election contest."[37]

Such a plan could not succeed without the cooperation of Democrats, however, and they were initially skeptical. DNC Rules and Bylaws Committee Co-Chair James Roosevelt Jr. pointed out that Bill Clinton had been elected twice under the current system, leaving many Democrats unconvinced that change was needed. As the committee's report indicated, "under the current rule on timing of the nomination process, the Party has successfully nominated candidates who have been victorious in the last two election cycles. Consequently, criticism about a front-loaded schedule has to be weighed against a process that seems to be working well."[38] Furthermore, urban liberals were concerned about the consequences for Democratic nomination outcomes of a system in which only small states would be given the task of weeding out candidates. The Democratic report expressed that members were "concerned about the lack of diversity among the early groups of smaller states. They sensed that the issues addressed by Democratic presidential candidates to appeal to the early small states would not help the candidate design a successful message with broad appeal in the general election."[39]

Talks between the parties had only just begun when the Republican reform effort collapsed. Mere days before the Republican Convention in Philadelphia, party officials reversed their previous support for the plan under pressure from the Bush campaign. Consequently, it never came up for a vote before the convention. The Bush campaign, which had previously signaled that it would not interfere with the reform process, never provided a full explanation for its change of heart. Some analysts speculated that Bush simply wanted to clear the convention of any prospect of controversy or disruption—a prospect that was very real, given growing opposition by large states like California and New York. Others believed that the campaign had reconsidered the practical political effects of the plan on a possible President Bush in 2004. Whatever its problems from other standpoints, front-loading is generous enough to incumbents that they might not want to abolish it.

Supporters of the Delaware Plan have vowed to return, though change cannot be passed until 2004, and cannot take effect until 2008. Even if Republicans revisit this reform and ultimately adopt it as a national rule, success will be far from ensured, since it will depend on the concurrence of national Democratic rules and implementation by the states. It is also unclear that the plan would have the intended effect of making nomination races more competitive. Candidates can lose political viability long before they lose mathematical viability. A string of defeats, even in small states with few delegates, can leave candidates with collapsing fund-raising and dwindling media attention. It may be that the problems of the current nominating system only superficially concern front-loading. Perhaps front-loading is simply another consequence of the system's primary-centered, media-driven, plebiscitary nature.

In the meantime, there will likely be ongoing talks between Democrats and Republicans about how to eliminate the awkward situation caused in 2000 by the adoption of differing primary windows by the two parties. Democrats, who were skeptical about the "small states first" plan, agreed that something should be done to align the windows by 2004.[40] Whatever the fate of front-loading, it seems probable that parties will attempt to exert more influence on their primary processes. Angered and frightened by John McCain's capacity to control the early primary agenda, many Republicans urged the banning of open primaries in 2004. It is worth noting that Democrats had tried that experiment in national party rules in the 1970s, but had ultimately backed off when several states, including Wisconsin, protested vigorously. It is unclear how much success a drive to close primaries will have, especially since many open primaries in the South were first promoted by Republicans eager to draw conservative southern Democrats into the GOP.

At the same time, the handful of states such as California and Washington that had utilized the so-called blanket primary will be forced by a U.S. Supreme Court decision to find a presidential primary method more compatible with party organizations. The blanket primary listed all candidates from all parties in the same column and allowed all voters, regardless of party affiliation, to vote for any of them. Delegates were to be distributed according to those voting results. When both national parties objected in 2000, California and Washington adopted a second, simultaneous primary for delegate selection purposes that was limited solely to party members voting for their party's candidates. Shortly after the California primary in

March 2000, the U.S. Supreme Court ruled that the blanket primary was an unconstitutional infringement of the parties' rights of association.

Political reform, brought to prominence by John McCain's surge in the early Republican primaries, has come out roaring after a summer of hibernation. As *Washington Post* columnist E. J. Dionne argued, "Political reform is a more important theme at the end of 2000 than it was when the year began. The reform agenda has now expanded beyond campaign finance reform to encompass electoral reform. . . . The paradox of the year 2000 is that the very frustration of the reform spirit could give birth to a more powerful reform movement."[41] Institutional change in the American system, when it occurs, is often the result of traumatic events that reorient the way people think about politics and political structures. The 2000 election and its aftermath were traumatic enough to call into question virtually every aspect and stage of presidential elections, from nomination procedures to campaign finance to voting and counting votes to the translation of votes into the Electoral College to the announcing of results by the news media. Some proposed reforms are likely to be enacted, such as funding for the modernization of voting and vote-counting machinery in some locales. Other reforms are probably dead on arrival, starting with abolition of the Electoral College. Most other proposals fall somewhere in between. Their chances of enactment depend on a contest between the heightened public concern in the aftermath of the 2000 election and the natural inertia produced by institutional entrenchment and competing goals. The prospects for reform will be a race against the clock as public interest wanes over time.

This is not to say that all, or even most, of the proposed reforms would be unambiguously beneficial. The merits of some are questionable. Others that are worthy when viewed singly are contradictory in combination, as "potential solutions often pit desirable goals in direct opposition."[42] Is reform defined as same-day registration, or measures against fraud? Is reform greater uniformity, or more states with early voting? Is reform allowing less money in politics, or more? Does reform mean more felons are allowed to vote, or fewer? If students of American politics have learned anything over the past 30 years, it surely should be that reforms seldom achieve all that they promise, and often produce a whole range of consequences that proponents did not anticipate or desire. Even if one can predict the results of a particular reform, one can never know until it is too late how that reform might interact with others. Nor can Americans simply ignore the potential long-term effects on broader structures of American government, such as federalism, of proposals like Electoral College reform and congressional subsidization of election equipment.

Reform, by whatever definition, is the watchword of the day—even if only for a day. In the throes of the political agony of November and early December, some commentators referred to the election of 2000 as a national civics lesson. If that analogy is apt, it seems a fair bet that even if the election is over, the semester has just begun.

Notes

1. John Harwood, "Fixing the System: Lessons from States Hold Hope for Reform," *Wall Street Journal*, December 22, 2000, p. A6.

2. Leigh Strope, "Voting reforms panel seeks improvement," *Denver Rocky Mountain News*, January 14, 2001, p. 45A.

3. Bryan Gruley and Chip Cummings, "Election Day Became a Nightmare, as Usual, for Bernalillo County," *Wall Street Journal*, December 15, 2000, p. A1.

4. Harwood, "Fixing the System," p. A6.

5. See Jim Abrams, "Review of Electoral Process Proposed; Members of Congress Suggest Panel to Study Voting System," *The Record*, November 16, 2000, p. A10; Eric Lipton, "Counting the Vote: The Process," *New York Times*, November 13, 2000, p. A25.

6. Harwood, "Fixing the System," p. A6.

7. Harwood, "Fixing the System," p. A6.

8. Harwood, "Fixing the System," p. A1.

9. Kathleen M. Sullivan, "One Nation, One Standard Way to Ballot," *New York Times*, November 15, 2000, p. A31.

10. Lipton, "Counting the Vote, p. A25."

11. David S. Cloud, "Felons Make Up a Large Part of the Missing Electorate," *Wall Street Journal*, December 18, 2000, p. A14.

12. Cloud, "Felons Make Up a Large Part of the Missing Electorate."

13. In Bernalillo County, New Mexico, for example, a touch-screen system is used at polling places and optically scanned paper ballots are used for absentee and early voting. When the scanning machine was misprogrammed, thousands of absentee ballots showed no presidential vote. Gruley and Cummings, "Election Day Became a Nightmare."

14. Andrew Nieland, "In Milwaukee, Activists Use New Tactics To Help Boost Voter Registration, Turnout," *Wall Street Journal*, December 18, 2000, p. A14.

15. Matthew Daly, "Chaotic presidential ballot system may lead to state, federal investigations," Associated Press State and Local Wire, November 20, 2000.

16. Manny Garcia and Tom DuBocq, "Unregistered Voters Cast Ballots in Dade," *Miami Herald*, December 24, 2000. http://www.miamiherald.com/content/today/news/dade/digdocs/110495.htm. In one precinct, won by Al Gore with 90 percent of the vote, someone voted under the name of Andre Alisme, a Haitian who died in May 1997.

17. The analyst, Robert Cook, pointed out that Palm Beach's double-punch rate was 4.4 percent, compared with 0.5 percent in the rest of Florida, though Duval County (which does not use the butterfly ballot) had more ballots double punched than did Palm Beach. In Palm Beach the rate of double punching was 10–15 percent in heavily Democratic precincts but only 0.5 percent in Republican precincts, and occurred almost

entirely in the presidential race (error due to genuine voter confusion should have been randomly distributed across races). Furthermore, only in Palm Beach County did Bush receive votes equal to less than 65 percent of registered Republicans, while in every other county in Florida he received more votes than there were registered Republicans. It was also one of only two counties in Florida in which he received fewer votes than Republican U.S. Senate candidate Bill McCollum. On the basis of this analysis, Cook concluded that Bush's actual votes in Palm Beach were about 15,000 short of his "predicted" votes. See Robert A. Cook, "Explicit Statistical Evidence of Massive Ballot Tampering in Palm Beach, Florida," http://reagan.com/HotTopics.main/HotMike/document-12.6.2000.1.html. See also C. Moore, letter to the editor, *Wall Street Journal*, December 5, 2000, who points out that similar fraud has occurred in Houston, which also uses the votomatic punch card system. As Moore pointed out, "reducing your opponent's vote count is just as effective as adding new ballots for your candidate, and virtually undetectable."

18. Cook, "Explicit Statistical Evidence of Massive Ballot Tampering in Palm Beach, Florida." Nor was Palm Beach the only county where it seemed that shifting vote totals during the recount were greater than one would expect on the basis of random error. See Jace Radke, "Statistics Point to More than Random Error in Florida Vote," *Las Vegas Sun*, November 10, 2000; "Evidence of Fraud in the 2000 Florida Presidential Election," http://www.fraudfactor.com/ffselcounties.html. In Pinellas County, for instance, Gore picked up 417 votes when election officials "tinkered with ballots before submitting them for a machine recount." In Gadsden County, the canvassing board examined a stack of ballots in a closed meeting, then emerged with 170 newly discovered votes for Gore. See John J. Miller, "'Our Campaign Continues,'" *National Review*, December 18, 2000, p. 36.

19. Gruley and Cummings, "Election Day Became a Nightmare," p. A1.

20. Glenn R. Simpson and Evan Perez, "As Absentee Voters Increase in Number, Fear of Fraud Grows," *Wall Street Journal*, December 19, 2000, p. A1.

21. Simpson and Perez, "As Absentee Voters Increase in Number, Fear of Fraud Grows."

22. See William Schneider, "Massive Immigrant Vote for Clinton?" *National Journal*, September 14, 1996, p. 1986.

23. Kevin Simpson, "Legal Threats Darken Vote-Buying Web Site," *Denver Post*, October 20, 2000, p. A7.

24. Simpson and Perez, "As Absentee Voters Increase in Number, Fear of Fraud Grows."

25. Cokie and Steven V. Roberts, "Election reform would help scrub away the tarnish," *Denver Rocky Mountain News*, January 7, 2001, p. 5B.

26. Harwood, "Fixing the System."

27. At the state level, several proposals have been offered like requiring identification at the polls, requiring Social Security numbers and citizenship verification on registration forms, and enhancing criminal penalties for fraudulent voting or procuring fraudulent votes. Some proposed federal reforms include amending the NVRA to allow easier removal of inactive voters from registration rolls, requiring identification for voting in federal elections, providing an easier means for states to identify federal felons, and permitting the use of Social Security numbers on registration forms.

28. The other clear case was in 1888, when Benjamin Harrison won the Electoral College despite losing the popular vote to Grover Cleveland. Two additional cases are often cited, though they are murkier. In 1824, John Quincy Adams was elected in the contingency election in the U.S. House even though Andrew Jackson had the most popular votes, but 6 of the 24 states still did not use popular vote to select electors, so no true national popular vote is available. In 1876, Samuel Tilden won the popular vote and lost the Electoral College to Rutherford B. Hayes, but large quantities of vote fraud on both sides and the awarding of the decisive 21 disputed electoral votes to Hayes by a national commission make this less than a clear-cut case. A final case is rarely cited, but a good argument can be made that it was another instance of the phenomenon. In 1960, while Democratic electors received about 113,000 more votes nationwide than did Republican electors, John F. Kennedy actually received fewer popular votes than did Richard Nixon. Half of Alabama's Democratic electors ran as an uncommitted slate—not a slate committed to Kennedy—and ultimately voted for Senator Harry Byrd. While the top Kennedy elector (of six) in Alabama received 318,303 votes, the top unpledged elector (of five) received 324,050 votes, making it, according to Theodore H. White, "impossible to determine the exact total vote." Additionally, an undetermined amount of fraud almost certainly padded Kennedy's national vote total. See Theodore H. White, *The Making of the President 1960* (New York: Atheneum, 1961), p. 423.; Walter A. McDougal, "The Slippery Statistics of the Popular Vote," *New York Times*, November 16, 2000, p. A35.

29. Tom Hamburger and Joni James, "Its Role in Question, Electoral College Picks Bush," *Wall Street Journal*, December 19, 2000, p. A22; "Poll Track: The Electoral College," *The National Journal*, November 18, 2000, p. 3667. A series of polls taken after election day showed a national popular vote supported by 57, 61, and 62 percent of Americans.

30. Additionally, it might be noted that the Electoral College was also justified by the Framers on the grounds of the superiority of representative over directly democratic institutions. This feature of the Electoral College, however, has long been nullified by the practice of electors pledged to the winner of their states' popular vote.

31. See Judith Best, *The Case Against Direct Election of the President* (Ithaca: Cornell University Press, 1971).

32. Richard E. Cohen and Louis Jacobson, "Can It Be Done?" *The National Journal*, November 18, 2000, p. 3659.

33. Center for Responsive Politics, http://www.opensecrets.org/index.asp. This figure includes DNC, RNC, DCCC, NRCC, DSCC, and NRSC.

34. This was true in each of the three big committees for each party—national committee, congressional campaign committee, and senatorial campaign committee. The biggest discrepancy came in House committees, where Democrats raised only 42 percent in hard money and Republicans 67 percent. Center for Responsive Politics, http://www.opensecrets.org/index.asp.

35. Robert D. Loevy, "Relevance and Irrelevance in State Presidential Primaries and Caucuses." Paper prepared for delivery at the annual meeting of the Western Political Science Association, San Jose, California, March 2000.

36. See Andrew E. Busch, "The Rise and Fall of the Rocky Mountain Regional Primary." Paper presented at the annual meeting of the Western Political Science Association, San Jose, California, March 2000.

37. Advisory Commission on the Presidential Nomination Process, *Nominating Future Presidents: A Review of the Republican Process*, May 2000, p. 36.

38. *Beyond 2000: The Scheduling of Future Democratic Presidential Primaries and Caucuses; A Report to National Chair Joe Andrew by the DNC Rules and Bylaws Committee*, April 29, 2000, Washington, D.C., p. 11.

39. *Beyond 2000*, p. 14.

40. *Beyond 2000*, p. 11.

41. E. J. Dionne Jr., "What McCain Started," *Washington Post*, December 29, 2000, p. A33.

42. Harwood, "Fixing the System," p. A1.

Appendix

The 2000 Election Vote

State and Electoral Vote	Turnout (% of Eligible Voters)	Bush Vote (%)	Gore Vote (%)	Nader Vote (%)	Buchanan Vote (%)	Other Vote (%)
AL (9)	49.99	941,173 (56.48)	602,611 (41.57)	18,323 (1.10)	6,351 (0.38)	7,814 (0.47)
AK (3)	66.41	167,398 (58.62)	79,004 (27.6)	28,747 (10.07)	5,192 (1.82)	5,219 (1.81)
AZ (8)	42.26	781,652 (51.02)	685,341 (44.73)	45,645 (2.98)	12,373 (0.81)	7,005 (0.46)
AR (6)	47.79	472,940 (51.31)	422,768 (45.86)	13,421 (1.46)	7,358 (0.8)	5,294 (0.57)
CA (54)	44.09	4,567,429 (41.65)	5,861,203 (53.45)	418,707 (3.82)	44,987 (0.41)	73,496 (0.67)
CO (8)	56.78	883,748 (50.75)	738,227 (42.39)	91,434 (5.25)	10,465 (0.60)	17,494 (1.00)
CT (8)	58.40	561,094 (38.44)	816,015 (55.91)	64,452 (4.42)	4,731 (0.32)	13,233 (0.91)
DE (3)	56.22	137,081 (41.81)	180,638 (55.09)	8,288 (2.53)	755 (0.24)	1,088 (0.33)
FL (25)	50.65	2,912,790 (48.85)	2,912,253 (48.84)	97,488 (1.63)	17,484 (0.29)	23,095 (0.39)
GA (13)	43.84	1,419,720 (54.96)	1,116,230 (43.21)	N/A	10,926 (0.42)	36,332 (1.41)
HI (4)	40.48	137,845 (37.46)	205,286 (55.75)	21,623 (5.88)	1,071 (0.29)	2,126 (0.58)
ID (4)	54.46	336,937 (67.17)	138,637 (27.64)	12,292 (2.45)	7,615 (1.52)	6,134 (1.22)
IL (22)	52.79	2,019,421 (42.58)	2,589,026 (54.60)	103,759 (2.19)	16,106 (0.34)	13,811 (0.29)
IN (12)	49.44	1,245,836 (56.65)	901,980 (41.01)	18,506 (0.84)*	16,949 (0.77)	16,024 (0.73)
IA (7)	60.71	634,373 (48.22)	638,517 (48.54)	29,374 (2.23)	5,731 (0.44)	7,568 (0.58)
KS (6)	54.07	622,332 (58.04)	399,276 (37.24)	36,086 (3.37)	7,370 (0.69)	7,152 (0.67)
KY (8)	51.59	872,492 (56.50)	638,898 (41.38)	23,192 (1.50)	4,173 (0.27)	5,352 (0.35)
LA (9)	54.24	927,871 (52.55)	792,344 (44.88)	20,473 (1.16)	14,356 (0.81)	10,612 (0.60)
ME (4)	67.34	286,616 (43.92)	319,951 (49.09)	37,127 (5.70)	4,443 (0.68)	3,680 (0.56)
MD (10)	51.56	813,827 (40.24)	1,144,068 (56.57)	53,768 (2.66)	4,248 (0.21)	6,421 (0.32)

State and Electoral Vote	Turnout (% of Eligible Voters)	Bush Vote (%)	Gore Vote (%)	Nader Vote (%)	Buchanan Vote (%)	Other Vote (%)
MA (12)	56.92	878,502 (32.50)	1,616,487 (59.80)	173,564 (6.42)	11,149 (0.41)	23,282 (0.86)
MI (18)	57.52	1,953,139 (46.15)	2,170,418 (51.28)	84,165 (1.99)	1,851 (0.04)*	22,928 (0.54)
MN (10)	68.75	1,109,659 (45.50)	1,168,266 (47.91)	126,696 (5.20)	22,166 (0.91)	11,898 (0.48)
MS (7)	48.57	549,426 (56.87)	400,845 (41.49)	7,899 (0.82)	2,237 (0.23)	5,640 (0.58)
MO (11)	57.49	1,189,924 (50.42)	1,111,138 (47.08)	38,515 (1.63)	9,818 (0.42)	10,500 (0.44)
MT (3)	61.52	240,178 (58.44)	137,126 (33.37)	24,437 (5.95)	5,697 (1.39)	3,548 (0.86)
NE (5)	56.44	433,862 (62.25)	231,780 (33.25)	25,540 (3.52)	3,646 (0.52)	3,191 (0.46)
NV (4)	43.81	301,575 (49.52)	279,98 (45.98)	15,008 (2.46)	4,747 (0.78)	7,662 (1.26)
NH (4)	62.33	273,559 (48.07)	266,348 (46.80)	22,188 (3.90)	2,615 (0.46)	4,361 (0.77)
NJ (15)	51.04	1,284,173 (40.29)	1,788,850 (56.13)	94,554 (2.97)	6,989 (0.22)	12,660 (0.40)
NM (5)	47.40	286,417 (47.85)	286,783 (47.91)	21,251 (3.55)	1,392 (0.23)	2,762 (0.46)
NY (33)	49.42	2,403,374 (35.23)	4,107,697 (60.21)	244,030 (3.58)	31,599 (0.46)	35,297 (0.52)
NC (14)	50.28	1,631,163 (55.96)	1,257,692 (43.15)	N/A	8,874 (0.30)	17,261 (0.59)
ND (3)	60.43	174,852 (60.66)	95,284 (33.06)	9,486 (3.29)	7,288 (2.53)	1,346 (0.46)
OH (21)	55.76	2,350,363 (49.99)	2,183,628 (46.44)	117,799 (2.51)	26,721 (0.57)	23,487 (0.50)
OK (8)	48.76	744,337 (60.31)	474,276 (38.43)	N/A	9,014 (0.73)	6,602 (0.53)
OR (7)	60.63	713,577 (46.52)	720,342 (46.96)	77,357 (5.04)	7,063 (0.46)	15,629 (1.02)
PA (23)	53.66	2,281,127 (46.44)	2,485,967 (50.61)	103,392 (2.10)	16,023 (0.33)	25,676 (0.52)
RI (4)	54.29	130,555 (31.94)	249,508 (61.04)	25,052 (6.13)	2,273 (0.56)	1,395 (0.33)
SC (8)	46.49	786,892 (56.85)	566,039 (40.89)	20,279 (1.46)	3,520 (0.25)	7,523 (0.54)

State and Electoral Vote	Turnout (% of Eligible Voters)	Bush Vote (%)	Gore Vote (%)	Nader Vote (%)	Buchanan Vote (%)	Other Vote (%)
SD (3)	58.24	190,700 (60.30)	118,804 (37.56)	N/A	3,322 (1.05)	3,443 (1.09)
TN (11)	49.19	1,061,949 (51.15)	981,720 (47.28)	19,781 (0.95)	4,250 (0.20)	8,481 (0.41)
TX (32)	43.15	3,799,639 (59.29)	2,433,746 (37.98)	137,994 (2.15)	12,394 (0.19)	23,846 (0.39)
UT (5)	52.61	515,096 (66.83)	203,053 (26.34)	35,850 (4.65)	9,319 (1.21)	7,088 (0.97)
VT (3)	63.98	119,775 (40.70)	149,022 (50.63)	20,374 (6.92)	2,182 (0.74)	2,955 (1.00)
VA (13)	52.05	1,437,490 (52.47)	1,217,290 (44.44)	59,398 (2.17)	5,455 (0.20)	19,814 (0.72)
WA (11)	56.95	1,108,864 (44.57)	1,247,652 (50.15)	103,002 (4.14)	7,171 (0.28)	20,744 (0.86)
WV (5)	45.74	336,476 (52.17)	295,497 (45.82)	10,680 (1.66)	3,169 (0.49)	2,303 (0.36)
WI (11)	66.07	1,237,279 (47.61)	1,242,987 (47.83)	94,070 (3.62)	11,446 (0.44)	12,825 (0.50)
WY (3)	59.70	147,947 (69.22)	60,481 (28.30)	N/A	2,724 (1.27)	2,574 (1.20)
DC (3)	49.12	18,073 (8.95)	171,923 (85.15)	10,576 (5.24)	N/A	1,322 (0.65)
Total	51.20%	50,432,517 (47.81%) 271 Electoral Votes	50,902,900 (48.26%) 267 Electoral Votes	3,084,542 (2.92%)	448,808 (0.43%)	617,011 (0.58%)

Source: Respective State Boards of Election and the Committee for the Study of the American Electorate.
*Nader was a write-in candidate in Indiana; Buchanan was a write-in candidate in Michigan.
N/A = Not on the ballot.
Bold = State won by Gore.

Index

abortion, 81, 88, 89, 105n53
Abraham, Spencer, 221, 228, 229, 230
absentee ballots, 196–97, 245–46, 247, 248
Ackerman, Bruce, 210n6
Adams, John Quincy, 262n28
advertising: against Bush by black groups, 165, 170n37; attacks on McCain by Bush, 96; Clinton–Dole race, 110; Clinton's scandal, 215; early introduction, 114, 130n6; negative, 87, 90; popular vote, 177
AFL-CIO, 72, 103, 223
African American voters, 155
Alesina, Alberto, 224, 238n25
Alexander, Lamar, 64, 68, 69, 75n18
Allbaugh, Joe, 63
Allen, George, 228
antigovernment philosophy, 42–43
anti-incumbent mood, 226
Apple, R. W., 101
approval ratings, Congress, 214, 223
Archer, Bill, 221
Arizona, 89, 91
Arkansas, 160
Ashcroft, John, 64–65, 221, 228
attraction model, 225

BAG. *see* Blame Al Gore (BAG) school
Baker, James, 177, 182, 188

ballots: call for uniformity, 243; irregularities, 180
Bancroft, George, 142, 168n10
Barak, Ehud, 38
Barnes, Fred, 117
Bartels, Larry, 25, 46n15
Bauer, Gary, 63, 64, 87
Bayh, Evan, 138
Beck, Michael Lewis, 25–26
Beck, Phil, 196
Beckel, Bob, 251
Beer, Samuel, 42
Benenson, Bob, 224
Bennett, William, 92, 100
Bernalillo Country, N.Mex., 260n13
Big Government, 37, 149, 152; factor in voter behavior, 227; reaction, 5; Republicans' reaction, 40–42
black voters, 97, 243; election of 1876, 2–3; patterns of support, 160, 163, 164–65, 170nn34–37
Blaine, James, 133
Blair, Tony, 38
Blame Al Gore (BAG) school, 25, 27, 31
blanket primaries, 53, 93, 258–59
Bliley, Tom, 221
Bob Jones University, 53, 89, 90
Boies, David, 177, 186, 188, 196
Bork, Robert, 100
Boxer, Barbara, 243

269

About the Authors

James W. Ceaser is professor of government and foreign affairs at the University of Virginia, where he has taught since 1976. He received his Ph.D. from Harvard in 1976. He has also held visiting appointments at Marquette University, the University of Basel, Claremont McKenna College, Harvard University, and Oxford University. In 1996 he was awarded "The Joint Meritorious Unit Award for Total Engagement in the Creation of the George C. Marshall Center for European Security Studies" by the U.S. Army. Professor Ceaser is the author of several books on American politics and American political thought, including *Presidential Selection* (1979), *Reforming the Reforms* (1982), *Liberal Democracy and Political Science* (1991), and *Reconstructing America* (1997). He is co-author with Andrew Busch of *Upside Down and Inside Out* (1993) and *Losing to Win* (1997).

Andrew E. Busch is associate professor of political science at the University of Denver, where he teaches American government. He received his Ph.D. from the University of Virginia in 1992. Professor Busch is the author of *Outsiders and Openness in the Presidential Nominating System* (1997) and *Horses in Midstream: U.S. Midterm Elections and Their Consequences, 1894–1998* (1999), as well as a forthcoming book on the Reagan presidency and numerous articles on elections, American politics, and Reagan. He is co-author with James Ceaser of *Upside Down and Inside Out* (1993) and *Losing to Win* (1997).